Philadelphia magazine's

S0-DZD-565

ULTIMATE
RESTAURANT
GUIDE

Edited by **April White**
Foreword by **Maria Gallagher**

Temple University Press
Philadelphia

Temple University Press
1601 North Broad Street
Philadelphia PA 19122
www.temple.edu/tempress

Published 2004
Printed in the United States of America

Cover and text design by Andrew Zahn
Photography by Zoey Sless-Kitain

⊗ The paper used in this publication meets the requirements of the
American National Standard for Information Sciences—Permanence
of Paper for Printed Library Materials, ANSI Z39.48-1992

Library of Congress Cataloging-in-Publication Data

Philadelphia magazine's ultimate restaurant guide / edited by
April White; foreword by Maria Gallagher.
p. cm.
Includes index.
ISBN 1-59213-146-8 (alk. paper)
1. Restaurants—Pennsylvania—Philadelphia—Guidebooks.
I. Philadelphia. II. Title.
TX907.3.P4W49 2004
647.95748'11—dc22

2004049794

2 4 6 8 9 7 5 3 1

To those with whom I have shared the most memorable meals: spaghetti and meatballs on Christmas Eve; lunch on the grill at camp; omelets in Africa; pepperoni and mushroom pizza from Paolo's; and boxes and boxes of clementines.

CONTENTS

FOREWORD

By Maria Gallagher

Philadelphia loves to eat. Give us a plate of roasted free-range Lancaster County chicken and a Jersey tomato salad, and we're happy; set a cheesesteak oozing with Whiz before us, and we're ecstatic. Our two best-known restaurants, Le Bec-Fin and Pat's Steaks, epitomize the range of our collective appetite. Our former mayor, now Pennsylvania's governor, is such a joyful omnivore that Wawa named a hoagie after him. We love eating so much that we'll even get up at 5 a.m. to watch other people do it: 20,000 spectators attended Wing Bowl 2004.

My education in Philadelphia food and restaurants began in the spring of 1976, the year I moved to a one-room apartment at 13th and Walnut and began working as an intern at Philadelphia magazine. Single and in my early 20s, I was precisely the type of customer who would feed the city's Restaurant Renaissance, though at the time my meager income couldn't feed it very much.

That year, the city's top fine-dining destinations included Le Bec-Fin, La Panetiere, the Garden, and Ristorante da Gaetano, but a group of young provocateurs—informal restaurants with a distinctly American style—were generating the most excitement. At Frog, Knave of Hearts, Lickety Split, Astral Plane, Judy's, Friday Saturday Sunday, and Under the Blue Moon, kitchens were turning out eclectic flavor combinations perfectly suited to the mismatched place settings and on-a-shoestring decor of their dining rooms. Cooks were often self-taught, or fresh out of Philadelphia's new culinary arts academy, the Restaurant School. Servers wore jeans. Blackboard menus were updated throughout the evening to accommodate inspiration—or expunge dishes that flopped. Many tastes of that time linger in my memory: Chestnut soup with chicken and cardamom at the Gold Standard on 47th Street near Chester Avenue. Swiss chard ravioli with tarragon cream sauce at Russell's at 17th and Lombard. Tall wedges of quiche-like shrimp, tomato and cheese pie at the Fish Market. The daring shad roe pâté at In Season on 13th Street near Pine. Frog's fiery Siamese chicken curry. The Commissary's carrot cake.

Most of these restaurants are closed now, but how we eat today dates directly from that transformative period, commonly called the Restaurant Renaissance. It was really a rebellion, led by restless individualists bored with the city's staid steakhouses, well-worn oyster bars, and hotel dining rooms serving predictable Continental cuisine. The unorthodox new restaurants were an extension of the anti-establishment sentiment generated by the Vietnam War, but they also reflected shifts in society occurring nationwide at that time.

Americans were traveling and tasting European and Asian cuisines in their native environments, often during year-abroad studies. Asian émigrés who fled conflicts in Vietnam and Thailand went to work in American restaurants, and later opened their own. Chefs began building menus around what was fresh and in season, spurning dried herbs and prepared products. In Philadelphia and elsewhere, jacket-and-tie requirements were jettisoned. Dinner became a destination, instead of a pit stop before a movie. Busy double-income couples and families were eating more meals away from home. Gays and lesbians came out, and went out.

After I began writing restaurant reviews for the *Philadelphia Daily News* in 1980, I saw firsthand how restaurants could re-energize a neighborhood, and how neighborhood gentrification could spawn restaurants. In the 1970s, the "in" spots were Society Hill, Queen Village and South Street; in the '80s, the scene shifted to Manayunk and Fairmount, and luxury hotels such as the Four Seasons, the Rittenhouse and the Ritz-Carlton. Center City, Rittenhouse Square, Old City and Northern Liberties boomed in the 1990s, driven in part by the opening of the Pennsylvania Convention Center and a proliferation of outdoor seating. Today, the new frontiers are Fishtown, East Falls, and Philadelphia's suburbs.

What began as a rejection of stuffed flounder and chateaubriand has matured into a significant chunk of the estimated $8 billion spent each year on travel and tourism pursuits in the city and its surrounding counties, according to the Philadelphia Convention & Visitors Bureau. Restaurants are now a key part of the city's marketing strategy. Before 1970, an event such as the Book and the Cook would have been unthinkable.

Thanks to immigrant cooks—and Americans who learned from them— we now have Thai, Korean, Vietnamese, Japanese, Chinese and Indonesian restaurants, as well as Mexican, Cuban, Puerto Rican, Colombian, Portuguese, Brazilian, Caribbean and Nuevo Latino. African, Middle Eastern and halal Muslim restaurants, opened to serve specific audiences, are now patronized by all. We have formal French and bistro French, regional Italian cuisine, restaurants that fuse flavors from many cultures, and restaurants that let us bring our own bottles of wine.

Ethnic grocers, the shops on South Philadelphia's 9th Street, the Reading Terminal Market, and gourmet purveyors like Caviar Assouline sell many of the exotic foodstuffs and condiments that we discover in restaurants, allowing us to play with them at home. Artisan bakers like Metropolitan Bakery and Le Bus have redefined our daily bread.

We're eating more adventurously, in large part because we can. Chili-dusted skate and gingered fried calamari with wasabi-lime mayo are among the most popular dishes at Alison at Blue Bell. A summer salad at Matyson combines icy watermelon chunks, crumbled feta cheese, red onion, local greens and eiswein vinaigrette. El Vez tops its roasted corn soup with a tiny quesadilla that incorporates a corn fungus called huitlacoche. Duck confit is so mainstream that it appears in a salad at Standard Tap, a bar in Northern Liberties. We can drink milkshakes made from the forbidding durian fruit at Pho Xe Lua in Chinatown, or bubble tea at Bubble House in University City. Fruit soup, a dessert menu darling of the '70s, is updated at Django to include tiny pastel scoops of house-made sorbet, made from several heirloom melon varieties.

Even our blue-collar foods have evolved. The cheesesteak begat the chicken cheesesteak and the tofu soy-cheese steak. In South Philadelphia, it's easy to find a meatless grilled vegetable hoagie, or a Vietnamese hoagie, filled with non-Italian lunch meats and cilantro.

Personalities have been as vital as food in shaping our restaurant scene.

Volatile, voluble Georges Perrier of Le Bec-Fin, in residence since 1967, is its most recognizable face (and voice). Consummate showman Stephen Starr has almost single-handedly refreshed Center City with the Continental, Buddakan, Tangerine, Jones, Pod, Morimoto, El Vez, Angelina and Striped Bass. Passionate entrepreneurs such as Steve Poses of Frog/Commissary, Judy Wicks of the White Dog Café and Jack McDavid of Jack's Firehouse bring their politics to the table. Legendary hosts like Frank Palumbo of Palumbo's, and John and Albert Taxin of Old Original Bookbinder's, paved the way for Neil Stein, although Stein ultimately lost most of his fashionable portfolio in bankruptcy court. Now, national magazines track our star chefs, Jean Marie Lacroix (Lacroix at the Rittenhouse), Marc Vetri (Vetri), Guillermo Pernot (Pasion) and Dominique Filoni (Savona).

Collectively, these tastemakers have fashioned a phenomenon that didn't exist in 1970, when Perrier opened a tiny restaurant called Le Bec-Fin on Spruce Street, nor in 1932, when Pat Oliveri served his first steak sandwich.

There is an unwritten rule that every story about Philadelphia food must include an anecdote about visiting Pat's Steaks. Here is mine.

Summer of 1976. On the eve of the Bicentennial, I'm at an American history-themed costume party in Haddonfield, dressed as Carry Nation, the hatchet-wielding temperance zealot—a deliberately ironic choice.

To fortify ourselves beforehand, we consumed mass quantities of rigatoni and meatballs at Strolli's in South Philadelphia. But by 3:30 a.m., we're all hungry again.

Someone suggests Pat's. Off we go to 9th and Passyunk, arriving around 4 a.m.

There's a line.

At that moment, I decide I can live happily ever after in Philadelphia.

Philadelphia magazine's
Ultimate Restaurant Guide

1 : THE **PEOPLE**

Forget the food. It's the chefs
and owners who add real spice to
Philadelphia's restaurant scene.

"Everybody Went to Bookie's"

Sinatra, Elizabeth Taylor, Frank Rizzo, Leonard Tose, Japanese tourists—and, oddly, David Bowie—drank, dined and schmoozed at Old Original Bookbinder's, and the Taxin family embraced them all

By Amy Donohue

Bookbinder's was born in 1893, a family-run tavern that over the next century grew into a sprawling 54,000-square-foot structure that took up most of Walnut Street between Front and 2nd. The place passed out of the hands of the Bookbinder family in the early 1940s when John M. Taxin, a produce merchant, bought it. Under Taxin, and later his son Albert, it became a martini-soaked mecca for celebrities, tourists, and a clubby crowd of Philadelphians who went there for long, boozy lunches, birthdays and anniversaries. The restaurant was officially known as "Old Original Bookbinder's" because in 1935, in a quintessentially Philly move, a rogue branch of the Bookbinder family boldly launched a rival fish restaurant, Bookbinders Seafood House, on 15th Street (thereby confusing generations of locals and tourists, and causing countless dining foul-ups when various parties arrived at diverse locations).

Victims of changing tastes, and decimated by the emergence of other power restaurants during the '90s (think Striped Bass and the Palm), both Bookbinders were recently shuttered. But with the Taxin family readying a smaller, more modern version of Bookie's, set in its old location in Old City, we've compiled an oral history of the great days (and nights) spent there. Unless otherwise indicated, when we refer to Bookbinder's, we're talking about the Old Original—remember, that's the one at 125 Walnut Street.

The 1940s through 1960s

John E. Taxin, a.k.a. "young John Taxin," and the most recent family member to manage the restaurant: "There was no Atlantic City when my grandfather, John M. Taxin, bought the restaurant in the 1940s. But big acts came to the

Latin Casino on Walnut Street, and they all came to the restaurant. We had a PR man named Arnold Stark, like a Damon Runyon character, he was a wizard. When Frank Sinatra was in town, Arnold would see that he got the *LA. Times* delivered to his hotel room every day. He'd deliver a cheesecake to the Oval Office for inaugurations."

Bookbinder's was so cavernous that locals preferred eating at the big round tables ringed by captain's chairs in the more intimate Presidents Room, a paneled lounge with a massive bar salvaged by the Taxins from an old Nevada saloon. Tourists got seated in the big dining room, which comfortably held 200—but John and Jean Taxin tried to visit every table, whether the diners were one-off visitors or three-times-a-week regulars. There was also a coatroom and a "holding bar" as you entered the restaurant.

Gus De Pasquale, waiter for 52 years: "I was 14 when I started as a busboy. When we first started, it was all girls working as waitresses, because of the war. In the late '40s, Jack Klugman waited tables with me—Quincy! Abbott and Costello came in around that time, too. Which was the fat one? Costello? He used to chase Frances, one of the waitresses, around the dining room. She was a little heavyset, and he liked to pinch her. And they'd insult the people at the next table."

Arthur Makadon, chairman, Ballard Spahr Andrews & Ingersoll: "I grew up with Albert Taxin, and I always went to Bookbinder's as a child on Sunday nights. My family would drive in, and it was a big deal. I always ordered the same two things, veal parmesan and strawberry shortcake. In those days, there were no other restaurants. It was that, Frankie Bradley's, and Arthur's steakhouse on Walnut Street. You always wore ties, and women got dressed up."

Elliott Curson, advertising executive: "There were only a couple of places to eat back then—the Hunt Room in the Bellevue, and the Vesper Club. Bookbinder's was two restaurants, really, one for Philadelphians and one for everyone else. If you walked into the restaurant and saw there were empty seats in the dining room but the bar was filled, you'd say, 'Well, there's nowhere to sit.' And you'd leave. It's like the Palm now, where you have to sit on the left. The Taxins were part of the fun, having Albert and his father come to the table and kid around with you. They had a coffeepot out front for the drivers waiting outside. I'd always get the bluefish, and they had great salads and martinis. It was expensive, but it was good."

Neil Stein, restaurateur: "It was the first restaurant here to have a 'big pound,' a huge wooden tank that could house 500 lobsters. The aroma was just fantastic. John Taxin and his cronies sat at the same round table in the bar every day at lunch and smoked cigars. And if you weren't there, your seat was empty."

Sharon Pinkenson, executive director, Greater Philadelphia Film Office: "When I was a kid, I remember going there with my whole family and being fascinated by the decor, and the photos and the lobster tanks. I felt like I was in a castle, and the women would always get dressed up and be very glamorous."

Neil Stein: "John Taxin used to go to the market himself to buy produce at 4 a.m. every day. They had four guys behind the raw bar shucking clams, taking the lobsters out of the pound and steaming them, right there. They also had a doorman—this was very unusual in a restaurant, and really nice. John would invite all the cabbies in at night for coffee and doughnuts, too."

Thanks to Arnold Stark's promiscuous cheesecake volleys, and John Taxin sending a car and driver to notable guests' hotels, by the early 1950s, celebrity sightings became a regular part of Bookbinder's lore.

Gus De Pasquale: "Elizabeth Taylor came in many times when she was married to Eddie Fisher. She sat at Table 33 in the bar, and she'd eat lobster. She came in one time in a dress cut down to there, and Eddie Fisher would go like this to try to cover her up." [makes motion of pulling a dress neckline up and together] "Then she'd put it back." [laughs]

Anthony Pantalone, maître d' and employee for 39 years: "Elizabeth Taylor was very pretty. Very approachable. And her earrings were down to there. Eddie Fisher? He was aloof.

"Mike Douglas's show was filmed downtown then, so he'd be done around two in the afternoon, and he had his corner booth in the big room. He'd always have a mild fish, like swordfish or sea bass. He'd bring Liberace sometimes—oh, my, Liberace was a good guest, very friendly. Frank Sinatra was good friends with Albert.

"The most impressive man I ever saw was Gregory Peck, an elegant man. He came in three times. John Wayne was loud, friendly, he patted everyone on the back. Big drinker, John Wayne."

Dennis Cogan, attorney: "During his presidency, JFK was in town for the Army-Navy game, and he went to Bookbinder's and had their bouillabaisse. He loved it so much that he asked Mr. Taxin for the recipe. Mr. Taxin said, 'I'm sorry, Mr. President, but we can't give out the recipe. But I'll fly the soup down to the White House whenever you want.'"

Frank Rizzo Jr., Philadelphia City Council member: "When my dad was at Bookbinder's, he'd always bring my mother home a slice of strawberry shortcake. Upstairs, they had great parties, you'd walk up those old, rickety wooden steps, the planks moved and shifted."

Ralph Roberts, chairman, Comcast Corporation: "It was marvelous. My wife liked the restaurant, and she loves lobster. The two places to go were the Warwick and Bookbinder's. The other Bookbinders on 15th Street was more convenient; I think that was the original family? It created confusion."

Alan Halpern, former editor of *Philadelphia* magazine: "If you asked a cabdriver 'Take me to Bookbinder's,' he'd invariably take you to the one that was farthest away."

The 1970s and 1980s
These were the heady days of big hair, strong drinks, coke-fueled nights and five-pound lobsters. Disco and Reaganomics only made Bookie's more popular. Albert Taxin, the second generation, was now running the restaurant. With his pretty, bubbly young wife Doris, he continued the tradition of glad-handing and table-hopping, and was soon as beloved as his father.

John Taxin: "My earliest memories are of being a little kid in the restaurant, and when you're a kid, things look even bigger. It wasn't your normal restaurant, it was 54,000 square feet—Striped Bass is about 6,000, so we were humongous. We had three full-time electricians, a full-time carpenter and a full-time painter—it was a city unto itself.

"My grandfather still came in every day, and my father and Jack Bronstein, who was a cousin, ran the place. My father had a way, even if something bad was happening, of going on the floor and smiling and saying 'Hi, how are you doing?'

"I still remember getting dressed up to meet President Nixon when he came in; they landed his helicopter across the street in a parking lot where the Sheraton is now."

Larry Kane, former KYW anchor: "In 1972, Richard M. Nixon flew into Philadelphia and had lunch at the Old Original, escorted by Frank Rizzo. There was a heliport nearby, and people were stunned that the President had flown in that day. I interviewed people in and around Bookbinder's and on Walnut Street. I always felt it was rude to walk into a restaurant and do an interview without an invitation. There was also a myth—I assume it's a myth—that live lobsters hated bright lights."

Frank Rizzo Jr.: "We'd go there as a family on my father's mayoral election nights, and we'd always sit in the main dining room at one of the big round tables. John Taxin and my father knew each other as boys, and they had a very personal relationship. My father helped them with their parking— they were struggling because there was no off-street parking down there."

Gus De Pasquale: "Mayor Rizzo used to ride down on his motorcycle when he was a cop, and when he came in as mayor, the whole dining room would stop and clap for him."

Dominic Sabatini, former president of Penn's Landing Corporation: "Anytime Monday Night Football was here, you'd see Howard Cosell come in before the game. There's a famous story that when Howard Cosell was doing Monday Night Football, he got drunk and went on the air—and that may well have been at Bookie's."

Meryl Levitz, president, GPTMC: "Albert Taxin was very sweet. He took such care of Doris. I was working with Doris at the Convention & Visitors Bureau, and he would always send food over and he'd always drop her off at work. They looked like the top-of-the-wedding-cake couple."

Doris Taxin: "If we saw a family that looked like they were having a special occasion, we'd go over and say, 'You're our deal of the day!' And we'd pick up the check."

John Taxin: "I was a huge fan of Dr. J, and he became a good friend of my father's. I remember once we all went on a vacation together, and I was in awe. We were on the golf course, and someone asked him if he would caddy. He laughed and said, 'I can caddy, but it's going to cost you a lot.'

"I always liked it when people came back and said hi to the cooks and the dishwashers. Julius Erving did that, Muhammad Ali did that, and Frank Sinatra. When Jerry Jones owned the Cowboys, he always came in, and one time he went upstairs to a Temple football recruiting event and let everyone try on his Super Bowl ring."

Marnie Witten, granddaughter of former Eagles owner Leonard Tose: "Bookbinder's was one of the only places that was open on Sundays, and it wasn't too far from the stadium, so my grandfather would go after the game. We'd always sit in the barroom—my grandfather loved to sit at the bar and have a drink and a smoke.

"The first time I ever met Julia [Tose, Leonard's fourth wife] was at Bookbinder's—we had a family dinner there so we could meet her. I was at a horse show on Long Island, and he sent a helicopter to pick me up and fly me back. We landed right there across the street at the helipad, and he was very excited for us to meet her. She was stylish and impeccably dressed."

Harry Weiner, former seafood vendor and current perpetually tanned man-about-town: "Practically all of the seafood consumed at Bookbinder's in the '70s and '80s came from me, so I was in there all the time, and Albert became my best friend. There were so many celebrities coming in there, and there was never a time when Albert or John didn't pick up the check. I remember once when Milton Berle was playing the Latin Casino, he jumped up on top of a table and screamed, 'If I can't pay my own check, I'm never coming in here again!' And he still didn't pay the check."

John Taxin: We used to joke that Leonard Tose and Harry Weiner had a bet as to who could get married the most. Down at the fish market, Harry had pictures of all five of his wives lined up in front of his desk. Harry was having one of his weddings here in the '80s, and Leonard dropped by and said, 'I'll get the next one!' I think they had one wife in common. One time during one of Harry's weddings, the place caught on fire."

Marnie Witten: "I was at that wedding, at Harry Weiner's wedding!"

Susanna Foo, restaurateur: "When I came over from Taiwan, I lived with a host family in Pittsburgh, where I went to school. We went to Bookbinder's on 2nd Street once, and it was an incredible event. We all had the lobster aprons, and their lobster was great. The Taxins were a nice family, and Mrs. Taxin used to come into my restaurant and give me helpful suggestions."

Anthony Pantalone: "My favorite moment was the night when David Bowie came in, during the tour with the big spider at the Vet. He brought his whole entourage in—40-plus people—around midnight. There were a lot of gorgeous girls, too. I remember he was a handsome guy with a beautiful multicolored shirt.

"There were a lot of gay people in the show, and they weren't even bothering with the girls. They drank champagne and stayed till 3:30 a.m. We didn't mind, because Albert paid us extra, and he'd do that kind of thing for celebrities like Bowie, and Frank Sinatra and Peter Allen. Then there was that big concert that was simultaneously here and in England—Live something? They all came. Madonna came in dressed as plain as plain can be.

"Seventy percent of business was out-of-towners, it kept us going, and a lot of Japanese guests. They'd spend. They'd get the biggest lobsters and steaks, because it cost nothing here compared to what they'd spend in Japan."

Rich Costello, president, Philadelphia Fraternal Order of Police: "They had a busboy who turned out to be a mob hit man, who was involved in hits in the '80s. It was a busboy by the name of Theodore 'Teddy' DiPretoro from Dickinson Street; he was a suspect in the assassination of Phil 'Chicken Man' Testa, who took over from Angelo Bruno." [DiPretoro pleaded guilty to that killing.]

Nick DeBenedictis, chairman, Aqua America (formerly Suburban Water Company): "They had the world's worst waiters. I never left there without having something spilled on me."

Hal Rosenbluth, former president and CEO, Rosenbluth International: "I'd go with my friends Alvin and Gary Block after Eagles games. I'd always see Leonard Tose there, and it was nice to unwind there with some hot chowder. I was a lowlife, not one of the luminaries, so I didn't have a regular seat. I'd schlep in in my jeans. It was upbeat, almost like the Roaring '20s. I'd also go to 15th Street when our office was on Walnut Street. We'd go to dinner after Top of the Tooz bar, assuming we could still stand. That place was more depressing."

Elliott Curson: "One time I went in after a movie and this guy said, 'Hey Elliott, know who I am?' I said, 'You look like Ron Perelman, but you're so thin.' He said, 'I am Ron Perelman, and this is my wife, Claudia.' That was two wives ago."

The 1990s onward

In 1989, the Palm opened. A few years later came Striped Bass, Rouge and Brasserie Perrier. Albert Taxin, beloved by his customers, died of a brain tumor in 1993. Poor luck hit the rambling old wooden structure, too, says John Taxin: "In my history, I remember three or four fires. I was very lucky [they weren't worse]." But regulars still carried the torch.

Evan Lambert, owner, Savona restaurant: "It was very nostalgic, with its photos on the wall and the traditional Northeastern seafood menu. There's a place in every city for nostalgia. When I think of Bookbinder's, I think of Sparks Steakhouse in New York: You walked in, and you felt like you were back in 1940."

John Taxin: "If somebody was having a function, Mayor Rendell would always pop in, and then he'd take a seafood salad to go."

In September 1999, the Inquirer *published a devastating review by Craig LaBan of both Bookbinder restaurants. Old Original came off worse, with its knee-buckling prices and boiled-till-rubber lobsters. Still, it had its loyalists. And the tourists. And the politicians.*

Marnie Witten: "My grandfather still went when it wasn't the place to be anymore. I remember being there with him just a couple of years ago, after Johnny Taxin was in charge. Suddenly his father was gone, and he took over."

John Taxin: "During the Republican convention, Bob Dole, former President Bush, Colin Powell and Mary Matalin came in. This was before September 11th, but we had Secret Service everywhere, and checking all the exits. Then an aide called the next day and said, 'President Bush would like to come in for lunch.' We were closed, I had a banquet booked, but what can I say to the former President? Then at lunchtime, Bob Dole came in, and we sent him up to the banquet by mistake—we thought he was there for the party."

Larry Kane: "Even in its latter days, the Bookbinder's bar was a gathering place for would-be and alleged power brokers. It was one of the smokiest bars in Philadelphia, too, and celebrities liked to eat dinner there, to smoke and seek some anonymity. And the Taxins didn't wince at me ordering chicken. I've always been a chicken man."

Meryl Levitz: "In the '80s, it was still considered venerable, but we got this speeded-up Restaurant Renaissance in the '90s. And all of a sudden there were all these new restaurants, and hotel restaurants got so good—there was competition everywhere.

John Taxin: "In 2001, our utility bills were $600,000. The infrastructure was really old. I started to worry about a situation like what happened with the Pier 34 collapse. We had five or six fires over a few years."

Jim Cuarato, city commerce director: "I heard it was closing on the radio when I was in my car. Instead of going to my office, I went right to Bookbinder's. Everyone who worked there was crying."

The Taxins are scheduled to reopen Bookbinder's this summer—a much smaller, completely renovated Bookbinder's, with 19 condos and eight apartments built in the old banquet rooms and in a new building set in the old alley behind the restaurant. Most important, the Presidents Room bar and paneling are intact and will be a centerpiece of the restaurant. This pleases most people (though not George Bochetto).

George Bochetto, attorney and former boxing commissioner: "I'm glad they shut down. I never really liked either Bookbinder's. I'm tired of all my clients calling and asking which one they should try when they come to Philly and which one is the real one."

Angel Ortiz, former Philadelphia City Council member: "I wish they'd bring it back again. I'd like to go there and eat some raw oysters."

Neil Stein: "What made Bookbinder's so successful in its day is precisely what makes it impossible now: its sheer size. There's too much competition now. Some things are not to be re-created, but to leave a great memory. If you think of the great seafood restaurants in Philadelphia, you have to think of Striped Bass as second, and Bookbinder's as first."

Published February 2004

As the Taxins completed renovations at the 125 Walnut Street location in the summer of 2004, construction was also under way at the 15th Street Bookbinders Seafood, which will reopen as an Applebee's.

What's Eating Georges Perrier?

After 30 years at the top, he's battling changing tastes, flashy competition, and the inevitable ravages of time— but he's not ready to throw in the toque just yet

By Ben Wallace

"Everybody want to fock Georges Perrier in the ass," Georges Perrier was saying. Lunch at Brasserie Perrier was winding down, and the owner's voice filled the bar. The voice was almost cartoonish; French-accented, octave-leaping, disdainful of syntax, it swung from soft, chiding singsong to asphyxiated growl to contralto screech. "Fock Georges Perrier in the ass!" the voice barked, as if Perrier were a fairground pitchman goading patrons to step right up and try their luck.

Customers drinking coffee glanced over at the 58-year-old man who just a few years before was almost never seen out of his chef's whites. Now, sitting at a table in the second-built of his three restaurants a few weeks before September 11th, he wore the finely striped monogrammed shirt, tasseled loafers and Cartier wristwatch of the businessman he had become. Perrier was meeting with his publicist and his graphic designer, talking about having new menus printed and griping that everyone—printers, florists, everyone—tries to gouge him on pricing. He looked around wildly. "Ohhhhh," he said. "Eeets Georges Perrier! Ah theenk I weel put mah deek in hees ass!" He scooted back in his chair, squared his hips to the table, and made a downward thrusting motion with one fist. "Ah yes," he said, "let's fock Georges Perrier in the ass!"

Perrier left the restaurant and hobbled east on Walnut Street. His usual hybrid of swagger and waddle—he isn't much taller than five feet—now featured a limp. In July, at the home of a friend of his girlfriend, he'd opened the door to what he thought was a bathroom but turned out to be the basement. He skied down a staircase, broke both his heels, and spent the next three months in a wheelchair. Three months later, it still hurt to walk.

Today, he was going to drive out to Wayne for a late lunch at Le Mas Perrier, the Provençal restaurant he'd opened a year before. After lunch, he planned to spend the rest of the afternoon getting ready for a political fund-raiser he was to host at his home that evening for gubernatorial candidate Ed Rendell. But first, he had some paperwork to do. He limped along Walnut Street toward his corporate offices, past Le Bec-Fin and the intersection with Georges Perrier Place, a kiss from his adoring adopted city on the occasion of its favorite restaurateur's 50th birthday, in 1993.

Upstairs at his office, he talked business with an administrative employee—details of upcoming banquets, catered weddings, that night's fund-raiser—then went into the small room where his desk sat. One wall boasted a framed Xerox of a *New York Times* article from 1974. Written by Craig Claiborne, then the newspaper's all-powerful food critic, the article put Le Bec-Fin on the gastronomic map. Accompanying the story was a black-and-white photograph depicting a leaner, darker-haired, 30-years-younger version of the man in whose office it hung. Now, Georges's hair was graying, showing flashes of silver and a streak of white. His midsection had sprouted a potbelly.

Elsewhere in the room, other laurels from Georges's career were on display. In the course of Le Bec's 31 years, national magazine surveys had deemed the restaurant the best in the country, and in 1976, Georges was inducted into an elite fraternity of the world's greatest French chefs. Of particular importance to Georges were the five stars Le Bec was routinely awarded by the Mobil Guide, putting it in a highly select circle.

Now it had been cast out. In January of 2000, without ceremony or explanation, Mobil removed Le Bec's fifth star. The demotion devastated Perrier just as he was embarking on the creation of Le Mas, a $3 million project. Stunned, he eventually made the wrenching decision to try to reinvigorate the kitchen of Le Bec by turning it over to a young French chef from New York, Frederic Côte. In short order, Perrier suffered other setbacks, including the breaking of his heels and the filing of two sexual harassment and sex discrimination lawsuits against him. (He has denied the charges, and the cases are pending in federal court.) But losing the star hurt the most. On a shelf beside his desk, Georges had propped the Mobil 2000 plaque awarding Le Bec its shrunken constellation, the phantom fifth star taunting him with what he had lost and what he hoped to recapture. He was considering ripping out Le Bec's longstanding Louis XVI appointments and redecorating in a more contemporary style. A portrait of Napoleon hung on the wall behind him.

Life was simpler when Perrier had only one restaurant and cooked every night. Now he is a CEO with a small empire to run, a personality customers want to see and talk to, a brand whose name opens wallets. He tries to visit each of his three restaurants every day, and he regularly hosts charity dinners at his home. Beside his desk, a folded-up padded table awaited his weekly massage. His chef's jacket hung on a wooden stand.

Georges sat, head bent over a stack of checks that needed his signature. Le Bec-Fin alone has 96 employees, to whom he pays more than $2 million annually. His total payroll encompasses 250 people—he is the patriarch of an oversized family. He doesn't talk about it publicly, but there are employees he has supported through rehab two and three times, and he has silently helped others in more generous ways. For years he paid for an employee's asthmatic son to travel each summer to the Alps to clear his lungs.

Georges began scrawling his signature on the checks. "What the fuck is that?" he said suddenly. "WENDY! What is that shit—US Bancorp! What's that?" His assistant, sitting in the next room, informed him it was one of his credit-card bills. He resumed flipping through the checks, signing his name with a ballpoint. "Fucking shit," he said. "WENDY!" She appeared in the door. "Who the fuck is Jennifer Belezzi?" A hostess at Le Bec, Wendy informed Georges, and yes, she was owed a week's vacation; she had been working for him for more than a year.

Georges finished with the checks, then drove his dark-green Mercedes sedan home to Haverford to pick up his assistant. He is a terrible driver. He had a Rolls-Royce once, but he totaled it. He views seatbelts as an imposition. Beneath his dashboard, he'd installed a radar detector. As he headed for his house, hitting speeds of more than 80 miles per hour, his stop-and-start driving unsettled the contents of his passenger's stomach, while Georges blithely honked at other cars, screaming "Asshole!," and complained about how many bad drivers were out there.

At his home, a formally decorated ranch house with a pool, he and his assistant, Liliane Nino, a middle-aged woman who worked for Air France for many years, climbed into an SUV driven by his chauffeur and headed for lunch at Le Mas. There, he would fuss over flowers, hook his arms through those of a pair of matrons to escort them on a tour of the restaurant, sign another stack of checks, discuss the restaurant's wine-by-the-glass program with a manager, and have a light lunch of warm lentil salad and mahimahi à la Provençal.

In the wake of his forced convalescence, during which he'd crawled around his bedroom on all fours and had to be carried downstairs at Le Bec by three employees, he was reasserting himself, as he had several times before in his career. In the early '80s, feeling Le Bec drifting, he'd fired the chef and resumed oversight; just two years back, he'd purged Brasserie Perrier of several employees following a period when he felt he'd ceded too much authority to a manager. Once more, he wanted to be in full command. "Now we work again," he said as he and Liliane rolled toward Le Mas. "We are working again. I am retaking control. I'm taking charge. The old Georges Perrier burn in fire now. This—" He held up a hand to command attention. "This is the new Georges Perrier."

On a Thursday evening a few weeks later, after the first dinner service at Le Bec-Fin, Georges went downstairs to eat at his Bar Lyonnais, which occupies the floor below Le Bec. His lawyer, John Pelino, was sitting at the bar with his wife. The three talked for a while; then a manager asked Georges if he was ready for his table. "Please, please don't push people," Georges said. "Don't be pushy. You very like my mother."

"You are crabby today," Karen Pelino said. "What are you crabby for?"

"I need sex," Georges said. He looked down the bar in the direction of a middle-aged blond woman who was sitting by herself. "Did you hear what I say, Lisa?"

"I heard you," the woman said wearily, as though she'd heard it before. Georges grinned and sidled up behind her chair, draping his arms around her neck. Then he took a seat at a table where Liliane and an old friend, Joel, were already sitting. They began talking about the troubled restaurant industry.

Georges's business, already suffering from the slump in the economy, had fallen even further after September 11th. More than half his banquet bookings for the month had been canceled. He understood why—he himself had scrapped a planned September trip to France to visit his parents—but that gave him little comfort. "I wanna take a gun, I wanna shoot myself," he said, "but it's not gonna do anything. I wanna jump out the window, but it's not going to do anything." He mused aloud, as he sometimes did, about opening a neighborhood restaurant and charging $10 an entrée.

The waiter brought appetizers.

"Are they okay in the kitchen upstairs, without me, for five minutes?" Georges asked.

"Yes," the waiter said.

"They okay? Eh? They okay?"

"We're okay," the waiter said.

After Georges lost his fifth star in January 2000, TV trucks showed up at the restaurant. He had what he calls "a nervous breakdown," then suffered a deep spell of depression. Despite wielding only a minute fraction of the clout of the Michelin guides in Europe, the Mobil guide is the closest American approximation to that tyrannical system, which over the years has driven French chefs to bankruptcy and even suicide. "I was devastated, because I have it for so long, and suddenly is not coming anymore," Georges said after finishing his order of steak frites. "You say, 'What I have done wrong?'" He began to act out. One night, eating at La Parisienne on the Main Line, he pronounced the coq au vin "an insult" and spilled a glass of wine on the table, prompting the owner to accuse Georges publicly of "insecurity and jealousy" and demand an apology.

As Georges talked about the lost star, his eyes teared up. He said he had been desperate to understand how this terrible event could have befallen him, and he undertook an internal investigation. He convened a staff meeting where he asked if anything had happened in service that could have brought this about. He said he wouldn't be upset; he just wanted to know. No one said anything. He consulted a medium in Chicago, an older woman named Beth whom he has been calling for several years for help in making decisions. (For instance, she gave him the go-ahead to do the Le Mas project.) Anytime he is considering making an important hire, he gives Beth the prospect's birth date, and she consults her zodiac. When it came to the lost star, Beth told Georges that someone who worked for him was responsible.

Finally, a friend at the Mobil guide called Georges and, in a breach of Mobil protocol, explained what had happened. It turned out Georges's astrologer was right. On the night when four Mobil officials ate at Le Bec, a waiter and a busboy had argued near their table. Three times, the Mobil officials asked the employees to take their argument elsewhere, as it was disrupting their meal. Georges's source at Mobil provided him with the date of the incident, enabling him to review the checks from that night and figure out who was working. Georges deduced which check belonged to the Mobil party, and his secretary was able to figure out who the busboy had been.

In the course of denying everything, the busboy said it wasn't his fault—the waiter had provoked the argument. Georges met with the waiter, who'd worked for him for 16 years, and said he couldn't believe that a customer had had to ask him three times to stop arguing. Georges couldn't understand this, he told the waiter, and he was also upset that the waiter had lied to him by not owning up to the offense. Georges said he wouldn't fire him, but one more mistake and he'd be gone. A couple of months later, a customer called to complain about pushy service from the waiter, and Georges dismissed him.

As part of a campaign to restore Le Bec to five-star status, Georges hired a new manager, Nicolas Fanucci, who had worked for Alain Ducasse and who vigorously set about updating and refining service at Le Bec. But when Mobil announced the awards again in January 2001, Le Bec still had four stars. "So, I been punish, I guess," Georges said. "It's not so much tough because I lost the star. It's tough for my ego. This is an ego thing. Because you say you not part of the family of the 18 best restaurants in the nation. Now, I'm four-star. I'm same as the Brasserie. I'm same as Neil Stein. I'm the same as Rouge. Rouge have four star. I mean, do you think I should be the same as Rouge? Four star to Rouge and four star to Georges Perrier? You comparing cauliflower to roses. Rouge can be very good, but don't compare to Le Bec-Fin."

With Mobil set to announce the stars once again in January 2002 and a new chef running the Le Bec kitchen, Georges thought he had a better shot this year. "I hope we will have it back," he said, "because it will bring some more happiness, a little bit, from my misery that I have since this. ... We will get the five star back. I know we will. We have work all year very very very hard to get it back. So if we don't get it back, then that proves to me we have not done good enough job."

After finishing his dinner with Liliane and Joel, Georges ran into the Pelinos again, this time outside Le Bec. It was 11 o'clock, and they were now with John Pelino's daughter Clare, Perrier's longtime publicist.

"You were cooking on the line tonight?" Clare asked.

"Yes, I was cooking on the line," Georges said. "Nobody believe I cook on the line, but I was cooking on the line."

Georges had spent the first dinner service moving restlessly around the claustrophobic Le Bec kitchen—seasoning a piece of red mullet, whisking a saffron sauce, keeping himself busy—but some things he could no longer do. Since 1995, when he reached into a Robot Coupe commercial food mixer to change a blade and cut four fingers to the bone, his right hand had given him trouble. Despite four hours of microsurgery and months of rehab, the finer knifework, like cutting the tomato diamonds that accompany his galette de crab, was now beyond him.

And he was lately something of a stranger in his own kitchen. In the spot on the hot line that had always belonged to Georges, Frederic Côte now stood. Georges had hired him away from Daniel Boulud, the renowned New York chef, after a three-hour phone conversation in which he'd sought Boulud's advice, and after Georges's astrologer had concurred that it would be an auspicious hire. Now, when line cooks said "Chef"—which for decades meant Georges—they were looking at his tall, dark-eyed, goateed young successor. As Côte and his crew busily plated updated versions of Le Bec classics as well as such new Côte creations as an olive soup and a potato brûlée, Georges had stood off to one side, sipping at a glass of Vittel water.

On the sidewalk outside Le Bec-Fin, the Pelinos begged Georges to come to their house to see the new kitchen Karen was near completing. After trying out different excuses—"I been up since 5:30." "You don't have any good wine"—Georges relented, but first told how he had come to the rescue at a charity auction at Fort Mifflin the night before. "They couldn't sell shit at that auction," Georges said, "and then they say, 'Georges Perrier, cooking demonstration for 10.'" When it didn't draw the minimum bid of $2,500, Georges upped the ante, saying he'd do it at his home, and for 20 people. That went for $4,000, and then Georges agreed to do another one for the underbidder, for $3,500, raising a total of $7,500.

"They're going to call you St. Georges," Karen Pelino said.

"Georges, that's huge," Clare Pelino said. "That's huge."

"I'm too good," Georges said.

"They should be kissing your feet," Karen Pelino said.

"Yes they should," Georges said, then thought better of it. "They should send me some customer," he said. "That's what they should do."

He got into his Mercedes—his driver had gone AWOL a few days before—and noticed a white slip of paper on the windshield. He had been ticketed on Georges Perrier Place. "That's not right," Georges said. "That's my fucking street. Fucking ticket on my street. Ridiculous I get a ticket. Piss me off." He pulled into traffic, still muttering. "I hate to get ticket. A ticket on my car. Stupid city." He spat out the window. "I'm annoyed. Annoyed. So annoyed. I don't care about the ticket; it's just the principle."

The following night, Georges didn't work in the Le Bec kitchen, on Chef's orders. It was a particularly busy Friday, the first busy night since September 11th—157 covers expected—and Côte had asked him to give the cooks some breathing room. So Georges shuttled restlessly around the restaurant, adjusting the thermostat ("Is it cold?"), giving a young line cook just back from doing a stage in Lyons a punch in the chest ("Do you learn something?"), answering the Le Bec phone ("I should be in reservation business"), and making cameo appearances in the kitchen. ("We busy tonight. ... Fire these fucking people! ... I need pickup! ... Go! Go! ... I hope you have lot of lobster. ... Holy cow! ... Chef, Table 8 is a friend of mine.") Then he switched to front-man mode.

Georges's presence in the Le Bec dining room had long been a part of the restaurant's appeal; people calling to make reservations would demand to know whether he would be there. Tonight, he greeted an Eagles executive, drank champagne with a society couple who'd been coming to his restaurant for years, seasoned the sauce at tableside for a couple of regulars who'd ordered the lobster press, kneaded the shoulders of a longtime customer and offered his recommendation of the lobster and the rabbit, toweled off a vacated table, abused the service bartender ("Your bar is pretty shitty tonight"), and otherwise kept himself busy.

Around 9 p.m., his girlfriend, Andrea, arrived. Tall, dark-haired and 32 years old, she wore a long, sleeveless black astrakhan coat, an expensive-looking silk blouse, and pointy heels. She and Georges embraced and went downstairs to have a glass of wine. They decided to have dinner at the Brasserie.

Domestic happiness was one of the pleasures Georges had sacrificed in his long marriage to the restaurant. He'd been married for 11 years to an American woman—they were divorced in 1982—with whom he'd had a daughter, Genevieve, now 28 and an actress living in Brooklyn. For many years, his relationship with his daughter was strained. Throughout her childhood, he worked from 7 a.m. to 2 a.m. and saw her only on Sundays, except for those occasions when she'd toddle around the restaurant. (Once, she fell into a pot of hot stock; she was immediately plucked out and swaddled in a tablecloth filled with ice.)

Georges felt guilty about the years when he wasn't around to raise Genevieve, and recently they had become very close, having had a candid conversation about Georges's lapses as a father. "I say, 'Za, I feel bad,'" Georges recalled. "'I love you, I always have love you. But I know I have not been a father that you expect, and I'm very proud that you came out the way you are. You are a wonderful daughter. And you have wonderful qualité. And when I have not give you what I can give you, like a normal father can give you, because I wanted to succeed so much, I sacrificed everything for the restaurant, and not enough for my family.' For years, I never took a day off. I worked seven days a week. ... But you know," Georges said now, reflecting on it, "restaurateur life is not a normal life. I don't think so, by any means, you can be a restaurateur and expecting living a normal life, 'cause it's not gonna happen if you care about what you doing." Then he seemed to have doubts again. "Everyone needs a parent when they young," he said.

Georges never remarried. Since his divorce, he'd had a string of young, pretty girlfriends. He seemed to have more in common with Andrea, a culinary-school graduate who once worked in the kitchen of the Four Seasons' Fountain restaurant and now advises wealthy people on their diets. She'd first met

Georges downstairs at the Le Bec bar, and they had been dating since April.

Earlier in the evening, Georges appeared anxious, but Andrea's presence seemed to relax him. As he perused the Brasserie menu, weighing what to have for dinner, Andrea teased him about his eating. "Diet is against my religion," Georges said. They ordered Belon oysters to start, and a basket of bread was put out. Since the opening of Le Mas, Georges's restaurants have made their own bread.

"C'est bon," Georges said.

"C'est très bon," Andrea said.

As they ate, Georges never stopped monitoring the room. From time to time, he got up from his seat and went into the kitchen to yell at the hustling crew—part cheering fan ("Go! Go! Go!"), part galley master ("C'mon. C'mon. Gimme fuckin' food! Pickup!")—before returning to his seat at the bar. Once, when he noticed a family that seemed to need attention, he flagged down the maître d' and asked what was going on. Another time, he left the Brasserie for 20 minutes to go down the street to Le Bec, where a customer was celebrating his 40th birthday in the mezzanine room; there, Georges performed a trick he has done many times, including on *Late Night with David Letterman*, opening a bottle of champagne with a saber in a single stroke.

As he sat with Andrea at the Brasserie bar, she ran her fingers through his hair. He seemed momentarily content. He smoked a Davidoff cigarillo. Around 11 p.m., he rubbed his eyes and said, "I feel very tired." On the TV screen above the bar, a Flyers game had given way to a Dennis Rodman interview. "Look at thees asshole," Georges said to the bartender, who happened to be the brother of actress Kim Delaney. "Patrick, how can a woman go out with a man like this?"

Andrea kissed Georges's forehead. Then he left to look in at Le Mas before going home to sleep.

Sometimes, to get away from the ever-encroaching distractions of his own business, Georges eats down the block from Le Bec at the restaurant of Susanna Foo, who has been highly acclaimed for her singular fusion of French and Asian cuisines. Like Perrier, she has published a glossy coffeetable cookbook. Their restaurants, along with Neil Stein's Striped Bass, are the mainstays of Rittenhouse Row. Unlike Georges, though, Foo has never expanded beyond her one restaurant, and she can still be found in the kitchen every day.

Lunching there a few weeks after his dinner with Andrea, Georges was having trouble finding something on the menu that he wanted to eat. "I cannot have spring roll, it's gonna be too greasy," he said. "Maybe I can have the steamed veal dumpling. I only eat the inside. And maybe I have the Mongolian lamb. And I will told them no, no, no, no nothing on the lamb. Just the lamb."

For three months after his accident, he was unable to exercise at all. He still hadn't been able to resume playing tennis, but in the past month, he had begun working out three times a week with a personal trainer, and three days ago, he'd gone on the Atkins diet. Already he had dropped from 173 to 165, he said, and he wanted to lose at least another seven pounds. "I start feeling better," Georges said, "and I'm start to feel my energy, and I start to feel I can walk again. I feel already I look great." He sucked in his stomach and patted it. "I got a pretty good control of my body," Georges said. "I have no bad habits. Yes, I love wine. That's a habit. I love good wine." He has about 1,200 bottles in his home cellar.

The waiter arrived with appetizers and put them in the wrong places. "No, you got it wrong, sir," Georges said. "Wrong. You could not work for me. Bad."

The waiter corrected his mistake.

"I forgive you," Georges said.

The physical and existential wages of being a chef began when Georges signed on as an apprentice. Born into a bourgeois family in Lyons, the son of a jeweler father and a biologist mother, he deeply upset his parents with his decision, at age 14, to become a chef. He left home and didn't return until his apprenticeship was over, three years later. The apprenticeship was hard. Wake-up was at 5:30 in the morning, and work ended at midnight. The chefs were tough. "They kick your ass, they hit you, they bang you, they dig you," Georges said, sitting on a banquette at Susanna Foo. "It was hard, really really hard. It was bad. It was too bad. I cannot talk nicely about it, because it was not nice." His left wrist still bears the scars of an incident when, late in getting a fire going, he tried to accelerate the process by pouring oil directly onto charcoal, burning himself badly.

Georges weathered additional abuse from his fellow apprentices, who came from working-class backgrounds and resented their middle-class peer. "It was traumatic," Georges recalled. "They have tough time to accept me. And they let me know and make me cause great pain, but I'm not going to discuss here. It was very difficult, and I have to fight very hard to stay. But I prove them wrong, because when the apprenticeship came [to an end], I was the number one apprentice."

Georges then worked at two of the great mid-century restaurants in France. La Pyramide, founded by the legendary Fernand Point in Vienne, was the first restaurant in France to win three stars from Michelin, and before Georges arrived it had already graduated such giants of modern French gastronomy as Paul Bocuse, Roger Vergé and the Troisgros brothers. Georges rose to saucier at the restaurant, then went to work at Oustau de Baumanière, a Michelin three-star in Provence.

Now, at Susanna Foo, he pushed his plate of lamb aside and pulled a gilt Le Bec matchbox from his pocket. The sulfur heads were pinched off, and Georges started picking at his teeth with a matchstick. Foo stopped by the table and asked about the lamb.

"Very good," Georges said, "but I, I, I'm on diet, so ... Wonderful."

"I wish I have a restaurant like this," Georges said, after Foo had walked away, "because, you know, there is five gram of meat." He pointed at the remains of his stir-fry, a hillock of purple cabbage and white disks. "It's only vegetables," he said. "I wish I have a restaurant like this."

He quizzically regarded one of the gummy disks. "What is this?" he said, poking it. "I gotta ask. Is like a starch. What is that?" He pulled at it. "What is that? Is a noodle? Eh?" He took the disk between his fingers and pulled it in opposite directions. "Very starchy. It's like ... élastique. I gotta ask the waiter." He flagged one down and interrogated him. "Thank you," Georges said, satisfied. "Chinese pasta."

Georges likes to stay up-to-date by reading other chefs' cookbooks. He said he admired Chicago chef Charlie Trotter's, and he had read the book by Thomas Keller, chef-owner of the French Laundry, three times. Located in the Napa Valley, the French Laundry, regarded by some critics as the best restaurant in America today, was the one restaurant Georges had never been to that he wanted to visit. "And he's a very nice man," Georges said of Keller. "I never met him, but I know some customer went there, and [he] says, 'We not have the pleasure to have Georges, but you can told him: "We want to thank him he has done what he has done toward the industry. Because of him, this is what we are now."'" That was nice of him. Really very nice man. I have never meet him. I love him."

Patrick Feury, Susanna Foo's chef de cuisine, came over to pay his respects to the master. "How are you," Georges said. "Nice to meet you." Feury mentioned that he'd had dinner at Le Bec a few nights earlier, and it had been wonderful. He was staring at the uneaten food on Georges's plate. "I'm sorry I didn't eat much, because I'm on diet," Georges explained. "And I can only eat meat. And I was afraid to ask to only have meat on my plate."

Georges had arrived at an age of heightened health concerns, and over the summer he'd driven to Washington, along with Jean Banchet, the 61-year-old former owner of Le Francais in Chicago, to visit their friend and fellow chef Jean-Louis Palladin, who lay dying of lung cancer in the hospital. Georges also co-hosted a fund-raiser in New York to help pay Palladin's health-care costs. "It is sad," Georges said, leaning back on the banquette. "Great chef. Great talent. You know, I think I learned that you have to enjoy the life. All the bullshit that we have every day means nothing. It means absolutely nothing. Today you are here, and tomorrow you can leave. So you gotta take the life a little bit not so seriously, much more relax."

"I'm sorry I didn't eat much," Georges said, on the street outside Susanna Foo. "But ... they were five gram of Jamison lamb. How much they charge for that? It was prix fixe? Five gram of meat." He chuckled at the thought.

The next Tuesday morning, around 7 a.m., Georges arrived at Pennock flower wholesalers in Germantown. He was with his assistant Liliane and Jean Banchet. Before Banchet left the kitchen of Le Francais a few years ago, it had five Mobil stars. Banchet and Georges are best friends; they talk every day on the phone. Now, Banchet was staying at Georges's house for two weeks. He had short black hair and a goatee. On this morning, he was wearing a black knit sweatsuit and Nike cross-trainers, while Georges wore baggy jeans, an untucked Academy of Music t-shirt and a blue fleece jacket.

Ever since Georges had decided he could save money by doing the flowers at his restaurants himself, he'd been spending a full day each week personally buying and arranging them. But Liliane was clearly in charge of the operation. At the Pennock warehouse, she gave Jean and Georges errands, and they went off to freezer rooms to count out roses and orchids and birds-of-paradise. Nicolas Fanucci, the manager at Le Bec, showed up to help transport the flowers, and everyone scattered. Nicolas took a carful to Le Bec, Liliane drove a load to Brasserie, and Jean Banchet and Georges got into Georges's silver Pathfinder and made the delivery to Le Mas. Then they headed for Center City.

They were having fun. As they passed a road crew on a tree-lined back road, Georges eyed a worker standing idle. The worker was dark-skinned and had a wispy beard. "Are you terroriste?" Georges asked through the glass, cackling madly. "He look like terroriste," Jean agreed, laughing. When they got into town, Georges went off to Le Bec to arrange flowers, while Banchet headed to Tower Records.

Later, Banchet arrived first for lunch at Brasserie. During his fortnight here, he would talk to Georges' chefs and managers, eat at his restaurants, spend time in his kitchens, then report to Georges. But his friendly advice extended to all areas of Georges's life, including romance. "I think he miss somebody at home," Banchet said. "He have to have somebody he love at home. This is what I think is most important." Banchet had been married to the same woman for decades; she'd run the front of the house at Le Francais. "You know," he said, "if you have nobody at home, you go home, you watch TV, you read the newspaper. This is boring, you know what I mean? Nobody to talk with." Banchet said he wanted to protect Georges. "I don't know if Andrea is the right one," Banchet said. "I don't know. I say: Find somebody simple, modest, low-key, which is not after your money. When they see all this, they see the house, they see the restaurants, I'm sure they say, 'Jeez, I don't have to work anymore.' I tell him: 'Don't look always for beautiful.' He like these young chick looks like a hooker."

When Georges arrived for lunch, he was clearly stressed. Sitting at the table with his friend Jean and his assistant Liliane, he squeezed his eyes shut, winched his head around on his neck, chain-smoked Davidoffs, and nervously worked a matchstick in his teeth. Liliane solicitously put a hand on his cheek. Georges and Liliane and Jean were speaking among themselves in French when a new waiter walked past. Georges asked who he was, and upon learning that he was working part-time at Stephen Starr's Alma de Cuba, next door, said: "Wonderful. Give him a job. Take him out of there. Take him out of there. Come here."

The waiter took a few tentative steps forward, and Georges began grilling him: Was Alma busy? During the week? It was? "Hmm," Georges said. "I'm impress. I'm very impress that so many people like starches." The Nuevo Latino cuisine of Alma de Cuba makes generous use of starchy fruits and root vegetables like yuca and taro and plantain. "I don't like starches," Georges said. "What, you gotta have everything for everybody? Only starches. How many starches." His face twisted into a sneer, and his voice turned demonic. "More starches!" he shrieked, pounding the table. "Get me more starches!"

A waiter took dessert orders.

"Starches, eh?" Georges said, having trouble letting go of the topic. Then he abruptly changed tones again. "No, no," he said, "it's a great restaurant. I like the restaurant. It's good." He chuckled darkly. Georges was upset because he had heard that Starr had described Le Bec-Fin as "stale" to a former Le Bec chef applying for a job.

"Steve Starr," Georges said, "Steve Starr." He chewed on the name as if it might be a rancid piece of meat. He was getting worked up. Suddenly he held up an index finger, and his eyes seemed to lock onto something no one else could see. "I declare war on Steve Starr!" he announced. Jean and Liliane were silent. "I don't give a shit," Georges continued. "It's true. It's a war. It's a fucking war. I declare the war! It's a war!"

He placed his declaration squarely in an honorable gastronomic tradition, invoking the feuds of his mentor, Paul Bocuse, who had once dismissed chef Alain Ducasse as a souped-up BMW beside his own well-engineered Mercedes. Of Michel Guerard, pioneer of a lighter, more diet-conscious style of French cooking dubbed "cuisine minceur," Bocuse snipped: "I'm a chef, not a doctor."

For 30 years, Georges had waged relentless war against imperfection and inconsistency, maintaining Le Bec as the longest-running act in French-American gastronomy. Now, he was fighting to reclaim Le Bec's fifth star, and in December, *Esquire* would name Le Mas Perrier one of the 23 best new restaurants in the country (which wouldn't stop Georges from firing its chef shortly after the magazine hit newsstands). Georges wasn't about to raise the white flag for a local theme-restaurant impresario.

"I think it's not fair for Steve Starr to say that to one of my chef," Georges said. "I really do. Because it reflect on me." Why not call Starr and clear the air? "Listen," Georges said, minutes after declaring jihad. "You want me to start a war? I start a war if I start to say something. I will have more enemies than I have friend. You know how many enemies I have? They hates my guts. Everybody hate my guts." Georges sucked in the last of his cigarillo, pressed it out in an ashtray, and went upstairs to continue making beautiful flower arrangements.

Published January 2002

Côte lasted barely 15 months in Le Bec-Fin's kitchens. In the summer of 2002, 32-year-old Cherry Hill native Daniel Stern, who had earned acclaim at L'Espinasse, Daniel, Mercer Kitchen, and the Ritz-Carlton at Half Moon Bay replaced him as Le Bec's executive chef. In addition to putting an American in the kitchen, Perrier hired a young sommelier, Gregory Castells, to revamp and expand Le Bec's wine cellar, and undertook a half-million-dollar renovation of the Walnut Street restaurant, replacing even the stemware. The drastic measures worked: Three years after Le Bec-Fin lost its fifth Mobil Star, it regained the honor, in January 2003—and retained it in January 2004. That month, Perrier fired Stern and announced his decision to return to Le Bec-Fin as executive chef.

The Last Neil Stein Story

Neil Stein says he isn't guilty. Neil Stein says he'll be fine. Neil Stein says he can beat this—the $6.7 million in debt, the criminal investigation, the pills. But does anyone believe what Neil Stein says anymore?

By Stephen Rodrick

hen Neil Stein betrayed the fish man, it was over. Restaurants, fortunes, wives, partners and drug addictions would come, go, and come again. The only constant was the fish. And for Neil Stein, that was just fine. He isn't a man who likes to listen. Besides, as he once told a friend, the fish never talk back. Fish made him money. Fish made him sexy. Fish made him a rock star.

It started when he was a boy. Fish as theater. Neil Stein watched his father grab carp right behind the eyes with his bare hands. It was a daily performance at Fruit Basket, the family's Mount Airy fish and produce shop. The child of two orphans, Neil Stein couldn't count on much. One thing he knew: It was the fish that allowed his father to gamble. It was the fish that gave his father an identity. In 1974, Stein took Dad's vision and opened Fish Market. It seems so simple now—fresh fish brought to a town accustomed to breaded and frozen.

Unfortunately for Neil Stein, there's more to life than fish. Eventually, he lost Fish Market, Rock Lobster and several other restaurants. There were two failed marriages. Kids who wouldn't talk to him. A coke problem. Partners who wanted out. Ten years ago, at 52, Neil Stein was living in a bare studio apartment. When he moved, he took along the shower curtain. He couldn't afford a new one.

And then, miraculously, fish saved him, rescued him from a life of oblivion where Prada and Armani would not grace his body. People came to Striped Bass for the fish, and they came in droves. In 1994, *Esquire* named Stein's baby one of America's top new restaurants. Seven million dollars poured in that year. Stein even turned down the President—said he didn't want to disappoint customers who'd made their reservations long before Bill and his Secret Service crew came to town.

Fish gave Neil Stein everything. Fish gave him the Porsche, the Rittenhouse Square apartment, the courtside Sixers tickets, the month-long vacation in St. Barths, and the omnipresent designer sunglasses. The fish paid for the Percocets he popped like Chiclets. The fish financed the spending sprees at Wayne Edwards and Barneys.

And it was the fish man who made it possible. Tony McCarthy was a man of few words, but those few words were bankable. It was Tony McCarthy, stand-up Jersey guy, who had the connections. McCarthy knew the Mainers seeking swordfish in the *Perfect Storm* waters off Newfoundland. It was Tony McCarthy who knew the Japanese trawler captains. They told McCarthy, who told Stein, about the bluefin tuna that the Spanish captured and kept in water cages. During mating season, the tuna would go crazy with hunger. The fishermen would feed them endlessly—the mariner equivalent of foie gras. Striped Bass was the only restaurant in America that bought the bluefin tuna whole, making Striped Bass's cuts the freshest in all the land. It was Tony McCarthy who let Neil Stein sell bluefin for $45 a pop. McCarthy filleted the fish at 5:30 in the morning, just as Stein drifted into an alcohol-soaked sleep.

Then Neil Stein got bored and forgot his past. All restaurateurs have megalomania coursing through their veins. They forget the defeats and remember only the glorious achievements. And Stein had more than a little Napoleon in him. He opened Bleu, a Rittenhouse Square competitor to his own restaurant Rouge, with a ridiculous kitchen setup that guaranteed pilferage and mediocrity. And then there was Avenue B, Neil Stein's Waterloo and Russian winter swirled into one soufflé of a disaster.

Avenue B opened on the Avenue of the Arts amid the Kimmel Center construction dust. The concept was all attention-deficit-disorder: giant Bordeaux clocks on the walls with an all-Italian wine list. An ever-changing menu with chefs-of-the-month. The guy with the golden touch was suddenly losing $60,000 a week. Stein thrashed like a drowning man. He hung a ghoulish series of semi-nude lithographs of Marilyn Monroe on the walls. Fittingly, it was her last photo shoot before she died.

Still, Neil Stein could bullshit. He's one of the great bullshitters of all time. He bullshitted the loan arm of the Delaware River Port Authority into giving him two $400,000 loans, money collected from area taxpayers for 266,667 trips across the bridges. The second came in November of 2002, after other banks were calling in their loans. He bullshitted busboys and sous-chefs into forgiving rubber paychecks while he frolicked in the Caribbean. He bullshitted so well that even *Daily News* editor Zack Stalberg bought his act and wrote an editorial column calling on the city and Stein's vendors to forgive his sins.

But it all fell apart when he tried to bullshit the fish man. As 2003 began, Tony McCarthy was owed in the low six figures. And if Tony McCarthy didn't get paid, there was a good chance he was going under. In early February, as McCarthy tells the story, he picked up the phone and reached the increasingly elusive Neil Stein.

"Neil, I need a check or I can't make payroll," said McCarthy.

"I understand. I'll have accounting cut you a check on Monday," said Stein.

Come Monday, there was no check. Tony McCarthy called Neil Stein's accountant.

"I have no authorization to cut you a check," the accountant said.

Silence filled the phone line. The fish man was at a loss.

"Where's Neil?" he asked.

"He's left for St. Barths."

Finally, the fish man was pissed. He slammed down the phone. The accountant reached Stein at his $1,500-a-day St. Barths villa, resplendent with its own pool and stunning ocean views. Stein called McCarthy back.

"We had an agreement," McCarthy said.

"What agreement?" Stein asked.

"You are a crazy man," McCarthy said, and hung up the phone. He immediately canceled the order.

Neil Stein flew back to Philadelphia. It's a testament to his bullshitting skills that McCarthy reconsidered and continued selling him fish. But it was too late. The rest of Neil Stein's world was crumbling around him. He was about to lose everything.

In March, three of Neil Stein's restaurants declared bankruptcy. Court documents show they owe $6.7 million in back taxes and debts to various employees and creditors, including Metrocorp, which owns *Philadelphia* magazine and whose COO is chair of the unsecured creditors committee for the bankruptcy. (He was not a source for this story.) In May, Avenue B shut its doors; Stein's employees never received their last checks. Then he completed the cliché: He checked himself into the Caron Foundation, Liza Minnelli's favorite rehab, for a $17,500 four-week stay. Tony McCarthy survived, barely. He's still owed more than six figures by Stein. He now sells fish to the creditors who run Striped Bass. He's paid cash on delivery.

A month ago, Striped Bass chef Terence Feury departed. While Stein and his partner, Donald Brody, attempt to devise a plan that will allow them to bring Striped Bass out of bankruptcy, how long it will be before the fabled restaurant closes or is sold is an open question.

And that may be the good news. On May 20th, agents from the Internal Revenue Service criminal division raided Stein's 15th and Walnut office, seizing records, according to court documents, "relating to allegations of tax violations, mail fraud, wire fraud, and bankruptcy fraud."

Shortly after Neil Stein emerges from the Caron Foundation, he is holding court at Rouge. As part of the bankruptcy agreement, Stein is now an employee at the restaurants he once owned. Already, when he requested a salary of $250,000 a year, Judge Kevin Carey slapped it down to a third of that. He holds no keys. He signs no checks. He is dressed in a checked Paul Smith shirt, and sips a cranberry juice. As usual, the hair is gelled back, displaying a terminally pink forehead destined never to recover from a thousand sunburns. His citrusy scent is the usual—Pomegranate, a $50-a-bottle women's perfume available from the boutique Fresh. His goutish right ankle has left him stepping gingerly.

The cramped bar is hopping. It is full of tired, sunburned middle-aged men; suave Euro-types; and, as Stein often describes them, 21-year-old girls not wearing panties. Tonight, Neil Stein doesn't show any humility. Instead, he shakes hands with a politician's smile, his eyes always on the next suitor. He whispers conspiratorially, "I was taking 60 Percocet a day. But now I'm ready to rock. I can beat this."

Of course, any doctor will tell you that 60 Percocet a day would kill a horse, much less a 140-pound man. But Neil Stein has always been the master of the exaggerated gesture. That's what makes him a success at selling a $6 piece of fish for $45. The next morning, Neil Stein sits at his regular table at the Rittenhouse Hotel's Lacroix. He dines on fruit, cereal, and the omnipresent cranberry juice. His Armani jacket lies on a nearby chair. Perhaps out of sympathy, the kitchen comps his breakfast. Stein is a little more subdued, but still defiant.

"Am I trying to say 'Fuck you' to the feds?" he asks rhetorically. "I would never say that."

He stares out across the Square toward Rouge. A few blocks away on Broad Street, auctioneers clean up after a public sale of Avenue B's equipment. "I totally believe that people who are guilty should pay the price," says Stein.

"But I also totally believe that I'm not guilty of anything." For once, Neil Stein takes off his sunglasses. He repeats himself: "Of anything."

Neil Stein is his father's son. Moe Stein was a fish man, and a sharp dresser. At the Fruit Basket, Moe would reach into the tank and pull out a carp. The hard-to-please Jewish ladies would appraise each fish like a fine jewel. They would hem and haw. Moe would roll his eyes. Then they would take the carp home and create gefilte fish, and everyone was happy. But Moe was also a chronic gambler who pissed away the Fruit Basket's profits on the ponies. When he died, there was nothing left. His only son seems hell-bent on being both better and worse than his father.

After a brief dalliance with minor-league baseball, Stein entered the restaurant business. In 1965, he borrowed five grand from a family friend to open Mimi Says, a Cheltenham supper club named after his first daughter. Not that he saw his little girl much. Just like his old man, Stein was a natural. His customers adored him. And just like his old man, Neil Stein was a natural fuckup. Married at 22 to Angel Milou, he had a son, Eric, and Mimi before he was 25. A lover of cards and the more-than-occasional wager on Eagles games, Stein took an impromptu four-day trip to Las Vegas in 1968 without informing Angel, who was caring for their infant son, Perry. When Stein got back, she gave him the boot.

What followed would become a pattern. Stein left—or was asked by a partner to leave—Mimi Says. Soon, the money was gone. His V-12-powered Jag was repossessed. For a few years, he scraped by with a catering business. Then, in 1973, he opened Fish Market, a homage to his father. Moe was going to be a partner, but he died on the first day of construction—Yom Kippur, the Day of Atonement. Still, there was Stein, just like his dad, cutting fish right in front of the customers. Retail and sit-down.

Located at 18th and Sansom, Fish Market was huge. In addition to fresh-off-the-boat seafood, Neil Stein brought something else to Philadelphia: dining as theatre. Food was cooked in an open kitchen. Patrons dined happily in a culinary ER resplendent with chefs screaming for more flounder and waitresses dodging and weaving through sizzle and smoke.

Stein rode the wave for a few years. He fathered another child, Maggie, with his second wife, Cindi. Again, he saw little of them. As with his dad, the dollars seemed to just slip away. His problem wasn't horses, though, or the Eagles, or cards. No, his loss leader was cocaine. Through the last half of the '70s and first years of the '80s, Neil Stein had a raging drug problem. His blue eyes often seemed at cross purposes. He started wearing his shades full-time. Everyone knew what was happening. His servers knew it. His customers knew it. Eventually, it cost Stein everything. Fish Market. Another wife.

In 1982, he came clean and got clean. Or partially. Stein bragged about doing it alone; no need for rehab or a 12-step program. In reality, he just substituted. Instead of snorting coke, he redoubled his martini consumption.

For Stein, this was progress. The rest of the '80s were relatively productive; his partnership with the Marabellas, the prominent Philadelphia restaurant family, led to a successful chain of Italian restaurants. But there was another falling-out, settled with the Marabellas writing Stein a check for $180,000. He used the money to buy a share of Rock Lobster, a merging of the Fish Market concept with a disco. Somehow, it worked. And, somehow, Neil Stein pissed off his partners. They bought him out.

Then he received a call from an old friend. Joe Wolf and Neil Stein went way back, to the sandlots of Mount Airy. Years after that, it was Stein who advised Wolf when he opened the Corned Beef Academy in the mid-'70s. Casting about for a new idea, Wolf heard that the owners of a building on the Ben Franklin Parkway were looking for a restaurant to serve as its anchor.

After his cocaine problems and multiple financial failings, Neil Stein wasn't exactly a good credit risk. That's where Joe Wolf came in—solid Joe Wolf, wearing a bow tie and meeting with the bankers. Meanwhile, Neil Stein worked on the concept. As usual, he had a good one.

Fish, nothing but fish.

It almost didn't happen. When negotiations for the space at 2601 Parkway failed, Neil Stein should have panicked. For him, cuisine and locale were inextricably linked. Grafting the Striped Bass idea onto another location was unnatural. But Stein and Marguerite "Meg" Rodgers, who has designed all but one of his ventures for two decades, stayed the course. A massive space was located at 1500 Walnut, a then-decrepit no-fly zone in Center City. Stein fell in love with its sheer scale—the 25-foot ceilings, the Moorish-themed architecture. As Rodgers set about designing Striped Bass, she kept one concept in her head: escapism. Inside Striped Bass—and not much has changed aesthetically over the past decade—something happens. It evokes a sense of serenity, of safety. The space transcends Philadelphia, or any city, for that matter. It feels as if a Demerol drip has just been attached to your central nervous system.

The space wasn't the only star. Passing over countless better-qualified chefs, Stein hired attractive, 31-year-old Alison Barshak, who had relatively little experience with seafood. "It doesn't matter," Stein told Wolf—and anyone who would listen. "I've got a drop-dead redhead. She's got it."

The restaurant was an immediate hit. There was the space, the fish—courtesy of Tony McCarthy—the sexy chef. With his cuisine, locale, partner, and chef in place, Neil Stein had everything he needed.

Except for the right clothes. Shortly before Striped Bass opened, with Joe Wolf's financial help, Stein moved into a Center City studio with his shower curtain and a few Italian suits, but just a few. Lacking funds, Neil Stein got creative. One Monday, he showed up in new duds. Joe Wolf wondered where the money came from. A month later, he figured it out. He opened Striped Bass's American Express bill and saw high charges to clothier Wayne Edwards. He confronted Stein.

"I have to look the part," explained Stein. "Don't worry, the money will come."

The money did come. *Esquire* named Striped Bass America's best new restaurant. You couldn't touch a table on a Saturday night unless you called six months in advance. In its first year, the restaurant grossed $7 million. Stein hobnobbed with the glitterati; he comped Bill Cosby so often that the comedian threatened not to return unless he could pay for a meal. Barshak courted the media, who ate up her hair and sound bites. Meanwhile, steady Joe Wolf tended the early crowd and monitored the books. Life was good.

Of course, that always made Neil Stein itchy.

To get to St. Barthélemy, whether you are a Rockefeller or Bill Gates, you have to take a 10-minute prop flight from nearby St. Martin. No jets are allowed. Only two and a half miles wide and 11 miles long, the island is home to scantily clad women and foie gras in almost equal amounts. It is Provence with palm trees.

For the very rich, there are the villas at the Hotel Le Toiny, the most exclusive hotel on the most exclusive island in the Caribbean. That's where Neil Stein wanted to stay. Situated on a bluff high above the ocean, Hotel Le Toiny has just 13 cottages, each with its own pool. Princess Di was turned down twice. She called too late. Gwyneth and Brad made it in (probably to Mr. Pitts's dismay; the paparazzi captured him, nude, on their balcony). In the morning, young men in starched white shorts and shirts set fine china on linen-covered tables next to the pool. For dinner, there's a five-star restaurant.

Neil Stein discovered St. Barths a quarter-century ago, and was seduced by its beaches, topless women and cuisine. He has been a guest at Hotel Le Toiny's villas since they opened a decade ago. For him, up to $1,500 a night was a slight price to pay for paradise. He would enjoy a luxurious breakfast, then jump into his Jeep and hit the beach. He also had his cell phone nearby. He'd call back to Philadelphia to check on reservations and kibitz with reporters. At night, he wined, dined, and danced on the tables at Le Gaïac, the island's coolest al fresco restaurant.

At first it was for two weeks, then three. Eventually, Neil Stein would spend the entire month of February on St. Barths. He and his current flame would tan and eat, while he took notes on St. Barths's restaurants, looking for ideas he could bring back home.

Back in cold, damp Philadelphia, it was the winter of 1997. People wondered how Neil Stein paid for his $30,000 vacation. After all, he was only drawing a salary of $250,000 before taxes. A month on St. Barths was a Rockefeller vacation, not one for a Philly restaurateur who rented his apartment.

For three years, Striped Bass had thrived. And thanks in part to Neil Stein, the neighborhood around the restaurant came back to life. Sure, there were bumps. In June of 1996, Alison Barshak departed, resigning by note. Stein and Wolf felt jilted, so they hired her ex-husband, Will Ternay, as the new chef.

The prim and proper Wolf had managed the books while Neil Stein gladhanded and kept his eyes on aesthetics, telling every woman who entered Striped Bass how beautiful she was. Round and round Wolf and Stein went. Stein wanted $12 cocktail glasses; Wolf pleaded for cheaper ones. Stein told Wolf he didn't understand. People came for the glamour and the fish. They didn't want to drink $12 martinis out of cheap glasses. Invariably, Stein won. And every month, Wolf would do the books. He would find lavish charges on the corporate credit card. Joe Wolf wanted out.

After three years, Wolf and Stein agreed their partnership was doomed. It was decided that whoever could raise the $800,000 buyout price first got Striped Bass. Conventional wisdom had Wolf raising the cash. Undoubtedly, Stein would move on to another concept.

The opposite happened. During the early Striped Bass years, an aged man would hobble into the restaurant. He wasn't a face. He wasn't a lawyer. All the waitstaff knew was what Neil Stein told them: Whatever Donald Brody wants, Donald Brody gets. Donald Brody wants lobster brought to his home, you do it. Eventually, they would learn that Donald Brody owns the Philadelphia Ticket Exchange, a prosperous business that has been selling Eagles and theater tickets above face value for 50 years. In his 70s, the jowly and stooped

Brody had been recently widowed and ran the business with his daughter. For Brody, Neil Stein was like a son. He had been friends with Moe Stein since the '50s and had known Neil since he was 11. After a series of conversations, Donald Brody became Neil Stein's sugar daddy. Agreeing to be the quietest of silent partners, Brody put up $800,000. Money in hand, Stein called Wolf. They arranged for a 6 p.m. meeting in the alley behind Striped Bass. When Stein told Wolf he had the money, Joe Wolf's eyes nearly bolted from their sockets.

Neil Stein wasn't through. With the Wolf buyout, Neil Stein gained control of Striped Bass. Now, Neil Stein could use the fish as collateral.

At first, the Striped Bass staff was overjoyed that Neil Stein had triumphed. Joe Wolf was a nice guy, but his dirty jokes and his wife's outdated gowns didn't lend Striped Bass the élan it needed to survive as a destination restaurant. Stein, in his Armani suits and sunglasses, was the showman. He knew people demanded theater at $100 a meal. And he gave it to them in spades.

However, Stein's one-on-one TLC didn't translate to the books. At most restaurants, senior staffers see monthly profit-and-loss statements. This allows them to understand where money is being wasted and take steps to bring costs under control. Under Stein's stewardship, that didn't happen, according to some upper-level employees. They say he zealously guarded financial statements, which Stein denies. General managers and chefs were left guessing which wines and dishes were best for the bottom line. Still, Stein would curse at them to cut costs. Managers joked that Stein loved telling them they were on the wrong road, then placing blindfolds on their heads and urging them to find the right road or else.

Stein didn't care. In 1997, while vacationing on Martha's Vineyard, he got a phone call: The wine store on Rittenhouse Square was closing. He flew back immediately. For years, Stein had had a vision for the wine store's location: a full-menu French bistro that would use the Square as an asset. Impossible, people told him. The space is too small. Where's the kitchen? Once a bar is installed, where will people sit?

Neil Stein said they would sit outside. As at Fish Market and Striped Bass, he conjured a concept that only appeared self-evident after its completion. Philly's mid-Atlantic climate made al fresco dining—with a little help from God and heating lamps—a seven-months-a-year proposition. Still, in 1998, there wasn't an outdoor table to be found in town. Stein thought that was idiotic. He skirted oh-so-close to the six-feet-of-sidewalk city ordinance. Not happy with the texture of the cement outside the restaurant he called Rouge, Stein simply poured his own, without pesky permits.

To Stein, it was simple: Pound the square peg into the round hole. Meg Rodgers constructed the bar using wood a quarter-inch thinner than usual; multiply that all around, and another body could be squeezed in. The tiny kitchen was a wedged-in cave. Striped Bass sommelier Marnie Old came up with a lean bar list for the limited shelf space. Want unusual vodka? Too bad. Go to a less fabulous place.

Again, it worked. From the day it opened, Rouge was packed. Neil Stein had gambled and won once more.

Unfortunately, he tried to go home again. In 1999, he reached 58, the same age as Moe Stein when he died. In a slice of kismet, Stein noticed that 122 18th Street, the original home to Fish Market, was vacant. He set out to reopen the space as a raw bar. Just like the old days, you could buy fresh fish retail or sit down for a meal.

Maybe it was fate; maybe it was the fortress-like doors that confronted customers. After six weeks, the fish counter was gone. The restaurant lingered for 18 months, but the resurrected Fish Market was terminal. Stein didn't really seem to care. When it closed in 2001, he dispatched a lackey to inform the staff. Remarkably, the fish had failed him. By then, Neil Stein's attention was elsewhere.

If one could point to a moment when Neil Stein lost his touch, it might have been on a blustery day in the fall of 2000. With Fish Market struggling, he grew restless for another project. He acquired space on the ground floor of the Sheraton Rittenhouse Hotel, just a block down from Rouge. For Stein, it was a no-brainer. Like Rouge, the space had a liquor license, frontage on the Square, inviting windows, and potential for outdoor seating. The longtime Francophile decided he would call it Bleu. Early in the construction process, a staffer paid a visit along with Hope Cohen, Stein's girlfriend. The more the staffer saw, the more agitated she became. "There is no way this can be a full-service restaurant," she said. "Someone has got to tell Neil. This is insane."

While the space had many superficial similarities to Rouge, there were significant differences. Rent at Bleu was nearly twice that at Rouge. Additionally, if the logistics at Rouge were difficult, those at Bleu were impossible. As his chef, Stein hired Shola Olunloyo, a precocious veteran of Le Bec-Fin and Blue Angel. Olunloyo designed a Le Bec-Fin-style kitchen for a diner-sized space.

While there was a floor-mounted stockpot and an eight-burner range, there was no room for dishwashing. Dishes would have to be rolled through the Sheraton's lobby to a common area, where they would be washed and com-mingled with room-service silverware, guaranteeing loss and delay. The grand kitchen also forced salad and dessert prep to be out of the chef's sight and control. Finally, the prep kitchen—where vegetables are cleaned—was in a different time zone. To get there, you had to go to the other side of the lobby and down two floors by freight elevator.

Aesthetically, there was the wart of a giant HVAC conduit in the middle of the restaurant. Not only was it a blight to be navigated around; it forced the bar to be designed with patrons' backs to the Square, the restaurant's pur-ported calling card. But Stein moved ahead anyway.

During her early visit, the staffer railed at Cohen for half an hour. In the end, Cohen just smiled. "This isn't our call," she said. "It has already been decided."

"Decided by who?" asked the staffer. "Where is it ordained that this has to be a full-service restaurant? By God?"

Unfortunately, God was occupied elsewhere. He'd fallen in love again, this time with a Spruce and Broad corner slot that had already claimed two restau-rants. That didn't dampen Neil Stein's enthusiasm. After all, he hadn't been involved. Even more than Striped Bass, Stein saw what he would name Avenue B as his legacy. Situated next door to the under-construction Kimmel Center, Avenue B, in his dream, was the anchor for the transformation of Broad Street to the much classier Avenue of the Arts.

However, with rent on the space a staggering $45,000 a month, Stein couldn't do it alone. Over a long lunch at Striped Bass, he persuaded Donald Brody to invest. He then enlisted Gabriel Marabella as a partner. Marabella's participation was odd. There had been bad blood when the Marabella family severed its relationship with Stein in the '80s. But Gabe Marabella was a con-genial man, and he had one quality that Neil Stein loved: money.

In January of 2001, Avenue B opened. After a few days, something strange happened. Nobody came. Philadelphia is a peculiar dining town. In New York, walking six blocks to hit a cool new place is nothing. But in Philadel-phia, persuading diners to take the 10-minute stroll from Rittenhouse Square to Avenue B was a daunting challenge. Not that the restaurant's schizophrenic appearance helped. While the menu boasted ultra-modern Italian, the decor was vaguely Asian, with some startling exceptions. As soon as the restaurant opened, critical praise was heaped on Old's all-Italian wine list. However, two giant clocks with the name BORDEAUX stamped in huge letters contradicted that.

Long a fan of New York's Gramercy Tavern, Stein attempted a similar two-menu plan—one for the bar, one for the dining room. Unfortunately, unlike the Gramercy Tavern, the space in Avenue B wasn't differentiated enough to justify the bother. Diners complained about not being able to order the calamari they could see on someone else's table 15 feet away. Stein also hoped to duplicate the outdoor dining of Rouge. However, on the first day of al fresco dining at Avenue B, dust from construction at the Kimmel Center forced him to comp everyone's meals. By the summer of 2001, the place was losing $60,000 a week.

Even before Avenue B's opening, Stein's empire was rotting from within. Court records show that his restaurants owed hundreds of thousands of dollars in liquor taxes and penalties from as far back as 1998. A disgruntled employee supposedly called the U.S. Department of Labor in 2000, alleging that Stein owed him and many others back pay. In September 2002, the wage and hour division of the Department of Labor ordered Stein to pay back wages and penalties totaling $55,379.41. Some employees say they've been paid in full. Others say they received some checks, but that they stopped coming. Stein says he's still paying but that he never did anything wrong to justify the investigation in the first place.

Avenue B just made matters worse. After a while, employees found their checks bouncing. This became such a problem that senior managers began paying employees their wages out of the cash till, with a $25 bonus for the inconvenience. The bounced checks took a human toll. A line chef says he saw two mortgage checks bounce, and his credit rating drop. At Avenue B, some senior staffers had to lend one employee cash so she could buy formula for her child. Frustrated managers say they begged Stein to clue them in on the company's financial condition so they could strategize how to reduce costs. Relations with longtime vendors also soured. As the restaurants fell further behind in their payments, the quality of produce and other goods started to deteriorate. Reasoning that the vendors were saving their best goods for paying customers, one ex-manager says, he began whispering to the vendors to demand cash on delivery.

And Rittenhouse Square regulars began noticing a change in Neil Stein. For years, a wineglass had been as much a part of his persona as the sunglasses. But this was different. He was slurring words, not making any sense. That was the pills.

Two decades ago, Stein started taking Percocet, a powerful painkiller, for a cut arm he suffered in the Bahamas. He quickly got hooked. Whenever he could, Stein convinced doctors to write him prescriptions. When he couldn't, he bought the drug on the street. Over the years, Stein would kick the habit, but by 2002, he was back to taking pills on a daily basis.

Meanwhile, things at Avenue B were getting downright weird. Stein bought a $30,000 Steinway piano without consulting his style guru, Meg Rodgers. Employees entered Avenue B one summer day and found a giant life-size poster of punk queen Grace Jones on the back wall of the restaurant. Horrified, the staffers convinced Stein's girlfriend, Cohen, to have him take it down.

Rumors swept Stein's inner circle that he was again using drugs. Meanwhile, the banks were growing impatient. In October of 2001, Hudson United Bank filed suit, claiming that Stein had defaulted on a $1.3 million loan by missing six straight payments.

Then Neil Stein caught a break. The Delaware River Port Authority had created a business-loan program administered by the Philadelphia Industrial Development Corporation. In 2001, Stein hosted some PIDC honchos at Avenue B and asked for a handout. One observer says that when a PIDC official dared to state the obvious—the huge risks of loaning money to a foundering restaurant—Stein grew angry, pounding the table with his fist, yelling, "Neil Stein is important to this town! If I go down, it can be on your heads." Stein calls this account "utter bullshit."

Through bravado or not, in October of 2001, Neil Stein received a $400,000 loan courtesy of area taxpayers. The loan with Hudson United was brought up to date. In July of 2002, he threw an extravagant wedding at the Four Seasons for his beautiful daughter Maggie, the only one of his four children with whom he has had a sustained positive relationship. And in February, Stein left for St. Barths and the Hotel Le Toiny.

The loan only bought Neil Stein time. The year 2002 was a long, slow death march. One ex-employee says that when he filed for unemployment, he was told the state had no record of his employment; if that's true, it would indicate that Stein withheld unemployment taxes but didn't pay them to the state. Stein says unemployment taxes were "absolutely paid to the state" and that he did nothing wrong.

In the spring, a manager informed Donald Brody of concerns about the company's bookkeeping methods. When word leaked back to Stein, the manager says, he was fired. Avenue B continued to gush red ink. Between menu and chef changes, the critically acclaimed wine list was junked. It was just as well. Due to unpaid vendors, favorite wines disappeared. The list dwindled to a point where servers were embarrassed to hand it out.

Last December, Stein hired PR maven Steven Grasse to throw a relaunch party. The theme was "The Rat Pack." The "showgirls" were moonlighting Delilah's Den strippers. It all seemed very 1997. A well-coiffed Stein worked the room like a nervous used-car salesman trying to peddle a Ford Pinto. The crowd was a slew of late-middle-aged couples wearing last year's styles. It was a creepy indication of how unhip Neil Stein had become.

Stein's personal life continued to careen along. In February, he was walking his boxer, Striper, on Walnut Street when he bumped into a stranger. Stein claims the man began cursing him. In the tussle, the man bit Stein's left thumb down to the bone. Bleeding profusely, Stein chased the man into Barnes & Noble. A side treat to Stein's subsequent hospitalization was another prescription for Percocet, to be coupled with his drinking. The already skeletal Stein began losing weight dramatically. He was in no condition to deal with a collapsing empire.

Remarkably, despite common knowledge of the restaurant's sickly status, the PIDC loaned Avenue B another $400,000 in November of 2002. But no amount of governmental largesse could save Neil Stein. In December, he may have sensed this; in a flurry of confusing transactions that the federal trustee characterized in the bankruptcy proceedings as "insider payments that raise serious questions and concerns," the trustee says that Stein moved more than $150,000 from his troubled restaurants to Meal Ticket Inc., the managing corporation for the restaurants. There, the money would be outside the immediate reach of any creditor suing a particular restaurant. On December 6th, Avenue B paid $34,410 in "rent reimbursement" to Meal Ticket. Between December 13th and December 20th, another $113,279 was transferred from Striped Bass to the Meal Ticket coffers, in part for management fees. On December 16th, Rouge paid Meal Ticket Inc. $4,850.20 in management fees. During the previous year, there were other transactions that the federal trustee describes as "troubling." Rouge directly paid Stein another $10,825.

In the early months of 2003, it all fell apart. In mid-January, around the same time that Stein boarded a plane for St. Barths, the Court of Common Pleas ordered him to pay another $1.36 million in back taxes. He didn't come back from the Caribbean until his conversation with the fish man, Tony McCarthy.

By then, it was much, much too late. On March 10th, after huddling with his attorney, Stein reluctantly agreed to have Striped Bass, Avenue B and Rouge file for bankruptcy. In addition to the $1.36 million in back state taxes, bankruptcy documents show, the restaurants owed $800,000 to the PIDC.

Finally, on May 20th, Stein announced that Avenue B would close in two weeks. As usual when his ventures failed, he didn't deliver the bad news personally. Gabe Marabella broke it to Avenue B employees. Loyal staffers dutifully served out the string. In a final indignity, they were stiffed for their last two weeks of work. When Avenue B workers showed up at Meal Ticket's offices to pick up their checks, management refused to open the doors. Some employees are out more than $2,000.

However, Meal Ticket was forced to open up its doors by someone else. On May 22nd, six IRS agents entered Stein's office. Stein claims they pushed him against the wall and seized boxes of records from Meal Ticket Inc.

"We got you, Stein," said an agent, according to Stein's account. "You're screwed."

"Fuck you," said Stein. "Fuck all of you."

Meanwhile, Stein attempted to increase his salary to nearly $250,000 a year. He had paid himself a quarter-million a year in the best of times. These were not the best of times. In bankruptcy court on June 4th, he agreed to give up his keys to the restaurants and lost the authority to write checks. Judge Kevin Carey set his salary at a mere-mortal $69,000 a year.

Conveniently, Neil Stein wasn't around for the last act. On May 28th, girlfriend Hope Cohen drove him in his Porsche to Caron, Pennsylvania, home to the Caron Foundation Rehabilitation Center.

They spoke little on the journey. Ten minutes into the check-in process, Stein begged Cohen to take him home. She made arrangements for the $17,500 payment and left. The nurses searched Stein and found 200 Percocets on him. They took away his shoelaces and anything that he might use to kill himself. For a week, Stein was left alone. A nurse would check on him occasionally.

"Please give me something!" he shouted. "Something for the pain."

Perhaps in poetic justice, Stein was forced to eat prepared hospital food. After a week, two fellow patients carried a crying Stein into the main complex. Gout had so inflamed his ankle that he could barely walk. His thoughts must have turned to the tranquility of St. Barths as he lay sleepless in a room with a snoring, bisexual crack addict.

Over the next three weeks, Neil Stein attended counseling sessions and came to know his higher power. After 30 days, he returned to Philly. Those around town to whom he owed money grumbled about his impeccable sense of timing: Wait until you're broke and wanted by every vendor, and then get clean. Still, in a city that once booed Santa Claus, his return was greeted with smiles, a schmoozy *Philadelphia Weekly* story, and pats on the head.

At the July 16th auction of Avenue B, Neil Stein disciples and sworn enemies picked at his carcass. Many of them couldn't help but flash schadenfreude smiles. After four desultory hours of pans and pianos—the Steinway went for $16,000 less than Stein paid for it—the crowd thronged around the Marilyn Monroe lithographs Stein had hung in hopes of resuscitating Avenue B.

All day long, a rumor had twisted through the cavernous space: The lithographs weren't the real thing. In a final sleight-of-hand, the story went, Stein had removed the originals. Potential buyers stared and squinted at the pictures. The general consensus was that if they weren't copies, the Monroes had been matted and framed by a four-year-old. Later, Stein would vehemently deny the pictures were copies. True or not, the rumor was a depressing sign.

As the Monroe pictures were auctioned away, cell phones buzzed and beeped. More than one restaurateur present had his cell phone's ring set to the first 12 bars of the theme from *The Sting*. It's fitting. Is Neil Stein any more or less of a con man? Stop in at Rouge, Bleu or Striped Bass. The man who used to be Neil Stein can be found haunting the restaurants he used to own.

On a late-August Friday night, Neil Stein is in the bar at Striped Bass. Behind the sunglasses, he looks tired. His fingernails shine from a recent manicure, but his tan has faded. He orders a glass of rosé, one of his favorites.

"Ninety days of sobriety out the window," says Stein, with a wan smile. "If I can have a glass of wine, that's great. If this leads me back to the pills, well, shame on Neil Stein."

He's had a rough day. He just had his first psychotherapy visit. In addition, he sees a drug and alcohol counselor at the University of Pennsylvania. Plus, he has frequent conferences with lawyers. Donald Brody still backs him; in July, he injected another $100,000 into Stein's sick restaurants just to keep the doors open. This month, Stein and Brody will present to their creditors a plan to bring Striped Bass and Rouge out of bankruptcy. If the creditors reject it, Stein's restaurants could be sold or liquidated before 2004.

"I'm not going to hide and have a drink," says Stein. "I'm going to drink right in front of everyone. I have nothing to hide."

Over the course of three hours, shades of the old Neil Stein sneak through.

He walks across his kitchens, sampling tomatoes and noticing a scrap of paper out of place on the floor. He proudly shows off the nudes hanging in the men's bathroom at Striped Bass.

"Look at her tits," he whispers. "Perfect tits."

On the way to Rouge, Stein describes his latest idea: a diner on Broad Street. "It could do $10 million," he says. "I mean a real diner, with stainless steel counters and the best meatloaf you ever had."

But Neil Stein may not have the freedom to pursue another restaurant, another dream. If he's indicted and convicted on tax-fraud charges, he could die in prison. For most of the evening, he is still full of bluster. However, his eyes well with tears when he considers the possibility of jail. It scares him.

"I don't know that I'm prepared to go to jail," he says. "But I'm prepared to face anything, because I'm telling the truth. Did we take money and use it somewhere else in place of taxes? Absolutely, but that's not a crime. We didn't pay them because Neil Stein thought, 'Well, we'll eventually get to them, and I gotta take money and filter it into Avenue B.' Well, that's not what they thought I did. They thought I put all those dollars in my pocket. That's not true."

As the evening limps along, Neil Stein begins to fade. At Rouge, the sun-glasses remain on. After a third glass of wine, his eyes drift shut and then pop open. There's a stop at Bleu for a nightcap. However, he's restless, ready to go. Back at his Rittenhouse Square apartment, boxer Striper greets him warmly. There's a back bedroom filled only with his accoutrements: shoes, designer shirts, and two dozen bottles of his favorite perfume.

For a few minutes, Stein lingers on his 16th-floor balcony. Below him, the nightlife of Philadelphia, a life he helped create, goes on without him. He rubs his eyes and takes Striper outside. As he walks through Rittenhouse Square, he notices that Rouge is still jumping, and smiles. He stumbles a bit. Someone asks if he's okay and will be able to make it home.

"Don't worry about me," he says. "Neil Stein will be fine."

Published October 2003

In December 2003, restaurateur Stephen Starr purchased the bankrupt Striped Bass and shuttered the landmark for renovations. Starr reopened the restaurant—his 10th property in Philadelphia—in May 2004. In bankruptcy proceedings, Stein also lost control of Bleu, but he continues to operate Rouge—and talks of his next Rittenhouse Square restaurant, or, perhaps, a chain of Rouge bistros.

The Reincarnation of Stephen Starr

How did a struggling concert promoter and club owner become Philadelphia's rajah of dramatic dining? And when is he going to start enjoying his phenomenal success?

By Larry Platt

So this is the spot, five years later. It's different now. Then, it was desolate and dark when he would drive past at night. "Should I do it? Who am I kidding? Am I crazy? I don't know anything about the restaurant business," he'd tell his wife, who says he has always second- and third- and fourth-guessed himself.

"You couldn't tell if he was being careful or if he was just a pussy," jokes Steven Grasse of Gyro Advertising, who came along on many of those pilgrimages to the corner of 2nd and Market in 1995.

But he'd been broke before, see, and he remembered the physical sensation of it, the nausea and the palpitations and the cold sweat when, his credit dried up, he'd had to pay for a delivery by ripping the twenty off his nightclub's wall—that traditionally merry reminder of an establishment's first sale, pinned right there next to the liquor license. He'd had many business incarnations—nightclub owner, concert promoter—and he knew about highs and lows. He knew the rush of bringing Madonna to town on her Like a Virgin Tour, but he also knew the degradation of auctioning off his club's P.A. system for pennies on the dollar before closing its doors for good. He'd vowed to himself that he'd never go broke again.

Still, Stephen Starr kept driving past this corner, drawn by his vision of a sleek martini bar in place of the nondescript diner that had stood there for years. He'd seen a subterranean resurgence of cocktail culture in New York and L.A., and part of him was sure that if he could design something in 1995 that felt like 1963, with lamps shaped like olives and Frank's crooning filling the air, he'd have a winner.

But with Stephen Starr, there are always doubts. "I remember saying to my wife, 'Walnut Street would have been better, don't you think?'" Starr says now, five years and an empire of restaurants later. He's at the corner, only it's bustling these days, at all hours. And he's wearing Armani and about to get into his two-week-old light-green convertible Jaguar to begin his nightly rounds of all his spots. He'll stop in at Buddakan, to hear the feedback a new chicken special is getting. He'll surreptitiously order two entrées at the Blue Angel, then rail at the staff because the sauce isn't "plentiful enough." At Tangerine, he'll worriedly stalk the kitchen. "This is what I do; this is the job," he'll say. "I check. I'm a checker."

For now, as he fires up the Jag outside the Continental, the spot that started it all for him—not to mention jump-starting Old City—Stephen Starr has found something else to obsess about: the car. "Oh, man, I just realized what this must look like," he says, closing his eyes, regretting showing me the ride. "Guy in his mid-40s, Jaguar convertible. What a total jerk I must look like. People are going to say, 'What a total asshole.'

"But the car is fun," he says. "I mean, I have no fun. None. I've always been the guy throwing the party and never in the party. I feel like Howard Stern sometimes, surrounded by all this glamour and beautiful girls and not having any fun."

He pauses, and then the king of Philadelphia's hippest scene begs, in a mock whine, "Can't you just let me have this little bit of fun?"

For years, the stars of the restaurant business in Philadelphia have been restaurant guys. Neil Stein and Georges Perrier grew up in the culture; their careers are steeped in early-morning visits to the market, where they'd smell the scallops and pick the leeks and lettuces.

But now comes Starr, 44, who has never mixed a drink and whose culinary skills begin and end with the sloppy construction of a tuna-fish sandwich. He wakes up every morning and, he says, still can't believe it. "Am I really in the restaurant business?" he asks himself.

The answer is that he's not—not really. Stein and Perrier are in the restaurant business. Starr is in the business of building the Stephen Starr Brand, just as he was as a club owner in the '70s, a concert promoter in the '80s and a radio talk-show host on WYSP in the early '90s. Now he's doing it with restaurants that are more than just restaurants—places to eat that are about more than the food, that are about, as he puts it, "a feel, a vibe, an experience," and that have come to embody a certain hip cachet by virtue of his attached name.

"Just the other night, someone said to me, 'Can you believe Stephen Starr has become the king of Philadelphia?'" says Steve Mountain, who competed against Starr back in the day, when Mountain had the Chestnut Cabaret. "And I said yes, I can. Because Stephen is tremendously competitive, and he knows that the restaurant business isn't all that different from the nightclub business. It's about knowing what's trendy and promoting it."

In addition to the Continental, Buddakan, Blue Angel and Tangerine, there will be futuristic automated-sushi spot Pod, expected to open next month at 37th and Sansom. Five more imaginatively themed eateries are in the works: For the next project, Starr is taking over Walnut Street's Le Colonial and turning it into a high-end Cuban restaurant with well-known chef Douglas Rodriguez, of New York's Chicama and Patria. It'll be called Alma de Cuba, "the soul of Cuba." ("Soul is hot now with the baby boomers," says Starr.) With Masaharu Morimoto, executive chef of New York's trendy Nobu, he plans to open Japanese restaurants here and in New York next March. Around the same time, he wants to create a hip back-to-basics comfort-food spot with entrepreneur Tony Goldman near 13th and Sansom.

And then there's the much-awaited restaurant at the W Hotel at NewMarket, brought to you by Starr, Will Smith, and Will's brother Harry. (The bar will be run by veteran Randy Gerber, Cindy Crawford's husband. "Will and Randy are the national star power," Starr explains. "I guess I'm the local star power.") A deal for a Starr restaurant in the Sundance Cinemas complex in West Philly fell through, though Starr did meet with Robert Redford at the Continental, telling the actor he loved him in the *Twilight Zone* episode Redford appeared in years ago. (Starr has every *Twilight Zone* on videotape.)

Even with all this expansion, Starr is not your typical restaurateur. He doesn't refer to diners as "customers," as would, say, Stein or Perrier. To Starr, they are his "audience," an audience he's been building for more than 20 years. Those who, in their youth, waited in line to buy tickets to Stephen Starr concerts at the Spectrum now make reservations at Buddakan and Tangerine. "My audience has grown up with me," Starr says, sounding like a restaurant-world version of P.T. Barnum—or, perhaps more accurately, Colonel Parker. Starr has long seen himself along those lines—equal parts discoverer, importer and promoter of pop culture trends.

Such was the case in the early '70s, when, as a student at Temple, he conned his way into network TV offices and, to no avail, hawked an improbable concept called "the music video," long before the advent of MTV. Or in the mid-'70s, when he cornered the likes of Jerry Seinfeld and Richard Belzer after their sets at Catch a Rising Star and the Improv in Manhattan and brought them to Philly because he was convinced that comedy clubs were about to be the next big thing. Such prescience was on display again in '95, when he successfully imported the cocktail culture that was already obsessing New York and L.A.

And now he's become the local champion of a dining trend that is sweeping the country: Call it "Experience Dining." Ultra-high-concept restaurants are suddenly in style—elaborate (sometimes tacky) places that eschew the often stuffy belief that decor and ambience ought to take a backseat to food. For years, the ethos of legendary chef Andre Soltner, of New York's Lutèce, reigned: Soltner was an artist, and the art that arrived on your plate sufficed. Now there's the Bellagio Hotel in Las Vegas, with its dozen Picassos on the walls and an $80 tasting menu, and San Francisco's Farallon and its undersea fantasy, complete with a pebbly ocean-like floor and giant sea-urchin chandeliers. The restaurant, and the scene, is now the art.

So Starr has given us his Arabian-nights fantasy, Tangerine, and Buddakan, with its shimmering waterfall and 10-foot-tall Buddha. Starr knew Buddakan's karma was good, he says, not when he first tasted the pad Thai, but on the day the cast-fiberglass gold-leaf Buddha was brought in on a flatbed, causing a group of slack-jawed Asian tourists to crowd around, clicking cameras feverishly. "You can open your refrigerator and cook a good meal," Starr says, sitting in his sparse Market Street office next to the Continental. "I want people to feel like they're not in Philadelphia or near their home in Huntingdon Valley when they come to one of my places. Let's face it—life is pretty mundane, for you, me or Cindy Crawford. So I want their night out to feel like they're getting away. I'm selling the experience."

As he talks, Starr flits around his office, showing off items that will soon occupy his latest fantasy. His Armani suit drapes a muscle-bound upper body, the product of daily morning workouts at the Sporting Club; still, as he scurries off to find his newest accoutrement, something about his shuffling gait and nervous banter makes him seem more harried homemaker than cutthroat businessman. He returns lugging one of the cone-shaped chairs that will soon occupy Pod; when you sit on them, they light up. "Remember the Woody Allen movie *Sleeper*? That's what I wanted. These are very *Sleeper*," he says proudly.

The reference to pop culture is no aberration; Starr immerses himself in it, peppers his speech with allusions to it. When he's told that Dan Rather has made a reservation at Tangerine, his first thought is to dig out and play R.E.M.'s "What's the Frequency, Kenneth?" When he devises a magazine ad for Pod, his stylistic model is the Beatles' *White Album*. He's a magazine addict, scouring the pages of *GQ*, *Paper* and *Face* for the next quirky trend. He and his brain trust—Continental manager Richard Roberts, V.P. of operations Michael Palermo, design consultant Owen Kamihira, and kitchen-operations overseer Bradlee Bartram—have cultivated sources from around the globe who fax cool menus to them every day.

Indeed, Starr sees himself as an A&R man—only instead of unearthing recording talent, he's discovering themes to enhance dining. Sometimes he's less of a talent scout than an importer, like a band that brilliantly covers somebody else's song and makes it their own. Buddakan, for example, came after the success of Asia de Cuba in New York, a similarly themed restaurant owned by Philadelphia native Jeffrey Chodorow, who also owns China Grill in South Beach. (Chodorow later bought the one restaurant concept Starr couldn't make work in Philadelphia—his Russian-themed Cafe Republic at dicey 22nd and South—and transplanted it to Miami in the form of the thriving Red Square.) Other times, the notions are all Starr, as with two he considered but discarded for the space that is now Tangerine: the Cuban eatery, complete with bodegas and shanties, that's going into Le Colonial; and a more kitschy place, featuring trailer-park ambience and playing off white-trash culture, serving down-home delicacies such as chicken-fried steak, that remains on his drawing board.

A typical Starr day begins at 8 a.m. and ends around midnight, and the only fun he has in it are the group sessions with his creative team, in which these themes are mulled over, tweaked, and either adopted or not. "The rest of the time, I'm an imposter," he says—a director masquerading as a businessman. But put him in a room with his brain trust, and Starr is transported back to what he always wanted to be, to what he still thinks he can become: a sitcom or movie creator. Then and there, his childhood dream is realized, and he's Rob Petrie from *The Dick Van Dyke Show*, head writer, creative force. "And [designer] Owen is my Morey Amsterdam," Starr observes, referring to Petrie's wisecracking sidekick, Buddy Sorrell. As for the rest of it, from the schmoozing he has to do at the restaurants to the closing of million-dollar loans from his venture-capital investors, that's not him.

"I'm an actor," he says. "I learned how when I was a kid."

Yes, his real name is Stephen Starr, and he grew up the son of a television repairman in Woodbury Heights, New Jersey, where he was addicted to sitcoms, pop music and the Phillies. He spent hours watching Dick Van Dyke and listening to the Beatles, absorbing the chords both struck in the popular imagination. When he found himself getting into schoolyard arguments with other kids about controversial Phillies slugger Richie Allen, he sensed that something bigger than baseball—something cultural—was at work.

"Richie Allen—it's Richie, not Dick—was my hero," he recalls. "And there was a small group of us who took our first stand on Richie Allen. Other kids would call him bad racial names, and the kids who loved him were the cool kids who became the hippies, who grew our hair long, who opposed Vietnam. The kids who hated Richie were the redneck assholes. I was eight years old in '64, but I knew standing up for Richie was something important."

When Starr was in his mid-teens, he and a friend dummied up fake press passes from London's *Melody Maker* magazine and, putting on British accents, conned themselves into concerts at the Electric Factory and Spectrum. "We'd be backstage, eating with the band," he recalls. "It was a great goof. Larry put on great shows." Larry is Electric Factory concert guru Larry Magid, now 58, against whom Starr would later compete. Sneaking into those shows may have been a typical teenage prank, but it was also a chance to soak up knowledge. Starr saw firsthand that the secret to a good show wasn't necessarily the music, just as a good meal isn't necessarily about food. The best concerts, he realized then, were those that morphed into spectacle, with an "energy" and "vibe" all their own—adjectives he'd later use time and again to describe his restaurants.

In his late teens, Starr spent his summers in Atlantic City, feeling, he says, like a character in a Springsteen song. Every day, he'd hawk cheap watches and gadgets to passersby on the Boardwalk. "That was selling," he says. "If you work in a mall nowadays, that's not selling. That's being a clerk. Back then, I had to convince tourists how wonderful this piece-of-crap watch was. That honed my ability, not to lie, but to sell. I learned all I ever needed to know about human nature on that Boardwalk. That people want to like something. You just have to say—it's okay, it's good to like this. You have to reassure them. I think that's where I learned how to act, how to play this businessman role."

As a communications major at Temple, Starr formed a production company and talked his way into a meeting with famed rock concert impresario Don Kirschner. Starr carried an empty briefcase with him and hinted about his many other clients who were already signing onto his big idea: music videos. Kirschner hired Starr to videotape local hero Todd Rundgren in concert at the Tower Theater. Even though the footage was never used, Kirschner paid Starr for it—his first music-industry paycheck.

After graduation, Starr used to trek to New York on weekends, where he'd laugh uproariously at the young comics doing stand-up at Catch a Rising Star and the Improv. He convinced the owner of a deli where he liked to eat lunch, Grandmom Minnie's at 3rd and Chestnut, to stay open on Friday nights, and brought in starving funny men like Jerry Seinfeld and Richard Belzer, who were desperate for gigs in the days before the comedy-club circuit. In 1976, he found a vacant building at 2nd and Bainbridge, and a bank gave him a small loan to fix it up. He opened Stars, which would become the Philly launching pad for comics Joe Piscopo, Sandra Bernhard and Bob Wuhl. Philly native Bob Saget started as a frequent member of the audience, and Starr watched him take the stage on open-mike night and gradually become a stand-up himself. It was a heady time. The comedy-club explosion mixed with the South Street renaissance, and Starr was in the thick of both.

As more comedy clubs opened up, Stars struggled, closing in 1980. "I could eat, but that was not a fun period," Starr recalls. "I had no money. I couldn't buy a car; I couldn't go out. Even today, these 20-year-olds who work for me don't seem to mind not having money. I don't understand it. They go to Europe, but they're broke. I'm envious. How do they do that? How do you have less money than me and still have more fun than me?"

"It was sad when Stephen fell on hard times," recalls one club insider from the early-'80s South Street scene. "He couldn't pay his bills, and he left a lot of vendors high and dry. But you always had the feeling he'd be back."

He opened Ripley Music Hall, a live-music venue at 6th and South, which whetted his appetite for putting on bigger shows. At the time, Electric Factory's mercurial Magid was a behemoth in the concert field. Starr formed the Concert Company and began promoting shows at the Walnut Street Theatre and the Academy of Music. By the mid-'80s, he'd surprised the experts and was surviving in the concert business. He brought Madonna to the Spectrum, and landed Steve Winwood, Lionel Richie, Guns N' Roses and Stevie Nicks. Electric Factory still outbid him for most top acts, but in every case, Starr drove up the cost of promoting big-name talent. He was doing well enough to open the Bank, a seminal dance club at 6th and Spring Garden. Meantime, he was earning a reputation as an artist-friendly promoter, in part because he always saw himself as a kindred spirit—a creative force in businessman's garb.

"The thing that stood out about a Stephen Starr production was the amazing attention to detail," says Bill Eib, former manager of Philly rocker Robert Hazard. "He knew that seemingly minor things mattered, that no matter how good the music was, if there was something wrong in the dressing room, the band would be pissed and the whole night could be screwed. Agents and artists liked him because he catered to them. And he was cool. Electric Factory had the established power, but Stephen was known for his style."

In 1991, Electric Factory made Starr an offer he couldn't refuse. In exchange for a buyout that one industry source estimates as at least in the mid six fig-ures, he agreed to stop competing against them. Afterward, Starr concentrated on running the Bank and hosting an early-Sunday-morning talk show on 'YSP that opened with audio of a man urinating. (I first met Starr when he called me to be a bleary-eyed guest on the show to talk about an article I'd written). His years hanging out with Belzer and Wuhl and Seinfeld served him well on the radio; he offered up a lot of shtick and high jinks at a time of day when most programming was mired in mind-numbing public-affairs pablum.

Meantime, Starr was among those with an idea for a large outdoor amphitheater on the Camden Waterfront, and he helped bring together all the players who would eventually make the E-Centre a reality—though he'd ultimately have to hire Center City lawyer George Bochetto and file suit against developer Malcolm Lazin to get his cut. (The legal action culminated in a settlement and confidentiality agreement.) Generally, though, Starr spent the early '90s working out obsessively and tending to his family. He and wife Debbie, an attorney—who met Starr when she was working at Grandmom Minnie's in the early '80s—married in 1989, and had a daughter, Sarah, two years later. (They live in Society Hill, and had a second daughter, Sophie, eight months ago.)

But then came the stalking of the little diner at 2nd and Market. In 1995, when Starr first asked the owner, a Greek guy named Pete, if he'd be interested in selling, he was met with a blank stare. "Are you crazy?" Pete asked. "What can you gross in a place like this? Four thousand a month, if you're lucky?"

During his late-night rides past the diner, Starr began repeating Pete's ques-tion—"Am I crazy?" Armed with the windfall from Electric Factory, however, he went ahead, and on opening night in October of 1995, the line to get into the Continental stretched down 2nd Street.

Today, five years later, he talks about adding restaurants near the Blue Angel at 7th and Chestnut streets, of turning that block and all of Old City into SoHo, to provide a counterpoint to the stuffy Upper East Side ambience of Walnut's Restaurant Row. But such grandiose plans seemed mere fantasy when Starr fol-lowed the Continental with a failed venture.

Starr spent his own money in 1996 to open Cafe Republic, a dark evocation of the last days of the U.S.S.R., thinking the hipsters at the Continental would eagerly trek uptown for vodka and caviar. For a time, they did. But the lack of parking and barren neighborhood at 22nd and South doomed the place. Unlike the Continental, Republic failed to spur development around it. "That was a wake-up call," Starr recalls. "It was like, 'Listen, shithead, not everything you do is going to work. So be careful.' It was a slap in the head, but not a death blow. And I take some comfort that the concept—even the very tattered Russian flags that were on the wall—lives on in South Beach in Red Square."

That was also, not coincidentally, the last time Starr would invest only his own money in a project. Because industry estimates say that close to eight of every 10 new restaurants ultimately fail, banks don't generally loan money for start-ups. Armed with the success of the Continental and a compelling explanation for the failure of Cafe Republic—location—Starr utilized the selling skills he'd first honed on the Atlantic City Boardwalk and struck a deal with a Philadelphia venture capital firm. For Buddakan, he raised $2.2 million; for the Blue Angel, $1.2 million; and for Tangerine and Pod, $2.8 million each, all while maintaining more than 50 percent of the equity.

Now, with plans for five more spots, four of them in Philly, the question faces Starr for the first time: Are we hip enough for this many Stephen Starr productions? "I used to be much more critical of Philadelphia when I was younger," he says. "I always wanted to live in New York. But now I think they're both the same, but the core of enlightened people—I hate the word 'hip'—is bigger in New York. But both places have parochial audiences that enjoy participating in these kind of trendy restaurants. In New York, you find 55-year-old guys wearing Prada shoes who live on Long Island. And most of the people who come to my restaurants are from the suburbs."

He pauses, smiles. It's the look of someone who believes he's found the next new thing. "That's why I'm excited about expanding into West Philly," he says. "Because there's an international feel up there. I was walking around there yesterday and saw tons of Asian people, and didn't once hear the word 'yo.'"

This is why he has a cell phone that vibrates: Inside the restaurants, he might not hear the ring when daughter Sarah makes her nightly call to him before she's off to bed. "Okay, Puppy, I love you," Starr says to her, hanging up as he makes his way through the kitchen at Tangerine.

His eyes dart about the room. A waitress carrying a dessert passes by, and Starr stops her and calls the chef over. "Is this ice cream too melted?" he asks.

"Yes," comes the reply.

The waitress about-faces to repair the error, and Starr seethes. "They know I'm standing here, they know you're a reporter, and still they're going to bring out a dessert with melted ice cream on it," he says, shaking his head. "That's my big accomplishment for the night, I guess. If you've just spent $200 on dinner, why should you have ice cream melted all over your plate?"

Moments pass, but Starr can't let go of the ice-cream faux pas. He doesn't like the Stephen Starr who flags the passing melted dessert, the actor playing the role of Big Boss Man. "I get frustrated, and I home in on things to the point that it's even ridiculous to me," he says, and then starts mimicking himself: "'Did you change that shrimp? Change that shrimp! Did you change that shrimp?' It's ridiculous. It's one thing, just stop it, it's not the end of the world. But when you look at the big picture, you have to be that way in order to make these places work."

The restaurant business rewards anal-compulsive worrywarts, and Starr admits to being that: He hates to fly, for example, because he doesn't trust that anyone knows what they're doing in any job. Clearly, the opportunities for anguish are overwhelming in a business where the performance of a 20-year-old waitress or hostess or dishwasher could make or break your $2 million investment. And now that Starr is expanding so rapidly, there are new causes for concern. How do you make sure the damned ice cream isn't too melted when you've got 10 restaurants? It's a conundrum he's mulled over with entrepreneur Tony Goldman. They agree that the whole business is dependent on hiring "checkers"—employees who are paid $200,000 and wear designer suits but whose job amounts to nothing more than being their eyes behind the scenes. "But I'd still rather put surveillance cameras with hidden microphones in every one of these places, and sit alone in a room somewhere and watch all day long," Starr says.

The bigger he gets, the more knotted Starr's brow grows. When does the playacting stop? When does he become what he's always seen himself as? Stephen Starr, it turns out, really wants to direct. "But I don't think I have to go to Hollywood to make movies," he says. "I think I can do it from here. Who knows? It sounds absurd, but maybe Will [Smith] and I will do something together."

For now, though, there are details to obsess over. We part company as Starr heads downstairs to check on the air-conditioning and the Data Beat computerized audio system that he painstakingly stocked with just the right background music for Moroccan-style dining. He mutters about the temperature in the dining room and fiddles with a thermostat. "Pretty riveting life, huh?" he says. He is a workaholic with very few friends ("My family are my friends," he says), and he is driven by a need to anticipate problems, by an obsessiveness that may be part his nature and part the nature of his business.

Upon opening the Blue Angel, Starr could have evicted the elderly palm reader above the restaurant, increasing the value of the building. "Donald

Trump would have booted her," says Continental manager Richard Roberts, who has been with Starr since his restaurant incarnation began in 1995. But Starr met with the aging psychic, who cried in front of him. He couldn't bring himself to play the part of the unfeeling businessman. "Stephen was moved," Roberts says. "He has great humanity."

But something else was at work, too. Starr is behind the wheel of his Jag when I ask about him and the palm reader. He pauses. "It was bad karma," Stephen Starr says at last, smiling slyly. "I could envision her slapping down one of those tarot cards and putting a hex on me, my restaurant and my family."

Published September 2000

Blue Angel's hex, it turns out, was the French backlash prompted by international events in 2003. Starr closed Blue Angel in March 2003, and six months later reopened the location as Angelina, a red-and-white-toile-covered Italian spot. In spring 2004, Starr brought his restaurant empire to 10—Iron Chef Masharu Morimoto's Morimoto, Nuevo Latino Alma de Cuba, and funky Mexican El Vez among them—with the reopening of Philadelphia landmark Striped Bass, helmed by Gotham chef Alfred Portale. At the same time, Starr had in the works three Philadelphia restaurant projects—including a Center City branch of his Continental lounge—and two New York locations, all scheduled to open within a year.

The Mysterious Mr. Chodorow

Today, he heads a global hipster dining empire. But first, New Hope's Jeffrey Chodorow had to go from being a Philly real estate lawyer to founding an iconic '80s eatery to enduring much darker times. A true rags-to-wasabi redemption story

By Amy Donohue

Jeffrey Chodorow was a little irked when he heard about Alma de Cuba, Stephen Starr's nuevo-hipster-Latino spot on Walnut Street, which opened in May 2001.

It was that name. Chodorow had opened the restaurant Asia de Cuba in 1997, at Morgans hotel in New York, and now owns three more ultra-sleek Asia de Cubas, in Los Angeles, San Francisco and London. You have to admit the name is similar. Asia de Cuba and Alma de Cuba look related, too, with their modern white furniture and glossy rooms. One might have assumed that Alma was a spin-off of Chodorow's place—which it isn't, since Chodorow and Starr aren't partners. So did Starr alert Chodorow that he was opening Alma de Cuba?

"No," says Chodorow, then laughs and adds, "I was a little annoyed about that. But I got over it fast." ("[Chef] Douglas Rodriguez named the restaurant," says Starr of Alma de Cuba, which means "soul of Cuba.") Chodorow has also noticed a similarity in the menus of Jones, Starr's new comfort-food place, and his own Hudson Cafeteria, the modern eatery in New York's Hudson hotel, one of about a dozen restaurants Chodorow runs in Ian Schrager's far-flung group of Eurotrash-friendly boutique hotels. Meatloaf, hearts of lettuce, and upscale macaroni-and-cheese appear on both (although at Jones the mac-and-cheese is $5, and at the Hudson, it's $15). Still, Chodorow insists, "I like Jones." "There's similarities in all comfort-food menus," says Starr.

Of course, Chodorow doesn't mind: Right now, he's the coolest theme restaurateur in the country, partnered with Schrager on the Blue Door, at the Delano in Miami, and on Spoon, the restaurant in London's Sanderson hotel. He owns four restaurants at Vegas's Mandalay Bay resort, as well as two Tuscan Steaks, in New York and Miami, and he's about to open his fifth

China Grill, this one in Mexico City.

Chodorow, who is 52, and Starr, 47, have known each other for years, since long before Chodorow was hoovering up $150 million a year in sales with his China Grill Management group. That's because since the early 1970s, Chodorow has been a Philadelphian, working here as a Blank Rome attorney and real estate investor before he evolved into a restaurant mogul. Naturally, Chodorow has been to Starr's places; his main residence, which he shares with his wife, Linda, and their two sons, is a 60-acre farm in New Hope. His best friends are Philadelphians, and despite his Philippe Starck-designed eateries, Chodorow's homes in New York City and Miami, as well as the Bucks County farm, have all been decorated by chintz-loving Rittenhouse Square decorator Bennett Weinstock.

But back to Stephen Starr. Lest you think it's only Starr reheating Chodorow's ideas, in fact the two gleefully feed off each other. (They even look alike, with their dark hair and brooding expressions and Prada-and-Armani wardrobes.) In 1997, Chodorow hired Starr to help re-create Philly's short-lived, Russian-themed Café Republic as Miami's Red Square. The two are friends—Starr himself says he sees more of Asia de Cuba in his own Buddakan, and through Chodorow, he bought much of its furnishings from Starck. Chodorow also says, "I'm doing a modern Japanese restaurant [in New York]. But not like Morimoto." Then he pauses. "Look, that's not to say there won't be some modern things you'd find at Morimoto."

Responds Starr, who's doing his own Morimoto in New York this year, "Oh, I don't care."

You might call Jeffrey Chodorow a stealth Philadelphian. "Our favorite place is the Pineville Tavern," Chodorow says of the modest roadhouse outside New Hope, known for burgers and beers and an eclectic crowd. "Very neighborhoody. We flew our managers from all over the world to Bucks County for a retreat. We did one dinner at Pineville Tavern."

Let's hope Ian Schrager doesn't hear about that.

"I opened China Grill as a hobby—I'm a foodaholic," Chodorow says in his rapid-fire patter on a recent Monday, bombing down Park Avenue in the back of a Town Car while his partner Neil Faggen, a Philadelphian, makes quiet phone calls in the front seat.

Chodorow is just back from Mexico City, where the new China Grill will open in January at the Camino Real hotel, and is off to Europe later this afternoon to visit his restaurants in London. Today, he'll drop in on a few of his New York restaurants during lunch; he has a two o'clock meeting with producers from a company that's proposing an Asia de Cuba-themed CD. He doesn't look like a foodaholic; he's buff in a black sweater and dark jeans.

At 40th Street and 3rd Avenue, Chodorow and Faggen, another former Blank Rome lawyer, jump out of the car—everything is at warp speed in the Chodorow universe—and beetle into the $8 million Tuscan Steak, leaving the driver idling outside. Chodorow, tall, with a signature scruff of beard and animated light-brown eyes under skeptical dark brows, smiles and says hello to his door staff and waiters, all gorgeous people with British accents. In the pale-green and beige dining room, with its huge windows and jazzy music, young business types are busily protein-loading. (*New York Times* restaurant critic William Grimes likens Tuscan Steak to "a big frat party.")

Chodorow was 37 when he launched his first restaurant, China Grill, in 1987, living on the New Hope farm with Linda, a former model; they'd just had their first son. He was then involved in a daunting number of ventures: the $50 million Philly real estate investment firm CoreGroup; radio stations in New York; and a group that in 1987 made an aborted $100 million bid to buy the New England Patriots. And in June of '88, Chodorow and partners spent $105 million to buy Braniff, Inc., a rinky-dink airline that struggled to get passengers onto its Islip-Orlando shuttles. Braniff would eventually lead to the bitterest chapter of Chodorow's career, including a prison sentence.

But that was all a lifetime ago.

A charming alpha male with a New Yorky, De Niro-esque accent though he was reared in Miami and educated at Penn, Chodorow is a master of reinvention (of himself, as cool restaurateur) and derivation (riffing on other peoples' restaurant concepts, making them hipper yet more populist). A lawyer surrounded by lawyers, Chodorow can also be very prickly, and spent weeks avoiding an interview. When I do finally meet him, he is smart and funny— as friends have promised—but during our day in New York, and in other conversations, he displays an effective method of deflecting and preventing questions he doesn't want to answer: In a likably manic monologue, he simply spews facts about how fabulous his restaurants are—which, indeed, they often are. "He's very successful in creating these social installations that attract beautiful, hip, happening people," the *Times*'s Grimes says of Chodorow. "The food doesn't matter so much, but the design matters a lot. And they've shown durability—restaurant years are like dog years."

Chodorow keeps a much lower profile than celebrity chef-restaurateurs such as Jean-Georges Vongerichten or Emeril or Molto Mario. Still, Grimes ranks

Chodorow high on the national restaurant radar: "For him to compile a track record of attracting young Manhattanites, he's beating a very tough game."

Chodorow freely admits that he modeled China Grill on Wolfgang Puck's Santa Monica hot spot, Chinois on Main. A glitzy, dark, 200-person restaurant in the CBS building, China Grill was a thoroughly '80s entity, and with its crispy calamari and deep-fried sushi, it out-Pucked Puck. "All the people I knew, including restaurant people, said, 'Don't take that space,'" Chodorow says of China Grill. But he began to see potential in the gloomy, narrow midtown place. He hired designer Jeffrey Beers to install futuristic light fixtures and tile the floor with whimsical bits from Marco Polo's journals, creating a sleek feeding station for celebrities (well, Diane Keaton and Malcolm Forbes).

By its second year, China Grill was grossing millions. It set a formula for Chodorow's future collection of 22 restaurants: dramatic spaces; short, catchy names (even if they don't really make any sense); huge portions designed for sharing; absurdly splashy opening parties. When Tuscan Steak's heat was on the fritz for its opening, Chodorow famously dropped $13,000 to buy pashminas for every female guest.

"Lots of the food should be framed, not eaten," the *New York Times*'s Molly O'Neill wrote of China Grill in '87. However, O'Neill had to admit that China Grill "as-polished-arena" was a huge success. The critics are rarely kind to Chodorow—which doesn't bother him. "In New York, there's a lot of political components, in my opinion, to reviews," says Chodorow. "Hudson [Cafeteria] got one of the worst reviews in the history of the *New York Times*. We started getting backlash positive press." (Indeed, Grimes calls Hudson Cafeteria's food "wretched.") Chodorow rattles on enthusiastically: "Regis Philbin's producer came in, and he called Regis and said, 'This place is great, you have to come here!'" (Chodorow's celebrity name-droppings are infrequent and of the B-list, Regis genre.)

"He's a kick," says Mario Batali, who owns the restaurants Babbo and Lupa in New York—rustic Italian spots that are the anti-Tuscan Steaks. Despite their differing philosophies, Batali admires Chodorow's places, and the two are friendly. "I once was about two minutes away from being on a boat with him in the South of France. We've passed like ships in Naples and on the Amalfi," Batali says wistfully. "I would have loved to get on his boat. He doesn't get a little boat; he gets a really big boat."

Chodorow doesn't do little anything. Jeffrey Beers, his designer, has become a master at translating kernels of Chodorow ideas (rum, half-naked girls, Brazil!) into crowd-pleasing faux worlds (Vegas's Rum Jungle). At Spoon in London, Chodorow's consulting chef is Alain Ducasse, perhaps the most famous French chef in the world. Ducasse, who owns the insultingly expensive restaurant at the Essex House in New York, will again pair with Chodorow on Mix, a $5 million bistro moderne in midtown, later this spring. (Paging Daniel Boulud!) Tuscan Steak's marble pizza counter will be re-jiggered next month to accommodate 60 kinds of antipasto and salumi, which are hugely popular right now at Lupa. (Paging Mario Batali!)

Back in the Town Car, Chodorow tells me about his new 200-seat bistro/pâtisserie in Mandalay Bay, called—paging Neil Stein!—Bleu Blanc Rouge, also designed by Beers. ("Really?" says Stein. "That's a really cool name.") There's an oyster bar, a wine bar, and a brasserie menu. Total price tag: $2.5 million just for renovations; there was a China Grill café, one of Chodorow's few failures, in the space before. "It was confusing to people between China Grill and the café," notes Chodorow, who'll fix things that don't work but never admits he might have had a bad idea.

Schrager, who's had unhappy divorces from previous restaurant/bar partners, now pretty much yields his dining spaces to Chodorow, no questions asked. Schrager initially admired Chodorow in the early China Grill years, and partnered with him first at New York's Royalton Hotel and then, in 1995, at the Delano. "We build and design the look, and then we hand over the space to Jeffrey," Schrager says.

At the Hudson Cafeteria, Chodorow and Faggen order lunch, but our goofy waiter doesn't seem to know who Chodorow is, and he's forgotten the details of the specials. Chodorow doesn't react—he genuinely doesn't seem to mind that the service is raw. In fact, staffers at all the restaurants we visit are quite informal and friendly with him, as he is with them.

Chodorow's personal magnetism is huge when he lets it unfold, especially when he's visibly excited by a restaurant accomplishment. "Oh my God, it's off the charts!" he raves about the design for the Ducasse collaboration, Mix, which opens in March in a vintage brick bistro space on West 58th Street in which the interior will be entirely sheathed in rose-tinted modern glass panels.

"Get a fish," Chodorow, in alpha-male fashion, tells Neil.

"Can I have the gumbo?" Faggen returns, good-humoredly.

"Okay, have the gumbo," says Chodorow, and orders shrimp in lobster sauce. Chodorow and his wife have just closed on a Hamptons house, where they'll install pieces they recently bought by Lichtenstein and Jeff Koons. Will Bennett Weinstock be decorating the Hamptons house?

"Oh boy," says Neil, rolling his eyes.

"Bennett's actually great," says Chodorow, and laughs. "If you saw our home in Miami, you'd know it was Bennett right away. But we're doing the Hamptons house in a more contemporary way—we talked to Philippe."

For a man whose business is to create trends, Chodorow is unexpectedly traditional. He is unflaggingly devoted to his wife and sons, which is one reason he is so reluctant to be a public figure. His Uzi-style assault of facts—"Asia de Cuba was the fourth most profitable restaurant in the U.S. last year. China Grill was the second!"—guarantees a sort of personal anonymity, though his sense of humor emerges.

Certainly he inspires (and invests) great love and loyalty in his longtime friends. Everyone in Chodorow's closest circle is a Philadelphian, like Faggen and their other partner, CFO Jack Polsenberg. His lawyer is Blank Rome's Craig Lord; he finances deals through Philadelphia Private Bank's Betsy Cohen. This loyalty—or parochialism, depending on whom you ask—has mostly served him well through the years, except during the time he owned Braniff. "Jeffrey has taken us places we never would have gone," Faggen says. The Chodorows hit Vegas, Miami, Europe and the Caribbean with Sharon Pinkenson, the film office czarina, and her husband, Joe Weiss, whom Chodorow has known for 25 years; this Christmas, they rented a house in St. Barths together. "The reason I don't want to open [a restaurant] in Philadelphia is because of my children," Chodorow explains. "When I'm home, I don't want to think, I'm 45 minutes from the city, let me run into town and check on the restaurant."

Chodorow's wife and sons "are of paramount importance," says Bennett Weinstock. This may explain Chodorow's voracious ambition: Presumably, he wants to provide his sons with a more secure environment than the one he had during his own strangely adult childhood.

Born in New York, Chodorow relocated as a baby with his mother, Lila, to Miami Beach when his father died in the early 1950s. "It was like living in Russia. We moved in with my aunt and her two children in a two-room apartment, my grandparents came down and they lived with us part-time," Chodorow recalls, rather fondly. Lila, a manicurist, would take little Jeffrey along on her dates to old-time Miami-cool spots like Capra's and the Studio.

Though Lila remarried when her son was nine, Chodorow, who was an Eagle Scout, says his childhood was "not affluent." But he was brilliant, graduating 10th in his class of 1,000 at Miami Norland Senior High School.

He'd seen around him in Miami examples of how stylishly life could be lived—with money. "When I was in junior high school, a friend of mine—well, his father—had a chauffeur, so the chauffeur drove him to school every day. So he picked me up on the way to school," he remembers, then laughs and says, "Even when my friend was sick, he'd still come to get me, because I depended on him."

In 1968, Chodorow left for Wharton. ("The first meal I ever ate here was La Terrasse; they had a $3 fixed-price meal," he recalls.) After graduating magna cum laude, he married his college girlfriend, Hope Gruber, who's now a doctor in Greensboro, North Carolina. He worked briefly in an accounting firm, then enrolled at Penn Law, where he was on law review, and graduated in 1975. Blank Rome's Craig Lord, a former judge of the Philadelphia Common Pleas Court who brought Chodorow into the firm's real estate department, says, "I remember him preparing special meals and actually cooking himself, and planning his trips around restaurants." Chodorow stayed at Blank Rome three years, leaving when he was 28—he'd seen that the real money was to be made as the client, not the lawyer.

Chodorow joined his former client Eddie Lipkin's National Property Analysts firm and began making deals—but only stayed a few months. Next, from his Dorchester apartment, he formed Commercial Properties Group, which later became CoreGroup, and began making deals of his own. Mentor Craig Lord came to work for *him*. Chodorow was a millionaire by age 30.

He was a risk-taker, one of the coolest guys in town in the late '70s and early '80s. "He was like any other rich 30-year-old kid—big cigars and motorcars," says his close friend Joe Weiss, a former attorney who until recently ran Packard Press. Weiss and Chodorow shared office space at 1822 Spruce Street, in the ornate mansion that is now Salon Royal Court (they sat where Cindy the manicurist now does toes), and made money, and partied.

Chodorow and Weiss and David Feld, then-flush owner of Today's Man, would groove around to all the cool places. These were the heady days of élan, the nightclub in the Warwick; "There was really no place else to go," protests Chodorow.

"I can take credit for arranging the fix-up," Joe Weiss says about the night Chodorow met his future wife, Linda. "Sharon Pinkenson—who's now my wife—owned Plage Tahiti, and she was having a men-only sale that night. Linda was modeling for Sharon. That's how they met." Despite their subsequent globetrotting lifestyle, Linda, a native Philadelphian, and Chodorow apparently saw something real, a person to depend upon, in each other.

In 1982, Chodorow "extricated himself," as Weiss puts it, from his first marriage. (Weiss served as his divorce lawyer.) The day after the divorce, Linda and Jeffrey married, and in 1987, they had the first of their two sons. It was an intoxicating life: One acquaintance remembers seeing the Chodorows in Venice on a gondola heading to the Cipriani, Linda drawing oglers all over the canal. "You've seen my wife's picture!" says Chodorow, calling her "the nicest person I know" and indirectly comparing her sweet-faced beauty to that of Nicole Kidman. Linda is said by friends to be a warm hostess, a wonderful mother, and a trusted adviser on his restaurants.

In his '80s incarnation, Chodorow also found time to hang out with Julius Erving in the South of France, throw parties (he once redecorated the Bellevue hotel as Rio de Janeiro), and idle at his second home in the San Remo on Central Park West. All this cost money, but Chodorow was then very flush from Core Group, which specialized in real estate syndication deals, among other interests. He and his partners earned as much as $50 million in the late 1970s and early '80s.

But in 1988, investors in real estate syndicates were slapped with surprise tax bills in the hundreds of thousands of dollars—which led to a vigorous round of lawsuits by them against syndicators. Chodorow later claimed that he had lost interest in real estate, and said the IRS had singled him out for reparations. He soon moved on to the airline business.

Chodorow was led to Braniff, Inc., by a 23-year-old from New Jersey named Scot Spencer. In June of '88, Spencer somehow persuaded Chodorow and New York developer Arthur Cohen to buy the airline. Spencer also convinced them that he should run it, despite his history of writing bad checks and other minor legal scrapes.

Under Chodorow and Cohen's holding company, the new Braniff, acquired for $105 million, brought in professional managers from Piedmont Airlines. But the untried Spencer was really running the show. Braniff lost more than $31 million in the first half of '89, filed Chapter 11 in September, then suddenly suspended flights in November.

The Braniff chapter took a weirder turn the following year, when Chodorow and Cohen decided to revive the airline again: In April 1990, they purchased the Braniff trademark and assets in bankruptcy court and in 1991 started flying once more. Inexplicably, Spencer was again Chodorow's Braniff boy Friday, serving as president of the airline. But by June of '91, the Department of Transportation had ordered Spencer out of the Braniff operation. In August, five weeks after its first flights lifted off, the airline filed for bankruptcy protection. Strangest of all, though he had been publicly dismissed, Spencer was still secretly at the reins—he was seen around the Braniff offices, and would return calls on Chodorow's behalf. The situation was disastrous: Braniff flights were constantly overbooked. In July '92, the airline suddenly stopped flying—a move that shocked its trustees in bankruptcy court.

The U.S. Attorney's office later charged Spencer and Chodorow with, among other things, conspiracy to defraud, alleging that Scot Spencer had never really stopped running the airline and that Chodorow had lied about Spencer's supposed nonexistent role.

Why Chodorow stayed involved with Spencer remains a mystery, one he isn't willing to address. It seemed Spencer had inspired the signature Chodorow loyalty. Chodorow pleaded guilty in 1995 to lying to the DOT about Spencer's involvement. (Two bankruptcy-fraud-related charges against Chodorow were dropped; Spencer was convicted of those charges and was sentenced to 51 months in prison.)

Chodorow served a few months in prison in 1996. "Nobody really understands what happened," he says intensely. "I mean, I lost a fortune there. And the only reason I did it was because I felt bad because when I did the airline the first time, we hired professional management and they ran the airline into the ground. And I felt terrible for the people, and I was determined to make it up to them."

Six years later, he remains surprisingly touchy about the situation, considering how well he's recovered—unlike, say, Ian Schrager, who's adopted a more unflinching stance about his own legal problems, which included prison. Schrager, who also has recouped rather nicely, says, "We've both had our bumpy times. We dusted ourselves off. You bond over it, because it's such an unbelievable experience."

Chodorow spoke to *Philadelphia* magazine on the condition that specific comments be included from friends about Braniff. Craig Lord's is: "Although I was a Common Pleas Court judge at the time, I am familiar with the case that was brought against Jeffrey, and in my opinion, both the process and the result were unfair to Jeffrey. Fortunately, Jeffrey had the courage and discipline to put this episode behind him and move forward to achieve extraordinary success as a restaurateur." Another, from Philadelphia Private Bank's Betsy Cohen: "Jeffrey Chodorow has always been a person of integrity. After I learned of his legal entanglement—just wrong, in

my opinion—I watched as he worked at ensuring that none of his obliga-
tions—financial or emotional—were neglected. I would lend and have lent
him money before and since." Chodorow's own final word on his guilty plea
is, "In the end, you have to make the decision that's best for your family, but
those who really know what happened know that the biggest casualty of
that event was the truth."

Despite the Braniff shit-storm, China Grill was still luring customers
with its crispy spinach and spicy calamari. It hadn't shocked friends that
Chodorow would get into the famously competitive, cash-incinerating
restaurant world—though no one would have guessed that China Grill
would lay the groundwork for his salvation. "I tried very hard to convince
him not to get into the [restaurant] business," Weiss says. "Which shows
you how smart I am."

Chodorow claims to have invented the most ubiquitous side dish of the
1990s: wasabi mashed potatoes. "In 1991, the restaurant lost money for the
first time. My accountant said, 'You had your fun. You have better uses for
your money.' All the other shit was going on," Chodorow says, adding that
Polsenberg advised him to shutter China Grill. "I said no, I really like the
restaurant. So I got personally involved there—and by 1992, it had made a
dramatic recovery." He ordered his chef to get mashed potatoes on the
menu, stat; the chef protested there was nothing Asian about spuds, so
Chodorow had a thunderbolt: wasabi!

Once Chodorow and his team began to focus on it, he says, the empire
built up quickly. A second China Grill opened in 1995, in Miami, and then
Schrager came calling. By 2001, there were 20 Chodorow restaurants; his
only failures were Miami's Red Square and the China Grill cafés. "When
I've done things that lost money, it doesn't affect me at all," Chodorow tells
me. "My habits are the same whether I've been up or down." He clearly
believes this, despite the recent $5 million Hamptons mansion purchase.
Perhaps what he means is that he's a born survivor, a scrappy Miami Beach
kid who's most at home with old friends despite his exceptional ability to
pinpoint trends.

Right now, Chodorow's thinking Spain. "I went to the Basque region
recently and had one of the most fantastic food experiences of my life," he
raves. "I've been to Gaminiz, the restaurant near the Guggenheim museum
in Bilbao, and we're planning a Basque restaurant in New York."

Chodorow is back in the car en route to Morgans hotel, where the most discreet of signs announces Asia de Cuba. Though it's a Monday afternoon, there's a fine buzz in this sexy room, with its long, glowing communal table and elegant, white-swathed booths. Even Neil Faggen looks relaxed here.

"When Asia de Cuba opened in 1997, there was another restaurant, Moomba, that opened within two weeks of us," Chodorow says. "They were the two hot openings of 1997. Three years later, Moomba closed. Asia de Cuba had its best year ever. The reason that happened is because we never forgot we're a restaurant. No matter how cool you make the place, if you don't have great food, the restaurant won't last." He laughs and tells me that in last year's Zagat guide, Asia de Cuba got a 23 (out of 30 points) for food. "The comment was, 'Food better than it needs to be,'" he says. "Who ever heard of that in a restaurant?"

Published January 2003

Jeffrey Chodorow took his place among well-known celebrity chefs and restaurateurs with his role as the financier behind Rocco's in NBC's reality show The Restaurant. *While Chodorow spent season two of the series wondering on-camera why the New York restaurant with the hot-shot chef was losing money, he also oversaw plans for a second Red Square, part of the $245 million expansion of the Tropicana in Atlantic City.*

2 : THE **INGREDIENTS**

Great meals start with great flavors—and Philadelphia's homegrown specialties are coveted by chefs around the country.

The Great Grape Hunt

California has its cabernets, Oregon its pinot noirs.
What, Chaddsford Winery's Eric Miller wants to know,
should Pennsylvania have?

By Benjamin Wallace

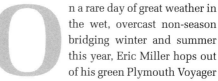

On a rare day of great weather in the wet, overcast non-season bridging winter and summer this year, Eric Miller hops out of his green Plymouth Voyager in the Brandywine Valley and looks around. With his sun-faded pink polo shirt, khaki shorts and hiking boots, Miller could be a counselor giving a prospective camper a tour ... of wine camp. He is surrounded by vines. Somewhere among them, perhaps, is The One, the grape variety that could do for Pennsylvania what cabernet sauvignon did for the Napa Valley. "That's cab franc over there," he says, pointing down a slope at rows of a grape typically used for blending. "And oh, we're doing a shiraz trial over there."

At Chaddsford Winery, the state's preeminent contribution to the industry, Miller produces wines both from obscure regional grape varieties like chambourcin and from famous noble varieties like chardonnay and pinot noir. They are tasty, impressive wines that often rise to the level of very good. Still, none is quite right.

That's why he continues to experiment, both in the "torture garden" in front of his house, where he first grows any new grape he's considering, and then in his vineyards, where those grapes that show promise in the torture garden matriculate. In this particular vineyard, we are surrounded not only by shiraz and cabernet franc, but also by pinot noir, barbera, chambourcin and vignoles. Has Miller found the perfect grape? "I'm getting there," he says.

He's been at this for 20 years.

It's from the old world that we inherit the notion that for every place there is a perfect grape: We know Burgundy for its peerless pinot noirs (pinot thrives on the loamy, clay-tinged earth and moderate temperatures of the region), Bordeaux for its exquisitely balanced cabernet sauvignons (cab flourishes there because of the gravelly soil and high, windbreak dunes, among several factors), the Loire Valley for its refreshing sauvignon blancs. From across the Alps, we enjoy similarly heaven-made matches in the fruity sangiovese reds of Chianti and the powerful nebbiolo-based wines of the Piemonte.

The stories of how these classic matchups came to be are mostly lost to history, but a handful survive through legend or anecdote. Take chablis: When Charlemagne wasn't busy beheading Saracens, he is said to have been the first to plant chardonnay in the now-fabled white Burgundy district of Corton-Charlemagne, and to have done so for mainly domestic reasons: The missus was on his case because as he moved into the golden years, red wine stains on his increasingly white beard were becoming an issue.

With the rise of New World wine regions such as California, New Zealand, Chile and South Africa, ambitious winemakers have quested after equally felicitous unions. Typically, the model has been to identify the Old World region most like the New World region, then follow its time-tested lead. On the West Coast, Robert Mondavi found that the Napa Valley had much in common with Bordeaux, and thus was born the California cab. In Oregon, pioneer Dick Erath experimented with 23 different varieties before determining that he was in one of the few places on the planet where the fickle pinot noir grape would take; today, some Oregon pinot noir bottlings command prices in excess of $100.

As prices from the best-known regions, such as Napa and Bordeaux, soar out of reach of the average sipper, "emerging regions" have become the hot growth area for wine sales. On the East Coast, which is only starting to emerge, there's a race on among the few states that have made any kind of name for themselves. Most successfully, New York's Finger Lakes district has won acclaim for its rieslings. Virginia, which has garnered some attention for its chardonnays, grandiosely dubs itself "the Napa of the East."

In Pennsylvania, the perfect-grape mantle is still up for grabs, but if we do have a perfect grape, it's likely that the man who discovers it will be Eric Miller. Chaddsford, which he owns with his wife, Lee, is by far the largest of the state's 86 commercial wineries; it sold 35,000 cases last year and appears on restaurant wine lists from D.C. to New York. Chaddsford is also, certainly, the most acclaimed Pennsylvania winery. In a 1992 *Wine Spectator* survey of American wines outside of California, Washington, Oregon and New York, its chardonnay won first place, and critic Robert Parker, too, has singled out its wines. Miller, one of whose four sons is named Tannin, is also the most experimental of Pennsylvania vintners, having tried all kinds of grapes, as reflected in the sheer number of different wines Chaddsford makes, around 18. "It's too many for a winery in this region," Miller says. "But it was a learning experience I had to go through."

Miller knows from imperfect grapes. He had an unsettled childhood, living for a year when he was 15 in Burgundy, where his father, Mark, an artist, traded paintings for wine. In high school back in Marlborough, New York, in the '60s, Miller filed the first long-hair lawsuit in the country, he says, after being kicked out of school for his shoulder-length mane; he was quickly reinstated. He then traveled the country playing guitar, before bad weather intervened. His father had traded in his paintbrushes for grape presses, launching a winery, Benmarl, in the Hudson Valley of New York. When a hurricane hit in 1970, Eric helped save the harvest, then spent the next 10 years as winemaker there.

Benmarl was, Miller says, "a 100 percent experimental vineyard." Mark Miller experimented with some 10 varieties before eventually making a commitment to creating wine exclusively from the esoteric French-American hybrid Seyval blanc grape. "He decided to be different for the sake of being different," Eric says. "It's better than pinot noir, but no one's going to pay for it."

When Eric decided it was time to strike out on his own, he and his wife studied the East Coast and were mainly interested in Long Island and Virginia. But passing through Pennsylvania, Miller decided he'd found a place that combined the best of both: Its moderate climate meant none of the roastingly hot Virginia summers, its inland position spared it from the coastal storms that bedevil Long Island, and the complex soils washing down into the foothills of the Brandywine Valley were more appealing than the gravel and silica underfoot on L.I.

The conditions struck Miller as like nowhere so much as Burgundy, and when he moved here, in the back of his mind he had the idea of making Burgundy-style chardonnays. His wife, the more practical of the two, was less interested in experimentation for experimentation's sake and more interested in building a solid business. But at first, obscure regional grapes dominated Miller's production. Cabs and chardonnays accounted for only five percent of the wine he made, while varieties no one has ever heard of, like Seyval and chambourcin and vignoles, made up the other 95 percent. This was mainly because those were the only grapes available, but Miller didn't mind. He was still learning the microclimate, working on the best ways to trellis and prune, figuring out how different varieties responded to the environment, and training nearby farmers to be consistent suppliers. (Miller himself grows only 20 percent of the grapes he uses.)

But there's the perfect grape, and then there's the perfect grape. Meaning, Eric Miller might decide that, say, the Niagara varietal, planted in northwestern Pennsylvania's vineyards, makes a stunning wine, one that affords a more perfect marriage than a better-known grape. But so what? The man has bills to pay, and when was the last time you saw a wine list teeming with Niagaras? A perfect grape must have commercial upside, not just aesthetic potential. To make money, and to stand a chance in the marketplace, you have to hit it big with one of the majors, the noble grapes, the cabernets and chardonnays and pinot noirs of the world.

When Miller got around to making the big reds and whites of his dreams, 10 years after he'd first arrived, the road didn't get any smoother. His one attempt to make champagne resulted in quick surrender: "I didn't like it at all. It was just a little stink-bomb." The area was too warm. He has given up on sauvignon blanc, too, after several failed attempts; our climate just doesn't have the dramatic temperature swings (warm days, cool nights) that lead to high acidity, a key component of quality sauvignon blancs. "If you don't have a shot at making a great wine, why do it?" Miller says. He has never even bothered to experiment with riesling. "This region is not for riesling," he says, chopping the air with his hand. "Period. It's too warm." He has tried zinfandel and viognier, neither with great success. Zin, thin-skinned and tightly clustered, succumbed to this area's humidity, attracting mildew and fungus.

Pinot noir has been called the heartbreak grape, and Miller is among those it has spurned. His first 10 years at Chaddsford, he made a pinot that was consistently bad, a thin and vapid little wine. One day, he discovered why: All those years, he'd been using a champagne clone of the grape, unsuitable for making a red wine. "That hurt me so much when I made that discovery," he says, "I got bitter and cleaned house. Twenty years ago, I didn't even know about clones. I didn't think to ask."

Along the way, he also learned that his original fantasy of Burgundy on the Brandywine was ill-conceived. "There are as many differences as similarities," he says with a sigh. "It's warmer here, there's less clay in the soil, there's more gravel."

Nonetheless, Miller has made estimable wines from several varieties. Among the regionals, his favorite red is chambourcin. His favorite white is vignoles, which retains its acidity despite the warm climate. Of the noble varieties, his pinot noir has come into its own, he has produced an award-winning chardonnay, and he has found cabernet to be a good fit here, its robust mouthfeel compensating for its low acidity. And he's still forging ahead with his experiments. Despite his earlier failures with zin, he has an idea for how to make the grape work in this area. A pinot grigio is also in the pipeline. But the grape he's most excited about is barbera, the Italian varietal used mainly as a blending grape.

He likes its thick skin, reliable growth patterns and saturated color, and "its acids and sugars are perfect for here." His enthusiasm makes it easy to imagine that one day, wine lovers will rhapsodize about Pennsylvania barberas the way they now speak of California cabs and Oregon pinot noirs, and about Eric Miller as the East Coast Mondavi. But even Miller has his doubts. "Will Americans be willing to accept Italian varietals and flavors?" he asks. "I don't know. If we can make these wines, I know we can overcome the Pennsylvania stigma."

Published September 2003

Chocolates
With a Conscience

Six years ago, John Doyle was a high-octane investment banker at a cutthroat New York City firm. Today, life is a little sweeter—though no less stressful

By Victor Fiorillo

I**t's a swampy late-August 94 degrees, and John Doyle and his fiancée, Germantown native Kira Baker, are zooming through North Philadelphia in their $600 un-air-conditioned 1992 Mazda 323, driving as fast as possible, windows down, to ensure the safe delivery of their temperamental cargo—350 boxes of the couple's handcrafted Jubilee Chocolates, praised on *Gourmet*'s February cover as that magazine's favorite chocolate.

It's a busy day. Earlier, they interviewed Liberian refugees for positions at their Feltonville factory. Then a pesky would-be consultant called, promising to make them millions, but Doyle insists he wants "slow, natural, organic growth." Then a potential investor rang. Doyle politely declined—investors don't get "organic growth" or refugees. Plus, he says, he hasn't borrowed any money yet, noting, "We've been bootstrapped all the way."

They still have to find time to pick raspberries. They need to figure out how they'll manage the product launch at Whole Foods Manhattan, less than a month away—at the same time that Baker will be reimmersed in doctoral studies at Penn.

There is also the small matter of Doyle finding a suit for their wedding next weekend. "I have to find something to wear, and I am not doing the tux thing," he promises. "There are just so many fucking details."

Details including the development of a new chocolate variety with a longer shelf life (their current product, devoid of preservatives, only lasts two weeks), and a trip to West Africa to verify that their chocolate suppliers aren't using slave or child labor. Making a profit while saving the world is no easy task.

There used to be more time to worry about refugees and human rights. Before the *Gourmet* coup in February, Jubilee produced only 4,000 pieces per month. This month, they are making 45,000, with orders coming in from as far away as Alaska and Hawaii—and Valentine's Day is fast approaching. Their sales grew from $10,000 in 2001, the year of Jubilee's incorporation, to $30,000 in 2002. Doyle expects that they will break $300,000 this year, and hopes to grow into a $10 million business in as many years.

Their success has forced the pair to relinquish control of certain aspects of the company. Just two years ago, it would have pained them to think of someone else making the chocolates. Now most are made by a full-time production worker who, Doyle admits, can work twice as fast as he and Baker combined. A recent photo shoot tried Doyle's nerves, since he had always photographed the chocolates himself. "Losing control is the hardest part of the business," remarks Doyle. "You've got to learn to let people do their thing."

Then there are the compromises. Recently, they decided to do away with their star-anise-flavored chocolate because, according to Doyle, "People just don't get it." They've stopped making the saffron-rosewater variety, except around Valentine's Day. If only Americans had French palates. They have been forced to hire a pricey food chemist in Atlanta to concoct a recipe for another product that will last for months, instead of the two-week shelf life of the original line, because most retailers won't carry Jubilee chocolates if they need to move them that quickly.

But there are certain principles on which Jubilee's owners say they will never compromise: using organic, fair-trade ingredients wherever possible; providing job opportunities at competitive wages to unskilled workers— they haven't figured this one out just yet; supporting local farmers; educating the public on these and other important social issues; and, of course, creating an exceptional product. These are all values the couple shares with another Philadelphia culinary success: Judy Wicks.

It was at a happy hour at Wicks's White Dog Cafe in West Philly that Doyle and Baker met in 1999. Having ditched the conscience-eradicating megalomania of Wall Street, Doyle had accepted an administrative position at White Dog, where his responsibilities included the sourcing of ingredients from area farms. Meanwhile, Baker was in a graduate program at Penn and overseeing an urban public-school gardening project. The couple wanted to start a business together that would not only be successful but would also produce positive social change. They saw upscale chocolates as their niche in Philadelphia.

The confections could be flavored with locally grown organic fruits, herbs and spices. Production would require tasks suitable for the unskilled people they wanted to offer employment. Plus, since most people review the insert describing the chocolates before digging in, communicating the story of Jubilee and the farmers behind the flavors would be easy.

Doyle and Baker had little culinary experience, so he apprenticed on Le Bec-Fin's pastry line and experimented in his tiny Powelton Village kitchen. They moved the operation to North Philadelphia's Wyoming Street, in the same building where Goldenberg Chews were once produced and where another chocolatier works, giving them access to more—albeit in most cases ancient—equipment. They developed eight varieties, all consisting of a hard chocolate shell enrobing a moist ganache of flavors like mint, lavender with honey, Earl Grey tea with orange-flower water, star anise, and raspberry.

Many of the flavoring ingredients came from local organic providers—the honey from a Philadelphia apiarist, the raspberry from Gap, Pennsylvania, and the mint from the urban garden tended to by students at Drew Elementary school. The cream was fresh from Lancaster.

The main ingredient, however, was neither organic nor local. Of course, chocolate doesn't grow in this region, and Baker says that the organic chocolates on the market today are significantly inferior to their choice: Valrhona.

For publicity, Doyle and Baker hosted free public tastings in West Philadelphia. Doyle collected hundreds of e-mail addresses and began marketing the chocolates through a newsletter with a down-home feel. The local newspapers picked up on their story, and then, in February, *Gourmet* pictured the chocolates on its cover, declaring, "We found our favorite chocolates."

The phones were jammed for days. Requests to join the Jubilee family poured in. Baker had to take off three weeks from school, and the couple and their friends worked around the clock to fill orders—400 boxes per day at their peak. The newsletter distribution increased to 5,000. Jubilee became a national chocolate company overnight, and taking over the world seemed easier than changing it.

Since February's boom, sales have tapered off. The chocolate season ends around Father's Day. But the Doyles, who recently returned from their honeymoon in Bordeaux, know that crunch time is coming, so they're back to finding more staff. Whether the refugees will work out remains to be seen. Jubilee has been down similar roads before, having hired the homeless and drug addicts. "We tried it, and it just didn't work," laments John. "But we're still very much committed to hiring people who really need work."

Other challenges lie ahead. With star anise on its way out, the Doyles need to perfect its replacement, Hawaiian ginger. Kira thinks it's too subtle. John thinks it's too strong. He's worried about improving the back-office systems before the holidays hit, while Kira, who turns 27 this month, is concerned about the origins of Valrhona chocolate. "In the end, you really don't know where it comes from," she admits.

The longer-shelf-life chocolate is in production. John says there are no preservatives and that the only difference is less cream. Though it's less rich, he claims to like it just as much.

John plans to begin drawing a salary shortly, since he hasn't been paid in over a year. The couple is looking into a Jubilee Chocolate Bus to be used for deliveries and field trips for urban children. And, using the Ben & Jerry's model, John is hoping to sell stock in the company to local residents.

Kira's dreaming of next summer, when she says they will start producing pâté de fruit in flavors like apple, mint and mango, and possibly Jubilee ice cream, both perfect solutions for the drop in summer chocolate business. John, seven years older and generally more cautious, isn't so sure.

"We're looking into both," he says. "But it's very important that we take slow, controlled steps. There are people with millions of dollars ready to invest in Jubilee, but we need to avoid an artificial growth. The best way to build business is slowly, naturally, and organically. Just like the chocolates."

Published October 2003

Thank You for Smoking

Bucks County's Max Hansen makes some of the best
smoked salmon in America. Who knew?

By Sasha Issenberg

Smoked salmon has been so many things in its brief but happy American life—immigrant sidewalk snack, white-tablecloth delicacy, mainstream supermarket treat—that it is little surprise to hear "artisanal" attached to it as well. The man throwing around the ubiquitous A-word is Max Hansen, who seems to be doing everything he can to discredit the stereotype of the salmon-smoker as an old Jewish man in an apron, hustling through a crowded room where piscine corpses dangle from hooks overhead. Hansen, 43, considers himself something of a gentleman smoker, having set up shop in the rolling hills of Bucks County, which has never been thought of as smoked-fish country. He works out of a very small one-story concrete-block building that looks as though its owner saw a medical examiner's laboratory and came back to his interior decorator and said, "I want that." It is spotlessly clean, outfitted with cutting surfaces and refrigerators, and kept at a chilly temperature, with dueling aromas of cleaning materials and pungent flesh. "When I am in that room, curing and slicing, there's something Zen-like about it," Hansen says. He calls the building "Salmon Land."

On a brisk, sunny day in early October, inside Salmon Land, Hansen, dressed in double-breasted chef's whites, opens a refrigerator and removes a side of salmon that he estimates weighs two and a quarter pounds. It comes to him as a "smokers cut," with the fat already trimmed and the pinbones gently removed so as not to break the flesh. It is a rich pink-orange, signaling a moderate fat content: The leaner a fish, the brighter its color. Fat lends flavor and the supple, melt-in-your-mouth quality of good salmon. Hansen settled on this farm-raised Atlantic salmon from Scotland after experimenting with salmon from Chile, Maine and Canada. He also tried an Icelandic salmon so fatty from the cold water that its flesh was a creamy pink. "It was like eating grease," he says.

Salmon Land typically handles 250 to 350 pounds of salmon a week. (Acme, the most venerable of the Brooklyn smokehouses, produces about

100,000 pounds weekly out of a 70,000-square-foot factory, and employs 145 people.) Hansen's output varies from week to week—and spikes during the period between Thanksgiving and New Year's—because he smokes on demand: for mail-order business, for his catering firm Max & Me, and for restaurant clients such as Montrachet in New York and Susanna Foo's restaurants in Philadelphia and Atlantic City. *Food & Wine* has called Hansen's handiwork the best in the country. For a decade, the French Laundry in Napa Valley has used Hansen's smoked salmon exclusively. "It's not as much a taste thing as texture," chef Thomas Keller explains. "It's like eating butter." He is, however, unable to compare it to others on the market. "I don't taste any more salmons, really," he says. "I haven't tasted another smoked salmon—other than airline salmon—in 10 years."

In the introduction to his new cookbook, *Smoked Salmon*, Hansen writes about his "personal quest to develop the perfect smoked salmon recipe." It hasn't been a lifelong quest, as Hansen never tasted smoked salmon until he was 18. It took a summer restaurant job in Martha's Vineyard for the boy from New Hope to be introduced to the delicacy, but he quickly made up for lost time. He moved to New York to help open the Cajun restaurant Memphis, just off a stretch of Broadway—it holds Zabar's, Citarella, Murray's Sturgeon Shop and Fairway, with Barney Greengrass one block over on Amsterdam—that can be considered the stations of the cross for smoked-fish devotees. Hansen began to sample and compare the different salmons, and studied, through the glass partitions of display cases, the skilled, delicate movements of those who sliced the pink carcasses by hand.

Hansen came to believe that he could make a better smoked salmon than those he ate in New York. "I found them too salty, too fishy, not smoky enough," he says. "It tastes great going in, but once it sits in your mouth for a while, it develops some unpleasant character." Hansen went to teach at the New England Culinary Institute, his alma mater, where a colleague gave him a book on Scottish smoking styles, and Hansen experimented with the school's smoker to design the perfect cure.

The result is a mixture that Hansen has used for 15 years, contained in a white garbage can on wheels. It includes kosher salt, pretzel salt and granulated sugar, in a ratio that Hansen says is roughly four parts salt to one part sugar. There are only a few variables in his business—the origin of the fish, the recipe, the temperature and duration of the cure, and the woods used in the smoking process—and so he keeps some secrets about the way in which he cures and smokes his salmon. "I don't want somebody with a ton of money to put me out of business," he says. "With food science what it is, someone can buy my salmon at a store and bring it to a scientist. They might not be able to find out the process, but they can find out what the ingredients are." One such secret is the precise ratio of the Max & Me salt-sugar mixture, although he will acknowledge that he includes neither brown sugar nor any herbs or spices, as other smokers do. He will say that he has an "unorthodox curing process."

After scoring the fillet's skin with a knife, just cracking the silvery surface, Hansen brushes it with cold water. He takes a handful of the salt-sugar mix and sows it over the fillet, covering the skin entirely with what looks like a dusting of granular snow. He sprays water on it, to make the salt stick better, flips it over, and repeats. With both sides covered in a slushy mix, Hansen places the salmon on a grill above a pan. This process is dry-curing, as opposed to brining, in which the salmon would be submerged in liquid. Smokers gauge the intensity of their cures by a "water-face-salt" ratio, which measures the proportion of flesh to cure. The law requires a minimum of four and a half percent—anything less is still considered raw. Hansen's is between six and seven percent—still less than many competitors', he says. During the cure, salt pulls moisture out of the fish and leaves flavor; the sugar is there only for taste.

After the fish has been sitting on the grill for 15 minutes, already a considerable puddle has developed in the pan beneath it—water that has seeped out. After 16 to 24 hours, Hansen rinses the salmon and lets it sit to dry. Then it's smoking time.

In 1988, Hansen returned to Bucks County. Without access to a smoker, he built his own. He took a refrigerator, sawed a hole in the top, inserted a stovepipe, and rigged a firebox on the side. The firebox produced smoke, and the stovepipe created a draft that pulled the smoke up over the fish. Hansen put the contraption on his porch. "It looked a little *Beverly Hillbillies*," he says, but he was able to reliably smoke salmon to his taste. He served it at catering jobs, and when it got raves, he realized he could market it. He bought a refrigerator and a vacuum-packing machine, and began to sell his salmon at $15-plus per pound wholesale. (The price hasn't changed much.) "It was like hitting oil," he says.

A few years ago, Hansen purchased a large professional smoker that can hold 49 sides of salmon at a time. In the smokebox, he uses a combination of hard- and fruit-woods: hickory, oak, cherry, apple, and "a couple others that should remain nameless." (Cherrywood isn't packaged for smoking; Hansen gets his by trading salmon to cabinetmaker friends for trash cans of cherry dustings and chips.) "What you're doing is just producing smoke, not heat," Hansen says. The salmon stays in the smoker—a fan circulates the smoke throughout the box—for three to six hours. "I'm trying to impart a nice, smoky flavor, but not so much smoke flavor that you can't taste the fish," Hansen says.

Max & Me salmon does have a clean, even taste that is certainly less fishy and salty than many of the salmons at the New York institutions Hansen used to frequent, and without the pungent, tonic-like quality some of them have. (It does, however, maintain a discernible taste of salt; every smoked salmon does.) Hansen's is less funky than the innovative preparations—wasabi and beet cures this season—put out by London's venerable H. Forman & Son.

Hansen lets the salmon sit for 48 hours after being smoked. Then he skins the fillet with a thin knife, and trims fat from the sides. (The skin and scraps are put aside for Montrachet, which uses them to make stock for a smoked-salmon consommé.) Hansen places the trimmed side of salmon on a gold-foil board and puts it inside a $30,000 electric-pneumatic-hybrid machine, which does its work far more delicately than a typical meat-slicer. In a matter of seconds, the salmon slides out the other end. On the gold board, the fish is outlined in oil, like a crime scene. After a week-long process of curing and smoking, the salmon is ready to be vacuum-packed—which Hansen says keeps the refrigerated fish fresh for two weeks—and sent by UPS anywhere in the country.

Every Tuesday, Hansen drives to New York to personally deliver packages of salmon to his New York customers. "It's like he's got his own vineyard—that's the way he treats his salmon. He still has the old values," says Montrachet chef Chris Gesualdi. While Hansen's there, he returns to the Upper West Side, to buy Ben's cream cheese and H&H sesame bagels, which he freezes the same day and then lightly toasts, to have with his salmon. He stops at the salmon counters, where so much fish is now pre-sliced and prepackaged, sold out of refrigerator cases. "They have 10 times more salmon than they ever did," he says, "because a lot more people have gone into the smoking business. You've got your varieties with different herbs, crusts and flavors." He is done experimenting. "I don't want to be a carnival act. I don't need to be a line of goods. I want to do one product to the best of my ability," Hansen says. "You can potentially age gracefully smoking salmon."

Published December 2003

Four-Star Farmers

Bucks County boutique grower Branch Creek Farm quietly
influences Philadelphia menus from Fork to the Four Seasons

By Amy Donohue

In Philadelphia's discriminating and inventive restaurant kitchens—places where ingredients are described on menus with precise and lengthy pedigrees—this will be the summer of baby okra. That is because Mark and Judy Dornstreich, since 1978 the proprietors of Bucks County's 21-acre Branch Creek Farm, became interested in okra over the winter while browsing through seed catalogs, and so will be growing it alongside their splendid lettuces, herbs and heirloom tomatoes.

The Dornstreichs are held in unique and holy regard by Philadelphia's chefs. Twice a week, their refrigerated van pulls up to the back doors of places like Angelina, Fork, Lacroix, Morimoto and Salt (and a dozen more restaurants around Philadelphia), loaded with carefully packed cardboard boxes of baby greens, herbs and vegetables. These might be the most fragile stems of seeded-two-weeks-ago baby celery, or diminutive French Breakfast radishes for a salad aux fines herbes served with yellowfin tuna hamachi at Lacroix.

Chefs, who are not always the most expressive men and women (sometimes they're downright crabby), become schoolgirlish when the Dornstreichs are mentioned. Many, like Francesco Martorella of Bliss restaurant and Thien Ngo of Fork, make regular pilgrimages to the farm, which is in Perkasie, 45 miles northwest of City Hall.

Martorella met the Dornstreichs in 1983, when he was sous-chef at the Four Seasons' Fountain restaurant. "I remember when they dropped samples off, I showed them to Jean-Marie [Lacroix, then the executive chef for Four Seasons] and said, 'Look at this stuff, it's unbelievable!'" says Martorella. He can throw any odd request their way: "I used to ask them to pick up all the cilantro seeds that fall off the plants—they have really intense flavor for duck sauces and stock," he recalls.

Fork owner Ellen Yin admires Mark's perfectionism in matters such as picking zucchini blossoms at dawn, when they are open and easiest to cook with. "In summer, we buy baby celery, pea tops, zucchini blossoms, Thai basil, sorrel. Their things are so good, they don't need to be overly complicated," she says. For a dinner last fall, Yin invited as guest of honor Amanda Hesser, the *New York Times* food writer whose book *The Cook and the Gardener* chronicled her stint as chef at a French château, where she depended heavily on the estate's gardener, M. Milbert. "The Dornstreichs are our Monsieur and Madame Milbert," Yin says, and so Ngo created a dinner based around Branch Creek's wares for Hesser's visit.

"Hey, sweetie!" Mark Dornstreich one recent chilly spring morning called to his wife, who was walking over to the barn/office from their white farmhouse. She responded with a radiant smile, very feminine with her long, wavy gray hair and delicate jewelry, her thin frame wrapped in overalls, flannel and boots. "When we started, organic agriculture was in no way part of American agriculture," Mark told me. "It almost had a political dimension to it."

On this day, Branch Creek Farm looked tranquil and muddy: Its namesake stream is as wide as a small river, a hundred yards from the barns and flanked by tall trees.

Mark Dornstreich was a professor of anthropology at Rutgers in the mid-1970s; one morning while traveling in India, he turned to his wife and said, "I think I want to grow vegetables for a living." This was unexpected: Both he and Judy were in their early 30s; Mark had grown up in Little Neck, Long Island, and Judy in Northeast Philadelphia, and the two met as undergrads at Penn. So there was nothing to predict this new passion, except perhaps that they had tired of living in cities, and both were sometime vegetarians. Mark enrolled in an intensive course at Emerson College in England, both apprenticed at a farm in York, and they chose a property in Pennsylvania partly because it was near Judy's family. "I live in my matrilineal territory," Mark said inside his barn office, "or, to be more anthropological, my matrilocal territory." Mark, who has dark eyes, a spare frame and a reserved manner, was dressed in jeans, boots and a trucker hat. (Probably he had his before Ashton Kutcher did.) Both he and Judy retain a bemused, hippie-ish air.

That is not to say they are easygoing; Mark in particular is quite intense. Over the years, the couple has survived droughts, weathered floods, been surrounded by McMansionettes—think Mel Gibson and Sissy Spacek in *The River*, but with baby mizuna greens. Their four children, who range in age from 17 to late 20s, worked all summer, too, when they would rather have been at tennis camp.

The steamy-windowed greenhouses, with their raised beds of dark soil supporting slender plants, were so pristine inside as to evoke a laboratory. Indeed, the six or so staff at Branch Creek, led by Mark and farm manager Greg York (the number expands slightly in summer), are hyper-vigilant about closing the doors quickly when entering and leaving, to prevent insects from hopping inside. The hand-seeded flats are filled with customized organic soil imported from Canada, and no chemical comes near them, though the flats themselves are given a mild Clorox rinse between plantings to prevent disease. Their contents range in color from the curly cress's pale celadon to rich green baby chard to deep-red micro amaranth. "The lettuces are so beautiful when they're planted," said Judy. "They're Mark's palette."

Branch Creek staffer Pastora Amador was harvesting a flat of 20-day-old kailan, a tender Asian green that resembles arugula in shape. She cut just above the soil so the fragile stems were left intact. Each leaf was impeccable.

"They're all the same thing," explained Judy of micro, baby and regular vegetable designations. "It's just how long something grows." Home gardeners' biggest mistake, she believes, is going for first-prize-at-the-fair size over flavor. She handed me a feathery stem of micro fennel, its pale bulb smaller than a pinky nail, tasting subtly of anise. When this same plant is grown outside this summer, it will be picked when the plant is about as thick as a finger, and sold as baby fennel. "Cut things young!" Judy urged. "The difference between a baby zucchini and a regular one is cutting early."

Inside unheated greenhouses called hoop houses, sturdier plants have "wintered over": dark spinach, lavender and chervil. In late May, thousands of seeds will be planted in fields that are black and dense from the rich topsoil that Mark marinates all winter: part composted leaves (the township collects them and dumps them at Branch Creek), part horse manure for nutritional value. Beginning this month, an incredible bounty will be flowing into Philly restaurants (and to Metropolitan Bakery's downtown stores). There will be BCF classics—heirloom and Green Zebra tomatoes; Silver Queen corn that comes in for one glorious month; edible nasturtiums; Eclipse, Mayfair and Knight peas; Bull's Blood beets; tiny squash; 20 varieties of lettuces; and that okra.

The Dornstreichs are incredibly methodical, knowledgeable and rigorous about soil, seeding, plant care and harvesting. But Judy doesn't use a computer, and all the ordering is done on the phone. They don't want to expand, and luckily for the chefs (if not for the Dornstreichs' real-estate values), their farm is in a floodplain, and thus largely unsuited for development.

Judy's calls to chefs aren't limited to talk of baby chard: "She and Thien have long conversations about what's going on in their lives," says Fork's Ellen Yin. Perhaps this is one of the reasons chefs' attachments to Branch Creek are so fierce, along with the pixie tomatoes and sorrel.

Published June 2004

Miracle of the Loaves

How Metropolitan Bakery makes the best bread in the city

By April White

Thump. Thump. Thump. Thump. *Thwack.*

A perfectly rounded ball of bread dough—just flour and water, mainly—lands in a willow basket, where it will be allowed to rise for 12 hours before baking. The willow basket gives Metropolitan Bakery's country white boule its subtly grooved surface. Here in Metropolitan's sparse 10,000-square-foot Port Richmond baking facility, co-owner James Barrett considers the loaf, then lifts it again, tucking and smoothing the pliable dough in a single fluid two-handed motion. *Thump*, against the lightly floured table. *Thwack*, back into the basket. Artisanal bakers show their unadorned talents through their country whites, and Barrett, age 40, molds his with painstaking attention to detail. He brushes some flour from the bakery's central worktable, further coating his already grayed black shoes. "Too much flour dries the bread out," he explains.

"Perfectionist," Metropolitan Bakery partner Wendy Born accuses him, with a friendly smile. "He's a total perfectionist," says Striped Bass chef Terence Feury. "James should be committed he's such a perfectionist," White Dog Cafe chef Kevin von Klause says. "That's why his bread tastes so good, why it's consistently the best."

Von Klause isn't alone in his assessment. Barrett's naturally leavened breads are on restaurant tables around the city—from Lacroix at the Rittenhouse, the Fountain, and Fork to Marathon Grill—and the bakery, which recently celebrated its 10th anniversary, has opened its sixth local retail location, at the Ardmore Farmer's Market. Von Klause has had Barrett's breads on the menu at the White Dog Cafe since pre-Metropolitan days, when Culinary Institute of America grad Barrett was the cafe's pastry chef and Born was a managing partner.

It was at White Dog that Metropolitan Bakery got its start. Barrett and Born became good friends and then, despite the poor city economy in the early 1990s, business partners, raising money from family and friends and even putting Born's house up as collateral to secure a loan. It was also in the White Dog kitchen that Barrett first developed the recipe and the bubbling starter that he still uses to make his country white. His starter—an ingredient essential for naturally leavened breads, produced without commercial yeasts—consists of flour, water, and Lancaster-grown Concord grapes, which draw wild yeasts from the air. It was birthed somewhere in the pungent, sour depths of a plastic tub, the size and shape of a trash can, that's now stored in a climate-controlled room in Metropolitan's Port Richmond facility. In a city without the strong bread tradition of places like Paris or San Francisco, and with many homegrown bakeries, including artisanal rival Le Bus, vying to put bread on your table, Barrett hoped that the distinction of using only wild yeasts—as well as the ritzy Rittenhouse Square location of the bakery's flagship store—would set his bread apart.

Barrett started his bread experiments by reading everything he could about naturally leavened breads. He tasted breads in Europe (the bakery name comes from the Paris subway) and around the country. And he read with the same hunger; *The Italian Baker* was his bible. He studied with Nancy Silverton, of La Brea Bakery in Los Angeles. "And I threw away a lot of bad batches of bread," Barrett says.

"We made an impression," Born recalls, laughing. "Our first customers thought the breads were burnt!" Born, age 51, is the face people associate with Metropolitan, the energetic blond with a baseball cap and a warm hello even at 7 a.m. "They were fully caramelized," counters Barrett. "There's a fine line between caramelized and burnt."

Flavored breads were the craze in the late 1980s—"Remember the Brazil nut loaf and cumin-red pepper rolls?" Born asks—but Barrett focused his efforts on the basics. "As a baker, you are judged on your country white bread," he explains. "It's harder to do the plain breads well." His recipes have changed only slightly, to adapt to the different baking environments he encountered as the operation moved from the White Dog to a small bakery in a Delaware office building, and then to the current spot under I-95. "I'm just tweaking," Barrett says. "Perfecting."

At Metropolitan's rustic French country bakeries—off Rittenhouse, on Pine Street in Washington Square West, on Market Street in Old City—those plain breads line the wall like floured works of art: the subtle cross-hatched pattern of the rosemary-olive oil rounds, the jutting points of a basket of baguettes, the pitted surface of an olive-thyme loaf. While Born makes her circuit each morning, checking inventory and greeting customers, Barrett bustles through the Port Richmond facility, which now operates almost 24 hours a day, with breads baked overnight for 6 a.m. deliveries.

Dressed in a Metropolitan-monogrammed, flour-faded denim shirt and checked chef's pants, Barrett pauses to listen to the bread mixer, which mixes the bread in small batches and short bursts. The scientist in him knows that the friction of the powerful machine will begin to heat the dough. It's rainy today, and unexpectedly warm, and he has an elaborate temperature control system in the warehouse, but the artist in Barrett knows that sometimes you just have to listen to the bread. This mix needs more flour. He's got a thermometer in his pocket, a heavy book of precise recipes, and a carefully timed process, developed over more than a decade of bread production. Still, he reaches into the nearby bread bin, poking at proofed white-bread dough. His index finger leaves a belly button there. He tears off a piece of the dough and stretches it until it's so thin, it's transparent. The dough doesn't tear. "This is ready to be shaped," he says.

In defense of Barrett's perfectionist tendencies, perfect shaping is not about looks alone. It's about taste, about distributing the yeast's gases evenly to produce a uniformly textured crumb and develop a crisp, unbroken crust. After 10 years in the bread business, Barrett can tell you how a bread will taste just by looking at it.

What emerges from the ovens, 48 hours after its humble beginnings as a pale blob, is an imposing boule, an almost perfect half-sphere more than eight inches in diameter. A gash running across the top and a dusting of browned flour give the surprisingly hefty loaf a homey, rustic look. Beneath the deeply caramelized crust, its carefully smoothed exterior now a rough landscape of tan mountains and browned valleys an eighth of an inch thick, lies the grain-flecked, creamy interior—the "crumb," in baker-speak. It is a lacy web of pencil-point air bubbles dotted with larger air pockets.

The loaf has a wheaty, somewhat sour aroma. The crust crackles slightly under the knife, but is hearty and chewy in the mouth, a bit salty, and rich with nutty flavors. The crumb is moist, resilient to the touch, and vaguely sour, with a hint of maltiness. "This tastes like what I imagine an ideal country white should," Barrett says. "That's the best test of a bread."

The bread's subtleties are why Born and Barrett haven't automated the baking process even as the output has increased 10-fold—and why the two partners haven't expanded beyond the Philadelphia region. "The bread is the boss," Born says.

Published June 2003

Hot Potatoes

In this golden age of the humble potato chip, there's no better place to be than right here, in the Potato Chip Belt

By Francine Maroukian

I have no interest in things automotive, never learned to drive, can't even refold, let alone read, a road map. But I am an enthusiastic traveling companion, willing to crisscross the country by car whenever I'm asked. I do it for the potato chips. Unlike chips manufactured by snack-food conglomerates (produced and distributed from facilities scattered all over the country), potato chips from smaller companies tend to stay within their own geographical locales, making them some of America's last real regional foods. It is possible to drive around this big, homogenized, everybody-in-khaki country listening to the same music and eating the same franchised fast food, and still score a different brand of potato chip in just about every state. In case you don't know it, Pennsylvania is a snack-food wonderland, and Philadelphians are sitting pretty, perched on the edge of America's mightiest potato-chip belt.

Celebrating their 150th birthday this year, potato chips were invented in 1853 by a cook named George Crum at Moon's Lake House, a resort in Saratoga Springs, New York—one of those "happy accidents" that occurred when a patron sent his fried potatoes back to the kitchen, complaining they were too thick. Potato chips are now America's number one savory snack, and Pennsylvania leads the country in production, an achievement that is less about diffusion and more a testimony to the state's "German heritage and entrepreneurial spirit," according to Tom Dempsey, vice president of sales and marketing at Utz Quality Foods, Inc., one of the largest and oldest local manufacturers (turning out about 50 million pounds annually). At Herr's, the local brand dominating the Philly market, director of marketing Daryl Thomas agrees: "People who lived in the area's farm communities were frugal by nature and looked for ways to generate additional income from their agricultural products. Potato chips were a natural spin-off, sold at farm stands and small local markets and even door-to-door."

Although other regional companies have been absorbed by national conglomerates (like the 1999 purchase of Massachusetts-based Cape Cod Potato

Chips by Lance, one of the world's largest producers of snack food), Herr's remains under the stewardship of founder Jim Herr, and Utz (originally Hanover Home Brand Potato Chips) is a third-generation outfit. But dedication to locally owned and operated companies is only part of Pennsylvania's potato-chip legacy: Kettle chips are a regional development gone national. Instead of undergoing a continuous fryer process that automatically turns out a constant stream of "regular" light, flat chips, kettle chips are made by a slower batch-by-batch method, under the artful supervision of "fry masters" who rely on their own techniques and timing to produce a variety of crisp, curled chips with a harder bite. "This is close to the way chips were made in the early 1900s," says Dempsey, "and Utz probably makes a broader range of kettle chips—four different styles in four different oils—than any other company in the country."

Chips seasoned to reflect a regional spice-palate are another benefit of smaller-company production, and there are people in far-off parts of the country who are crazy to get their hands on chips that Philadelphians take for granted—a feat that's not so easy. Like other American regional foods crafted to specific tastes (small-batch smokehouse bacon, for example), potato chips may be available via mail order, but the high cost of shipping such a perishable and fragile product is a major factor in keeping regional chips confined to their own neighborhoods. Long before terrorism turned air travel into a crapshoot of inconvenience, I was under orders to carry crab-boil-spiced chips—a singularly homegrown flavor that seems exotic to those who live outside of the Baltimore area—to snack-deprived friends whenever I visited them in Los Angeles.

For me, what's interesting about regional potato chips is not just what's in the bag—it's the bag as well. Potato chips were scooped out of barrels or sold in bulk tins (now collectibles available on eBay) until 1926, when Laura Scudder, founder of Scudder's Chips in Monterey Park, California, ironed sheets of wax paper into paper bags, filled them by hand, and ironed them shut. By inventing the first individually sized serving bags, Scudder not only helped to preserve freshness; she pioneered the idea of potato chips as self-service convenience food. In 1933, machine production of preprinted waxed glassine bags (with inks that didn't run or fade) began at the Dixie Wax Paper company in Dallas, Texas, and for the first time, potato-chip makers could safely and cheaply use the outside of the bag to let their customers know what was inside. Branding was born.

Smaller companies don't usually rely on advertising focus groups and marketing experts. They go with their gut, and "estate" potato-chip bags can be viewed as a form of American folk art: highly individualized and wildly inventive, often unwittingly employing a kitschy retro-design that features a bannered sales pitch. ("Gee! They're delicious!" boasts a bag of Pennsylvania's Kay & Ray's chips.) Today, Herr's may rely on I.Q. Design Group, a New York City-based company specializing in heritage food packaging, but according to I.Q. partner Bob Avino, the company has a strong idea of how its product should look: "Although they want their packaging to evolve, they know they are a regional, family-owned brand, and that's the message they stay with—the 'feeling' that they want to pass on to their customers."

But one universally accepted hallmark of progress is the potato itself. "Chipping" potatoes, a different variety from "table stock," are horticulturally adapted (through a natural rather than a chemical process) to be round like baseballs, without "eyes" or other deformities that make peeling difficult. The chemical makeup is also different, with a lower sugar content, to prevent caramelization (surface browning of natural sugars) during the frying process. "Our Russets Kettle Classics chip is made with regular russet potatoes," says Utz's Dempsey, "and when people see them, they think they are burnt. But that's what 'table stock' potatoes look like when their higher content of natural sugar has caramelized." Although Pennsylvania leads the country in production of "chipping" potatoes, devoting 70 percent of the state's potato acreage to them, both Utz and Herr's buy their potatoes seasonally, starting in the spring in Florida and moving up the Eastern Seaboard, to get the freshest potatoes (which make the freshest chips).

The bottom line is that at a couple of bucks a bag, chips may seem like small potatoes. But they're a big, complex business, mixing the power of a $6 billion industry with the vulnerability of flowers—delicate and characterized by their geography. And it's not just the trucking expense that keeps them close to home. Smaller companies strive to have their chips on your supermarket's shelves 24 hours after manufacturing. So enjoy them—and respect them.

Published May 2003

Caffeine High

Why Alain Ducasse, Martha Stewart and Georges Perrier all buy their coffee in Philadelphia

By Benjamin Wallace

A few years ago, Jean-Philippe Iberti, co-owner of La Colombe Torrefaction, the superstar Philadelphia coffee roaster, was invited to dine in the kitchen of Alain Ducasse's three-star restaurant in Monte Carlo. When he arrived, Ducasse said, "So you're the coffee guy," and set five cups of coffee before him. Iberti tasted the first and correctly guessed its identity: Brazilian. "Bam!" recalls his partner, Todd Carmichael. Iberti then guessed the next three—Colombian, Zimbabwean, Kenyan—correctly, identified the fifth as a blend, and was able to name two of its three component beans. "Bam! Bam! Bam! Bam!" Carmichael says. "It's like a game show. You're freaking out."

Carmichael and Iberti were guests on that occasion of Philadelphia chef Jean-Francois Taquet, who in those days made something of a hobby out of trying to stump Iberti. Once, at Taquet's home on the Main Line, the chef took two pieces of bread into his garden, then returned and handed them to the La Colombe owners to taste. The best Carmichael could come up with was "something herby." Iberti, the son of a produce dealer, was a bit more precise: "You rubbed it with tomato leaf." Bam! Taquet swore.

"J.P. gets this unusual pleasure from his taste buds," Carmichael says, "like there's this superhighway of nerves from his tongue to his brain."

La Colombe is best known to Rittenhouse Square strollers as the smoky, high-ceilinged café just north of 19th and Walnut with the good-looking baristas and motley clientele of students, artists, professionals and chess players. But while the café (along with its sibling in Manayunk) is the single biggest customer for the company's coffee, its sales represent only 10 percent of the 95,000 pounds roasted by La Colombe every month. The roaster's main business is supplying more than 800 restaurants in Philadelphia, New York, and other cities. La Colombe is served by the leading French chefs in New York, including Jean Georges Vongerichten and Daniel Boulud. Alain Ducasse selected it for his restaurant on Central Park South only after pitting it against the products of 14 other roasters—including Italy's legendary Francesco Illy, who flew in for the tasting. And ever since style doyenne Martha Stewart sampled La Colombe coffee at Jean Georges, she's been serving it in her Connecticut home. All these people are willing to pay two and a half times as much for La Colombe—seven dollars per pound wholesale— as they would for other premium coffees. Why?

Before arriving here in 1993, Iberti and Carmichael lived in Seattle. Iberti was studying flight engineering, and Carmichael was taking a break from selling yachts in the South of France; both tended bar in rival Seattle cafés until they joined up and decided to open their own place. In Seattle, the preferred taste in coffee is bitter verging on charred. In Philly—where the partners chose to base their fledgling café and roasting business because of the city's European, walk-around feel and the lack of competition—they discovered that the locals put a lot of sugar in their espresso. "People here were afraid of espresso" is how Iberti puts it. Iberti and Carmichael responded by designing a soft, gentle, almost molasses-flavored espresso called Nizza. New York, where high-end customers quickly proliferated after La Colombe signed up Le Bec-Fin and the Fountain in Philadelphia, demanded yet another flavor. "New York has this idea that they like really strong coffee, but really, they don't," Carmichael says. The result: Phocea, an espresso that hits the tongue with a punch but is actually quite mild. Corsica, the blend served in the Rittenhouse Square café, is what Carmichael calls "our flagship drip coffee." Iberti designed it to have enough strength to stand up to the eight ounces of milk and seven spoonfuls of sugar a philistine Philadelphian might add, yet still deliver a rich coffee flavor. Iberti, the tasting Zen master, is a purist: He drinks only espresso; a cappuccino has never passed his lips. Carmichael, his manic finance and operations partner, has reined in his previous daily consumption of 25 cups of espresso and now drinks only a handful of various coffee beverages every day.

The fourth La Colombe blend, Beaulieu, is the pair's luxury riff on the light-roast, high-acid style of supermarket coffees like Folgers and Maxwell House. They don't even sell it wholesale, because restaurants would get sticker shock. The fifth La Colombe blend is Monte Carlo, a decaffeinated coffee.

The La Colombe roasting plant is a two-story brick-and-steel warehouse in Port Richmond, with a basketball hoop mounted outside for downtime summer games. Inside, the chill of a January day gives way to a robust coffee aroma that seems to change by the minute, from chocolate to mint to toast. Here, the process starts with raw beans, scrawny green pebbles that arrive by truck twice a month. Hemp sackfuls lie around, stamped with the names of the beans' disparate ports of origin: Malabar, India, Costa Rica, Papua New Guinea. Since Iberti and Carmichael launched the business in 1993, they have homed in on the precise peak times for different regions and farmers, and now pinpoint their procurement of different beans to varying times of year.

Once the beans arrive, they are blended. Coffee, like wine, is made in two basic forms: as a varietal (a single-bean coffee, comparable to a single-grape wine such as a chardonnay), and as a blend (à la bordeaux). Two years ago, La Colombe bought out a varietal roaster, New Harmony, and now markets those coffees under the Phoenix brand. But the bulk of its business is the five blends. Each represents a different balance of bitterness and acidity, the dominant taste variables in coffee. La Colombe follows the traditional course of blending before roasting, to better meld the beans' distinct flavors into a coherent whole. And La Colombe workers do so manually, maintaining constant visual and tactile contact with the beans.

Unlike many commercial roasters, La Colombe recirculates the air given off by the roasting coffee, to enhance the beans' flavors. And while commercial roasters "flash-roast" their beans in a lightning five minutes, La Colombe takes a leisurely 12 to 15 minutes, the time window it has determined makes for the best roast with the most knitted-together flavors.

Following roasting and cooling, the beans are packaged. Iberti and Carmichael, who restores tractors for fun and is nicknamed "MacGyver," put a lot of energy into this. They've found that sealing a premeasured "dose" of espresso within a paper "pod" is helpful for reassuring nervous hotel food and beverage managers that espresso costs won't percolate out of control. La Colombe also takes the unusual step of holding its coffee in the warehouse for four or five days so it can "settle," allowing the "greenness" of the beans to die off.

All this attention to detail and nuance puts La Colombe in the first tier of coffee roasters; it is one of a handful of high-end artisans who care passionately about coffee. When Corby Kummer, author of the java bible *The Joy of Coffee*, spent time in Philadelphia last summer, he hung out at the café, where he was impressed by the freshness of the coffee and the company's passion for the quality of its beans. "It's a big deal when someone cares as they do," Kummer says.

Kummer notes, too, that La Colombe hews to a dark, European-style roast that's rare in the northeastern U.S., and also offers New York restaurants all the advantages of a local supplier. In fact, the true secret to La Colombe's success may be the extraordinary degree to which it gets involved in how its coffee is handled. Rather than wait to respond to orders from restaurants, La Colombe practically manages the restaurants' stockrooms, keeping track of where more coffee is needed and when. The idea is to get restaurants to switch from thinking of coffee as something like dried pasta, that can be left to languish in a storeroom indefinitely, to perceiving it more like meat or fish. "We don't want our coffee on shelves more than a week," Carmichael says. "There have been jokes that the restaurants should have timecards for us and our employees."

Patrick Gioannini, general manager of the acclaimed restaurant Jean Georges, says that La Colombe "probably" doesn't taste superior to the handful of other great coffees; what really sets it apart is all the hands-on customer service, the weekly visits to the restaurant's kitchen, the training of restaurant staff and vigilance about quality and consistency. "Even if the price is a little higher," Gioannini says, "we prefer to go with them. Long-term, it's better for us."

And maybe there is something elusive about the La Colombe taste, some ineffable quality that people can't quite articulate but recognize when it's vaporing up their noses and sliding across their palates. Marketing manager Nicolas O'Connell points out that when La Colombe competed for the business of some of Ian Schrager's boutique hotels in a blind tasting of 30 different coffees, the company was unable to exercise its usual control over the coffee's preparation—yet still won. "We didn't have a speech about our coffee," Iberti says of snagging La Colombe's key customers. "We did this." He holds out a cup of espresso.

Published March 2002

Brewery Town

Philly may once again be turning into the nation's beer capital

By Victor Fiorillo

Until two months ago, I never drank beer.

Having always considered myself a refined cocktail man, I could be found on the average Friday night sipping a martini, Manhattan or sidecar at the Ritz-Carlton Rotunda Bar. Oh, there were the occasional indiscretions—a two-dollar Pabst Blue Ribbon at Bob and Barbara's, or a golden bottle of Corona in my hand as I scanned a pulsating dance floor—but these lapses were merely that. So when I bellied up to the famed Belgian beer bar at Monk's a few months back with an out-of-towner and ordered some spirited concoction, my friend, a self-professed beer geek, said, "You've got to be joking. You live in Philadelphia, and you don't drink beer?"

Then, from a choice of 15 draft beers, he ordered the only non-Belgian: a pint of Yards ESA, all the way from Kensington—yes, Northeast Philly.

He was in the loop on the Philadelphia beer boom, a recent explosion of impeccably handcrafted local beers chronicled in magazines like *Gourmet*, which stated that Philadelphia "may now be America's best beer town," and by renowned English beer critic and author of *Ultimate Beer* Michael Jackson, who penned an online column titled, "Why I Would Rather Be In Philadelphia." This renaissance of excellence among breweries like Yards, Dogfish Head and Flying Fish is reminiscent of a time when beer was more important here than cheesesteaks and soft pretzels could ever be—a time from William Penn through the beginning of Prohibition when Philadelphia was producing some of the country's best beers.

As it turns out, my Monk's companion had attended the 25th Great British Beer Festival in London in August, where two Philadelphia-area brews, Victory HopDevil and Heavyweight Perkuno Porter (from Ocean, New Jersey), won gold and silver medals in the American Beer Tasting competition, beating out at least 20 other stateside beers. Even though I've been a bartender, I had never heard of these breweries; I was under the impression that the only "Philly beer" was Yuengling.

There's a lot more to it than Yuengling, which is less of a Philly beer than I thought. Though it has become synonymous in Philadelphia with lager (ask any bartender), and the draft we drink here comes from "America's Oldest Brewery" in Pottsville, in 1999 the Yuengling family opened a massive complex in Tampa, and that is where much of the bottled beer—the Yuengling that most people drink—is produced. And while Yuengling sells seven beers, it actually makes only two beer "concentrates," and uses color and flavor additives to create the lineup. This has Philly beer snobs turning their noses in the air and looking elsewhere for their local beer.

Many have found it at Yards Brewing Company, the only manufacturing brewery in Philadelphia proper. Now eight years into the game, Yards moved earlier this year from its tiny Manayunk digs into the 40,000-square-foot Kensington factory formerly occupied by Weisbrod & Hess Oriental Brewing Co., which closed its doors in 1938. What started as a 10-barrel-a-week venture between two college buddies has become a 10,000-barrel-a-year enterprise handcrafting 10 distinctive and generally conservative brews, including the always reliable Extra Special Ale (ESA) and India Pale Ale (IPA), and one truly adventurous option, the Love Stout, made using 150 whole oysters, shell and all, in each batch. Ed Friedland of Edward Friedland Co., the area's largest distributor of craft beers, moves the equivalent of about half a million bottles of Yards each year, and the demand is increasing. "To anyone with any local loyalty, Yards is it. It's the only beer being made in Philadelphia," explains Friedland, "and they hit on all the major styles, so they have a flavor for everybody."

Beyond the city limits, the options become a bit overwhelming, with well over a dozen distributing breweries—not including the many brewpubs—operating within an hour-and-a-half drive of City Hall, in places otherwise unexceptional, such as Phoenixville and Downingtown. But you can avoid the trip by checking in at the Standard Tap, a tavern in next-to-be-hippest Northern Liberties that serves only draft beer, and only that which has been manufactured within a 75-mile radius, but not in another metropolitan area—the definition of "local" as determined by owners William Reed and Paul Kimport.

In this hometown beer mecca, where the accoutrements include original 1950s Bakelite hand pulls and a dizzying array of specialty pipes, valves, meters and gaskets—all designed to give customers the perfect pour—selections include offerings from all of these local breweries on a rotating basis.

A couple of the more promising liquids that may grace your palate at the

Tap include the predictably hoppy Victory HopDevil out of Downingtown—Victory's flagship beer, accounting for 52 percent of its annual sales among 19 recipes—and a surprising underdog from Phoenixville, Sly Fox Dry Stout, which, says Reed, frequently sells as well as the Yuengling products.

"Craft beer-lovers in Philadelphia had to rely on imports for many years—then we started doing it correctly at home," says Bill Covaleski, Victory's brewmaster, who entered the arena in 1996 and hopes to produce 14,000 barrels this year out of the old Pepperidge Farm bakery that houses the brewery. Victory products are distributed in 14 states, and requests come in from Japan and Canada. Victory's Golden Monkey is a slightly more daring choice than the HopDevil, with hints of coriander and an alcohol content of 9.6 percent.

Sly Fox is slightly harder to find, as the company self-distributes, keeping most of its product for customers at its brewpub and sending the balance to a handful of local bars. But it is worth seeking out. When I made a recent visit to the Tap with Jim Anderson, NPR's beverage correspondent for *A Chef's Table* and the man behind beerphiladelphia.com, our bartender placed a pint of Sly Fox Dry Stout in front of me, at Jim's suggestion.

"But I hate Guinness," I protested, since the Sly Fox looked the same: dark as death, with the head and nitrogen cascade so familiar to Guinness fanatics.

"So do I," replied Anderson, who refers to Guinness Stout draft, the one everyone raves about, as "sour and flaccid ... the biggest scam going."

Shocked that a certified beer guru could defame the one beer that has probably started wars, or at least really big fights, I brought the Sly Fox to my lips and immediately found myself in beer heaven, a place I never knew existed. The stout slipped down without a hint of the bitterness of Guinness, revealing a chocolaty backdrop with a velvet texture and a complexity that I would normally have associated with a fine wine. In fact, Anderson, who teaches beer- and wine-tasting courses, says that "nine and a half out of 10" wine lovers who try Sly Fox for the first time ask, "This is beer?"

Our founding fathers would be proud of what's happening in Philadelphia, insofar as beer is concerned. As far back as 1683, William Penn wrote of the liberal beer consumption at his estate. By the mid-18th century, there was a tavern in Philadelphia for every 25 men. Most early-American beers were dark, English-style brews. But massive German immigration brought with it a new lager yeast, changing the face of beer-drinking (and -making) in Philadelphia and then throughout the country.

By 1890, Philadelphia's first beer boom was in full force, with more than

90 breweries in the city (not counting another 100 or so in the vicinity)—more than any other American city at the time. But after Prohibition, only a few breweries in the Philadelphia area were still operational, and most of them had outdated equipment. The big beer barons like Pabst and Busch quickly swallowed up the market, and only a handful of breweries produced beer in this area for most of the 20th century. Pasteurization and refrigeration allowed beers to stay fresh longer, and the handcrafted dark brews of the City Tavern's heyday gave way to the pale, comparatively watery mass-produced beer that still reigns supreme in the States today.

There wasn't a watery, mass-produced, pasteurized or even refrigerated beer in sight at Jim Anderson's Real Ale Rendezvous 8, held in October at the Independence Brew Pub across from Reading Terminal Market. Beer aficionados came from as far away as Toronto and North Carolina to sample specially prepared local brews poured from spouts hammered into the kegs that sat atop the bar.

Hundreds of devotees tasted a 15.5 percent-or-so alcohol barley wine (still technically a beer) from Delaware's Dogfish Head Brewery; special batches of Victory ESP and Yards Love Stout; a porter from Stewart's, another Delaware brewer, that tasted like very burnt diner coffee; and about a dozen other options. While they weren't drinking, the beer geeks traded tidbits about Philadelphia brewing history, homebrew tips, and questions like, "So, what was the first beer you ever drank?"

One beer-bellied gentleman wearing a shirt that read BREWERS DO IT BETTER pulled me aside when he saw me chugging a half-pint of Iron Hill's Scotch Ale and reprimanded me, saying, "I'll bet you wouldn't do that with wine."

He held a half-empty glass containing a dark elixir up to the light, swirled it around, brought it to his nose, inhaled deeply—then guzzled it rapidly.

Grinning, with a slightly glassy-eyed expression, he said, "This is beer. It's meant to be swallowed, not sipped, so it's got to taste good. And Philly beer tastes damn good!"

Published December 2002

3 : THE **RESTAURANTS**

What's for dinner? *Philadelphia* magazine's food writers have more than 200 suggestions.

Is Philadelphia a Great Restaurant Town or What?

We asked *Esquire*'s renowned food critic to tell us how Philadelphia stacks up

By John Mariani

I still get it all the time: "I'm going to Philly next week. Aside from Le Bec-Fin, anyplace else I should eat?" When I'm asked about other cities—New York, Los Angeles, Atlanta, Chicago—the question is posed very differently: "There are so many great restaurants there—can you help narrow them down?" For reasons that range from mere naïveté to pure ignorance—and not a little snootiness—Philadelphia's remarkably diverse restaurant scene hasn't registered with Americans in the tantalizing way other cities' have. Which rightfully annoys Philly's restaurateurs, and certainly bewilders me. As someone who eats out for a living in at least 25 U.S. cities each year, I can attest that Philadelphia has for a long time been one of the best dining-out towns in America, with exciting restaurants opening every year.

Indeed, in the more than two decades I've been compiling *Esquire's* annual "Best New Restaurants of the Year," 23 Philly restaurants have made the list. In 1994, Striped Bass topped it as "Restaurant of the Year," and in 1999, Guillermo Pernot of ¡Pasión! was my choice for "Chef of the Year." Back in 1993, I pronounced Le Bec-Fin the best French restaurant in America—a choice I still wouldn't back away from. And in 2001, Le Mas Perrier in Wayne (now Le Mas) made my *Esquire* list of the best new restaurants for the way Georges Perrier has combined new turns on traditional dishes with a casually chic atmosphere. Then, in 2003, Jean-Marie Lacroix joined the list with Lacroix at the Rittenhouse.

I have such wonderful memories of eating around town, from the moment I tasted my first Philly cheesesteak to my first bite of a Levis hot dog (which then went for 60 cents) and slurp of "Champ" soda. I gained a strong sense of Philadelphia's historic hospitality in the genteel dining room at the Garden. I was enchanted with the funky charms and eclectic menu of the White Dog Café, and with the chicken salad and carrot cake at the Commissary. Café Nola was serving Creole and Cajun food long before other cities picked up on the trend, and the roast pig and pastries at Magyar Hungarian Restaurant and Bakery were among the best Eastern European food in America.

Two decades ago, the city's restaurant scene could be summed up in a few lines. Now there's Georges Perrier; Susanna Foo and Patrick Feury (Susanna Foo and Suilan); Bruce Lim (Max's); Francesco Martorella (bliss); Alison Barshak (Alison at Blue Bell); Terence Feury (The Grill); Martin Hamann (Fountain at the Four Seasons); Jean-Marie Lacroix; Jack McDavid (Jack's Firehouse); and Guillermo Pernot, to name a few of the city's talented chefs.

Still, Philadelphia rarely leaps to people's minds as a restaurant destination the way New Orleans and San Francisco do. The (largely New York-based) food media hasn't helped much. In 2001, *Gourmet* magazine's list of its top 50 U.S. restaurants gave the nod to only one in Philly, ¡Pasión! (at number 34), while of more than 100 restaurants in 70 cities chosen by *Bon Appetit* as "Our Favorite Places," only one Philadelphian—¡Pasión! again—made the cut. No Philadelphia restaurant has garnered *Wine Spectator*'s prestigious Grand Award for having a world-class wine list.

So where does Philadelphia rank among other American cities as a serious restaurant town? I think pretty high for its size and population. New York, Chicago and Houston dwarf Philadelphia in those categories and draw much larger crowds of tourists who regard restaurants as major attractions. But Philly has so much to offer on just about every level and with such local flavor that it is easily in the Top Ten, beating out cities such as Miami, Boston, Washington, Dallas and Las Vegas. That Philadelphia's restaurateurs have legitimate gripes—the most chronic complaint I hear from restaurateurs and food writers here is that the locals simply don't support the city's better restaurants the way Bostonians, Chicagoans and Atlantans do theirs—is only to suggest that there is work to do. But I can't think of a city in America where you get such a neighborhood feeling about the restaurants, from South Street to Rittenhouse Square, none more than a few blocks' walk from one another, and with a range of price and style from low to high.

I'm never at a loss for a good meal in this town.

The Reviews

REVIEWS BY : Daniel Bergman, Teresa Banik Capuzzo, Amy Donohue, Kathleen Fifield, Victor Fiorillo, Maria Gallagher, Lawrence Goodman, Sasha Issenberg, Rebecca Kenton, Lauren McCutcheon, Blake Miller, Daniel Morell, Roxanne Patel, Richard Pawlak, Caroline Tiger, April White, Jason Wilson and Stephen Yeager.

ADRIATICA, *217 Chestnut Street; 215-592-8001.* Adriatica's vast 156-seat space is defined by exposed brick and dark-wood accents, and boasts three separate dining rooms. Despite a few awkward tables near the bustling open kitchen, it's pleasant to sit here on a warm evening, with doors opened onto Chestnut Street. There's an attractive bar with ambient techno, as well as a lobster tank, a raw bar, and a small retail fish market off the alley. Moroccan-born chef Mustapha Rouissiya's Mediterranean menu is full of value, but the menu could offer bolder flavors; the 150-bottle wine list offers an excellent and ambitious mix. ● $$$

Key to Symbols:	
○	Breakfast
◐	Lunch
●	Dinner
⊙	Sunday brunch
✪	Late-night menu
⯒	BYOB
⊖	Cash only

Average Entrée Price:	
$	under $12
$$	$13 to $20
$$$	$21 to $30
$$$$	more than $30

ALISA CAFÉ, *109 Fairfield Avenue, Upper Darby; 610-352-4402.* After two decades of minding the stove at Alisa Café in Upper Darby, Tony Kanjanakorn is hinting that retirement may not be far off. That's as good a reason as any to revisit, or discover, this endearing budget-priced BYOB, named for the chef-owner's daughter. Can there be a better duck dish than Tony's crispy duck with a green peppercorn-studded wine sauce, a steal at $16.95? Closed Sunday and Monday. ● ⯒ $$

ALISON AT BLUE BELL, *721 Skippack Pike, Blue Bell; 215-641-2660.* Contemporary American cooking, Alison Barshak-style, is a celebration of the melting pot. Big, bold flavors are her trademark, and while those tastes may be derived from Asia, France, Italy, Greece or Mexico, her 65-seat BYOB in a tidy business plaza is unmistakably American. Alison at Blue Bell is worldly, yet relaxed—the kind of place where Veuve Clicquot flows freely at a six-top, while the dress code runs to Talbots and Ralph Lauren. Arriving customers—many of whom have driven from Center City for a seat at this sophisticated suburban bistro—greet the chef-owner, a homegirl from Lafayette Hill, with a hug. Closed Sunday and Monday. ◐ ● ♦ $$$

ALMA DE CUBA, *1623 Walnut Street; 215-988-1799.* Alma de Cuba, Stephen Starr's darkly glamorous, red-glowing tri-level hit, is a big show full of fun, rich flavor, fat and more fat, and some unconventional starches. But this isn't to say the cooking isn't serious; it is. Coco shrimp soup is a take on a dish so popular in Honduras that the kitchen claims a hit song was written about it: Shrimp are sautéed in olive oil with some onion, then simmered in fish stock sweetened with coconut milk, given a hit of heat with jalapeño and garlic, and finally brightened with a squeeze of lime, for an excellent balance of sweet and sour. On some nights, such kitchen pyrotechnics may be more than you want. In such instances, head for the first-floor lounge. Slinky-low beige Ultrasuede couches, flattering candlelight and, of course, several of those knockout Alma Coladas—that's often enough. ● $$$

AMEA, *1990 Route 70 East, Cherry Hill; 856-874-0063.* AMEA, chef Eric Gantz's version of a neighborhood BYOB, isn't in his neighborhood. It's on a strip-malled section of Route 70 in Cherry Hill that doesn't look like anyone's neighborhood. But inside AMEA, you'll find the casual, friendly vibe all Center City BYOBs covet. Energetic and efficient, Gantz is in the restaurant's open kitchen, serving a Mediterranean menu starring simple dishes like a daily special of grilled whole red snapper with olive oil and capers. In the dining room, it's often a full house, with birthday-party guests singing over warm chocolate cake, or a boisterous all-female book club lining the plush banquettes. And for wine to go with Gantz's decadent rack of lamb, patrons can trot across the courtyard of the Village Walk Shopping Center to CorkScrewed of Cherry Hill. Closed Monday. ● ♦ $$

ANGELINA, *706 Chestnut Street; 215-925-6889.* This being a Stephen Starr restaurant, there is a dazzling design hook—a busy red-and-white toile pattern that covers virtually every surface in the 110-seat dining room except the fresh-faced servers. But executive chef Christopher Painter, previously posted at Starr's Tangerine, is an old hand at cooking to compete with the scenery: tuna tartare lustily packed with piquant capers, black olives and zesty mustard; rosemary sausage served over green lentils with a tomato sauce touched with cinnamon; crisp-crusted shrimp and arugula pizza, no thicker than a cracker, gilded with olive oil; wide pappardelle ribbons, the ideal conveyance for a meaty Bolognese ragu. Adriana Paveglio's desserts incorporate something for everyone—a not-too-sweet buttermilk panna cotta with fresh berries; a decadent frozen tiramisu with alternating layers of espresso-soaked ladyfingers, espresso ice cream and mascarpone ice cream; a raspberry and fig crostata with caramel sauce; a delightful cookie plate with a cup of cold espresso for dipping. Closed for lunch Saturday and Sunday. ◑ ● $$$

ARPEGGIO, *Spring House Village Shopping Center, Spring House; 215-646-5055.* At Arpeggio, a wood-burning oven produces thin-crusted regular or whole-wheat pies with exceptionally fresh-tasting tomato sauce and dozens of topping possibilities. Pizza is just one aspect of a large Med-eclectic menu at this family-friendly BYOB, with grilled kabobs, salads, sandwiches, and more than a dozen pastas. Save room for chocolate hazelnut gelato. Closed Monday. ◑ ● ▮ $$

AUDREY CLAIRE, *276 South 20th Street; 215-731-1222.* Owner Audrey Claire Taichman has a no-reservation policy Friday and Saturday nights at this small, cash-only Mediterranean BYOB. In the summer, patrons clutching brown-bagged wine bottles mix and mingle on the sidewalk, hoping for a seat by the wide-open windows; in the winter, they kill time across the street in the bar of Taichman's 20 Manning. Regardless of the season, don't miss the Jewish apple cake—Taichman's grandmother's recipe—advertised on the blackboard dessert menu. Each plate holds two hefty slices, topped with a dollop of fresh whipped cream. The cool sweetness of the cream enhances the nutmeg and cinnamon, and chunks of fragrant apple add tang and texture to the moist cake. ● ❸ ▮ $$

AUGUST, *1247 South 13th Street; 215-468-5926.* Nothing about cash-only August screams "Italian"—and that's a good thing for a spot in Bella Vista, just steps from South Philly's old standbys. Owners MaryAnn Brancaccio and Maria Vanni call their cooking style "Italian fusion"—pasta-stuffed spring rolls, lamb chop lollipops, a don't-miss-it house-made cream cheesecake with a crust so rich it's almost indistinguishable from the cake—and serve it from an open kitchen, the centerpiece of the warm, dimly lit dining room. Closed Sunday and Monday. ● ❸ ⬧ $$

AZAFRAN, *617 South 3rd Street; 215-928-4019.* Nuevo Latino cuisine can be an everyday option at Azafran, the cozy, well-established Bella Vista BYOB. Many credit Azafran ("saffron" in Spanish) with kicking off the Nuevo Latino explosion when it opened in 1997, and it's still one of the best. Azafran offers ceviche—a two-dish tasting that changes daily—and inimitable chicken preparations. The justly famous pulled chicken arepas (roasted and shredded chicken seasoned with onions, olives, peppers and raisins) are served with a great corn cake that's firm on the outside and hot and soft inside. Azafran's intimate, casual atmosphere, brightly colored dining room, upbeat music and delicious churros always deliver a tropical vibe. Closed Monday. ● ⬧ $$

AZURE, *931 North 2nd Street; 215-629-0500.* It's a safe bet that Azure owner Bob Bitros likes to vacation in the warmer climates of the South, Southwest and Caribbean. The flavors of those locales predominate on Azure's very vegetarian-friendly menu of inexpensive "vacation cuisine"—and there's Bob, dressed in a Hawaiian shirt, Bermuda shorts and loafers, no socks. He's seating customers, serving drinks, even busing tables at his Northern Liberties spot, anxious to ensure that everyone is enjoying the culinary holiday. Detours to Italy—addictively crunchy-then-creamy polenta fries and fragrant olive oil-almond-orange cake—and Greece are also on the itinerary. ◑ ● ⊙ $

BAHAMA BREEZE, *320 Goddard Boulevard, King of Prussia, 610-491-9822; and 2000 Route 38, Cherry Hill, 856-317-8317.* This Caribbean-style eatery mimics an island getaway, with its villa-like white facade, tin roof, dark wood and wicker furniture, and palm trees. Huge helpings of coconut-breaded Island onion rings will help soak up oversize frozen cocktails like the Bahama Ritas and Mojito Cubanos. But entrées give Bahama Breeze its signature island-dining appeal: Jumbo sea scallops are pan-seared with lemon-cilantro pesto, asparagus and pasta; Jamaican grilled chicken breast is paired with cinnamon yam mash, roasted squash and Cuban black beans. We're definitely on island time here: The wait on a Saturday night is close to two hours. ◑ ● ✪ $$

THE BAMBOO CLUB, *the Pavilion at King of Prussia; 610-265-0660.* With its hand-painted murals and Pacific Rim cuisine, the Bamboo Club is a sensory escape from the crowds at the Pavilion at King of Prussia. Since its flagship

average entrée price: $ under $12 $$ $13 to $20 $$$ $21 to $30 $$$$ more than $30

opened in Phoenix in 1994, the Bamboo chain's original owner and former designer, Debbie Bloy, has traveled the world in search of the newest dining and design trends for its seven locations, and she's decorated each with exotic-looking black bamboo, Asian sculptures and lush foliage. Spicy crackling calamari—flash-fried calamari in Thai-chili barbecue sauce, served with fresh vegetables—is a signature appetizer; Hong Kong steak is ignited tableside with brandy and mushrooms. You can also sample flights of the restaurant's 100-bottle wine list, but we'd rather try a Hong Kong Hangover, a blender drink of rum, raspberry liqueur, blackberry brandy and strawberries. ◐ ● $$

BIRCHUNVILLE STORE CAFÉ, *1407 Hollow Road, at Flowing Springs Road, Birchrunville; 610-827-9002.* Bring a fine wine and telephone ahead for explicit directions to the haute-rustic Birchunville Store Café, because it's very easy to get lost en route to this former general store in Chester County, especially after dark. Your reward will be whatever has moved the muse of French-born chef-owner Francis Treciak that day—foie gras, diver scallops, or perhaps an exquisite venison chop—to be savored at a table on the rear porch, or in the sponge-painted, pottery-furnished dining room. Open Wednesday through Saturday. ● ♦ ◉ $$$

BLACK BASS HOTEL, *3774 River Road, Lumberville; 215-297-5815.* Sinuous River Road (Route 32), on the Pennsylvania side of the Delaware River, is lined with inviting cottages. The Black Bass Hotel—three miles north of New Hope, or a one-hour, 15-minute drive from Center City—offers the added enticements of open-air or screened-in riverside dining, plus a vast collection of commemorative crockery issued to mark the birthdays and weddings of Britain's royal family. Charleston Street crab casserole is embedded in the menu, but chef John Barrett offsets such Continental classics with modern lunch options like chilled lobster-mango spring rolls, and a Cuban pork sandwich that's a riot of flavors: cinnamon, cloves, cumin, cilantro, pickled jalapeño, ham and melted Monterey Jack. Excellent house-made fruit pie or retro pineapple upside-down cake can conclude your stay—unless you're lucky and have booked one of the nine rooms upstairs. ● ◉ $$$

THE BLACK SHEEP PUB & RESTAURANT, *247 South 17th Street; 215-545-9473.* If ever a building looked like it wanted to be a pub, it's this one, a National Historic Landmark where, to the delight of Black Sheep owners Matthew Kennedy, James Stephens and Gene LeFevre, most cell phones don't work. So the Emerald Isle natives have a real get-away-from-it-all pub on their hands, with 18 Irish whiskies, 30 single-malt scotches, and scores of beers available from bottle or tap. There's a true-pub-plus menu: fish and chips with vinegar, of course, but also a popular Guinness stew, and chicken and mushroom pie. The main floor here is devoted to the bar and the crowd; the basement features darts and a jukebox, and the top story is a place to sit down to a tablecloth and no smoking. ◐ ● ☉ $$

THE BLACK SWAN, *127 Ark Road, Mount Laurel; 856-866-0019.* This strip-mall BYOB boasts a healthy (all menu options are available in low-cholesterol, low-sodium and low-calorie versions) New American menu. The most popular item, though, isn't the healthiest: calf's liver wrapped in prosciutto. Among Chef Francis Hannan's specialties: filet or strip steak dressed up with compound butters, such as roasted red pepper and garlic or herbed mustard. Closed Monday. ● ⬧ $$$

BLISS, *220/224 South Broad Street; 215-731-1100.* Bliss, the first independent venture for Philly veteran chef Francesco Martorella, is a Zen of blond-wood and blue-glass. Martorella's tour of Philadelphia's top kitchens (Four Seasons, Brasserie Perrier, Ciboulette and Pod, among others) is apparent in the sleek spot's seasonal menu of contemporary Asian, Italian and French flavors, like crispy ginger chicken (or red snapper) with baby bok choy; peppered duck breast with savoy cabbage and port-wine sauce; and porcini-dusted salmon with couscous perfumed with truffle oil. Closed for lunch Saturday and Sunday. ◐ ● $$$

BLUE SAGE VEGETARIAN GRILLE, *772 Second Street Pike, Southampton; 215-942-8888.* The nondescript exterior of Blue Sage makes what's going on inside even more surprising—the place is buried in a characterless mini strip mall. But through the door, jade-green dishes are being plated with mixed organic greens adorned with sun-dried berries and sunflower seeds; with mango slices and watermelon meat; with plantain fritters sagging beneath piles of chunky guacamole—and those are just the appetizers. Chef Mike Jackson and his wife, Holly, serve healthful comfort foods: green apple-pumpkin risotto; triangles of tender polenta surrounding a khorma—or stew—of red lentils, squash and leeks. Noticeably absent is the "wheat meat" and tofu that most vegetarian chefs depend on. Closed Sunday; closed for dinner Monday. ◐ ● ⬧ $$

BLUEZETTE, *246 Market Street; 215-627-3866.* Owner Delilah Winder learned soul food in Virginia kitchens and introduced it to Philadelphia with two Delilah's Southern Cuisine food stands. At Bluezette, Southern standards get dressed up. The menu ventures south of the South, through the Mississippi Delta to the Caribbean, following African trade routes. Lobster is jerked and served alongside fufu in a tropical broth, and shrimp and grouper swim in a subtly spicy creole sauce. Closed Monday. ● $$

BONK'S BAR, *Richmond and Tioga streets; 215-634-9927.* Connoisseurs of hard-shell crabs will achieve no-frills nirvana at Bonk's Bar, a family-run corner tap-room in Port Richmond. Matterhorns of meaty Maryland hard-shells are pre-sented on plastic trays with a steaming slosh of spicy boiling liquid, a secret recipe guarded by three generations. Closed Sunday. ◐ ● ◓ $

BOURBON BLUE, *2 Rector Street, Manayunk; 215-508-3360.* A N'Awlins fanta-sy, Bourbon Blue is the first in what could be a restaurant renaissance for this riverfront neighborhood. (Manayunk recently ended a half-decade-long mora-torium on new eateries.) With seating for 180, the Balongue Design-renovated dining room evokes a French Quarter balcony, with high ceilings, exposed brick, and the requisite wrought iron. The menu offers indulgent, seasonal Big Easy-style food: crawfish étouffée, hearty jambalaya, cornmeal-crusted catfish, and some less expected dishes—like alligator quesadillas. The experience is completed, minus the humidity and the beads, with a Hurricane cocktail (limit two per customer!) and the Crescent City soundtrack of live jazz, blues and funk featured in the canal-level lounge. ◐ ● ☉ $$

BRASSERIE PERRIER, *1619 Walnut Street; 215-568-3000.* Happy hour for the well-heeled creates a traffic jam of classic cocktails—the sidecar, a lime twist on the typical lemon-and-brandy concoction, is popular—in the sidewalk café of this Walnut Street spot. Beyond the revolving door, the Art Deco bar serves up an excellent steak frites at the bargain price of $16. And in the dapper din-ing room, an equally well-dressed but more sedate crowd finds just what they expect from a Georges Perrier restaurant: contemporary French dishes matched with polished service and a lengthy wine list. (Guests can BYOB on Sunday evenings.) Closed for lunch Sunday. ● $$$

BRIDGE CAFÉ, *8 Bridge Street, Frenchtown; 908-996-6040.* Fifty-six miles north of Center City, one of the most scenic spots along the Delaware River can be found in Frenchtown, New Jersey. The vine-shaded deck of the Bridge Café, a casual BYOB alongside the Uhlerstown-Frenchtown Bridge, affords a ringside seat to the 1 p.m. Sunday rush hour comprised of strong-armed kayakers, tight-bunned cyclists, dog-walkers, and guys brandishing fishing poles who never seem to catch anything. An earnest folkie covers Joni Mitchell and Bob Dylan songs during brunch for a denim-clad clientele ranging from toddler to AARP. Big burgers, hearty salads, and iced coffee drinks with names like "The Nutty Professor" are popular. ◑ ● ○ ⬗ $

BUCA DI BEPPO, *309 Old York Road, Jenkintown, 215-885-6342; 258 South 15th Street, 215-545-2818; and 1 West Germantown Pike, East Norriton, 610-272-2822.* Buca di Beppo's pledge of "Immigrant Cuisine" audaciously revises American history: The only immigrants with a cuisine this extravagant might easily find themselves tired and poor, but never hungry. Buca di Beppo guarantees its diners an unduly exuberant dining room—a festival of Italo-kitsch, walls coated with mass-produced heirlooms—and large quantities of food. The chicken cacciatore entrée describes itself as "seven pounds of love"—that is, a whole chicken and four pounds of mashed potatoes. The remarkable thing about the cacciatore isn't the weeks of leftovers it can birth, but the simple fact of the dish: how much better it is than it has to be. Open for lunch Saturday and Sunday. ◑ ● $$

BUDDAKAN, *325 Chestnut Street; 215-574-9440.* Although the communal table under the colossal gold Buddha is a coveted dining spot in Stephen Starr's first real blockbuster restaurant, my favorite place to eat is the upstairs bar, where you can watch the whole social theater unfold. Without benefit of stage or band, Buddakan buzzes like a nightclub. And the food, delectable Asian fusion dishes constructed as avant-garde architecture—edamame ravioli, duck breast with roast garlic five spice jus—is a show all by itself. Closed for lunch Saturday and Sunday. ◑ ● $$$

BUFFALO BILLIARDS, *118 Chestnut Street; 215-574-7665.* Any casual pool player in Center City can tell you that there are few tables this side of Delaware Avenue where you can shoot a few games and not have to swim with the sharks. Enter Old City's Buffalo Billiards, part of a chain of upscale (for pool halls) pool halls that's been racking them up in D.C., Austin and Nashville for years. For the Philly version, billiards moguls Mark Handwerger, Geoffrey Dawson and Curt Large refurbished 118 Chestnut into a bi-level hall with 14

average entrée price: $ under $12 $$ $13 to $20 $$$ $21 to $30 $$$$ more than $30

pool tables and three dartboards. The beer selection includes Bass and more exotic brews like Allagash, a white beer from Maine. The kitchen produces burgers and wings you can grab and bite while waiting for your shot; the ambience takes its cue from a West that's more Roy Rogers than Wyatt Earp, but the cowboy kitsch adds an unpretentious zing to the decor—like a dash of habanero. ● ✪ $

BUON APPETITO TRATTORIA & BAR, *1540 Ritner Street; 215-551-8378.* Forty-year-old Ciro Rendina, a son of Naples, holds forth in Buon Appetito, a former bar in South Philadelphia, ably assisted by his wife, Maria, who waits on every table. All is as it should be: The fish are pristine, the sauce red, the parking impossible. Impeccable ingredients, an affordable wine list and a passionate proprietor in this unassuming spot set the stage for a memorable meal: fried zucchini blossoms stuffed with ricotta and salami; chicken soup with tagliatelle noodles; capellini with lump crabmeat in tomato sauce; veal piccata; grilled veal chop. The daily early-bird deal—three courses for $19.95 between 4 and 7 p.m.—is a fine value. Closed Monday. ● ♦ $$

CAFE CLASSICS, *816 North Easton Road, Doylestown; 215-489-3535.* Finding the blues north of Memphis is challenging, but this nonsmoking gem in Bucks County does it right. Among walls adorned with golden trombones, Blue Note LPs and artwork from the original Cotton Club, sassy owner Eileen Schembri books the smoldering music. The diverse seasonal menu can include duck confit, deliciously messy barbecue ribs, crab-asparagus ravioli, and fiery andouille jambalaya. Cool down with a planter's punch or Lambertville's River Horse Hop Hazard Pale Ale. Closed Monday and Tuesday, and closed for dinner Sunday. ◐ ● $$$

CAFÉ FRESKO, *1003 Lancaster Avenue, Bryn Mawr; 610-581-7070.* Casual, cash-only Café Fresko is the debut for chef Demetrios Pappas, whose family is behind many Main Line hangouts. It brings to the suburbs chef Lassine Sylla, formerly of Tangerine, and her Mediterranean fare. At this simple BYOB, wild striped bass is paired with wild mushroom-filled herb crepes; rack of lamb is crusted with pistachios; and mussels swim in a saffron broth. Closed Sunday. ◐ ● ✪ ♦ $$

CAFE LIFT, *428 North 13th Street; 215-922-3031.* One of the first restaurants in the Loft District, Cafe Lift has a lofty brownstone setting that mirrors the look of the former-warehouse apartments surrounding it, and attracts a crowd of young neighbors. (Lift is open Tuesday through Friday for lunch and BYOB dinner, and for brunch only on the weekend.) At noon, have a simple grilled chicken-and-sharp-provolone panini, hot and luscious off the panini press, or Thai coconut soup with shrimp and crab; at night, chef Michael Pasquarello presents specials such as ziti puttanesca and walnut-crusted black bass with a white truffle sauce, with background tunes of indie rock or European pop. Closed Monday; closed for dinner Saturday and Sunday. ◐ ● ☉ ▲ $

CARAMBOLA, *Dreshertown Plaza, 1650 Limekiln Pike, Dresher; 215-542-0900.* Carambola recognizes our primal attraction to grilled foods, serving up grilled pizzas, grilled shrimp (destined for a risotto), a grilled center-cut pork chop, and a whole grilled fish. Trendy ingredients abound on the exuberant menu; the wine-savvy crowd, with intriguing bottles in tow, is exuberant, too. ◐ ● ▲ $$

CARMAN'S COUNTRY KITCHEN, *1301 South 11th Street; 215-339-9613.* Flounder and other freshly caught Jersey fish surface frequently on the brunch menu at Carman's Country Kitchen between May and October, when salty proprietress Carman Luntzel commutes from her Long Beach Island houseboat. At other times of the year, look for seasonal produce or Italian Market finds on the menu. The entrées, like Carman, are thoroughly over-the-top—she might pair soft-shell crabs with scrambled eggs and home fries, or plop a big scoop of ice cream on French toast. There is one outdoor table: on the flatbed of Carman's red pickup truck. Open Thursday thorugh Monday. ○ ▲ ❾ $

CARMINE'S CAFÉ, *5 Brookline Boulevard, Havertown; 610-789-7255.* Chef/owner John Mims hails from New Orleans, and his cooking has brought Louisianans out of the woodwork to this little checkerboard-floored former deli. It is a foie gras lover's dream come true: Besides the wildly popular appetizer, served sautéed over frizzled Vidalia onions with deglazed balsamic butter sauce, there's foie gras debris in the risotto and the dirty rice. There's also a duck of the day, a concept that should sweep the restaurant world. Never has cash-only/BYOB/no-reservations seemed so luxuriant. Closed Monday. ● ▲ $$

CAPITAL GRILLE, *1338 Chestnut Street; 215-545-9588.* It's part of a chain, but no local chophouse does a better job. Though the menu is standard beef-and-potatoes, everything is done exactly as it should be. A dry-aging room helps turn out steaks that are especially complex; when a sirloin is prepared here, the full flavor puts one-note versions at other steakhouses to shame. Closed for lunch Saturday and Sunday. ◑ ● $$$

CHERRY STREET CHINESE VEGETARIAN RESTAURANT, *1010 Cherry Street; 215-923-3663.* For more than a dozen years, Cherry Street has been serving General Tso's and sweet-and-sour, only with wheat gluten in place of the chicken, and soybean substituting for beef, pork and shrimp. Thanks to the deep-frying and the sauces, you can't tell these from their real-meat prototypes—so for a more unique experience, choose a "chef's specialty." "Mushroom mushrooms" is rice noodles stir-fried and topped with five types of sautéed mushrooms; "twin mushrooms winter melon roll" is thin layers of melon rolled around asparagus and black mushrooms, then steamed; jade (green) or rose (pink) dumplings have wrappings flavored with, respectively, fresh-squeezed spinach and carrot juice. The eclectic clientele includes med students, aging hippies and nose-ringed hipsters. ◑ ● ♦ $$

CHEZ COLETTE, *17th and Sansom streets; 215-569-8300.* This is 1930s France in Technicolor: At Chez Colette, warm Mediterranean colors stretch from the brightly printed valances to the lapis-blue carpet, and gleaming blond-wood tables are lit by starry spotlights. The menu—more Philadelphia French than traditional French—features local ingredients and regional specialties, including Maine lobster and Maryland crabcakes. ○ ◑ ● ◉ $$$

CHEZ ELENA WU, *910 Berlin Road, Voorhees; 856-566-3222.* This ballroom-like space, with its marble foyer and linen-draped tables, its French-accented Chinese food and refined desserts, is just as likely to be a special-occasion destination as a choice for a casual meal. Those ribs are glazed with sesame honey, as elegant as they can be and still be called ribs. Fresh ingredients and a clean touch make the Chinese classics sing, and the French accent turns dishes like honey walnut shrimp with apples and crab puffs into things of beauty. Located in the same complex as the tony Ritz 16 theaters, this is a great Act 1 of dinner-and-a-movie. ◑ ● ♦ $$

CHLÖE, *232 Arch Street; 215-629-2337.* Through a storefront window trimmed with tiny white lights, Chlöe's parchment-wrapped candles glow softly. On one side of the narrow dining room, a shelf displays antique kitchen tools. Fresh-faced servers bustle between tables, delivering plates piled high with hearty fare, opening bottles of Yuengling, uncorking bottles of syrah. In the kitchen, chef-owners Mary Ann Ferrie and husband Dan Grimes excel at new American favorites, such as grilled Caesar salad, panko-crusted goat cheese over mixed greens, and rare ahi tuna with tropical Asian trimmings. But their genius reveals itself in their upscaled comfort foods: grilled pizza topped with fig jam, gorgonzola, pancetta and thyme; bourbon-soaked pork chop with macaroni and cheese; warm banana bread pudding. Closed Sunday and Monday. ● ♦ ◉ $$

CHOPS, *401 City Line Avenue, Bala Cynwyd; 610-668-3400.* This isn't the Palm—we're in Bala Cynwyd—but Alex Plotkin is here. And where longtime Palm manager Plotkin goes, the dry-aged steaks, full-bodied wines and power players follow. Chops is Plotkin's first foray into restaurant ownership (with partners Larry Brown and Billy King), and he's sticking to what he knows very, very well. Expense-account standards like filet mignon and swordfish chops are served in a dark-mahogany dining room with tin ceilings; booths are set with Riedel stemware. But this end of City Line is more accustomed to the prices of Friday's and Chili's (the location was formerly Marabella's), so Plotkin has adopted a simple philosophy: "I want to give people a lot for their money." That includes a California-heavy wine list with more than half the bottles under $50; the popular 10-ounce New York strip for $24; and 10-ounce martinis for under $10. Closed for lunch Saturday and Sunday. ◑ ● $$$

CHRISTOPHER'S, *108 North Wayne Avenue, Wayne; 610-687-6558.* Christopher's is California-casual, with large windows overlooking North Wayne Avenue, plus exposed brick walls and terra-cotta-colored walls. Sure, you'll spy young Main Liners on dates at the bar, but most tables are filled with parents and kids enjoying the $5-and-under children's menu. The friendly wait staff is trained to serve quickly—a kid necessity—and menu choices include pasta with butter, hot dogs and Jell-O; the kitchen will even cut the crusts off a grilled-cheese sandwich. More adventurous eaters might try a pizza topped with caramelized onions, Granny Smith apples and mozzarella with a balsamic reduction. Adult-size entrées are $11 to $20 and range from meatloaf to vegetarian lasagna to grilled whole fish. ◑ ● ⊙ $$

CITRUS, *8136 Germantown Avenue; 215-247-8188.* Walk too quickly down the Hill, and you'll likely whiz past this little place wedged between those Chestnut Hill stalwarts, Flying Fish and Bredenbeck's. Citrus's narrow storefront rarely reels in folks who aren't looking for it. But step inside, and you'll find yourself in a tranquil 18-seat dining room. Oil paintings and sketches of local scenes hang on walls painted pale lime, and neither servers nor diners seem particularly rushed. The slightly bohemian atmosphere matches the healthful array of vegetarian and seafood dishes. This light eating leaves plenty of room for dessert: moist gingerbread, traditional éclairs, cinnamon-dusted apple strudel, and lemon meringue tarts, all of which have begun to lure a dedicated teatime crowd. Closed Sunday and Monday. ● ▮ ❸ $$

CLAUDE'S, *100 Olde New Jersey Avenue, North Wildwood; 609-522-0400.* Claude Pottier's namesake 90-seat BYOB is now in North Wildwood, having moved south after seven seasons in tony Stone Harbor. Pottier's food seems to grow more sophisticated and elegant each year. A cosmopolitan flair that's natural and unstuffy pervades the restaurant. The corner entrance opens into a funky bistro-feeling room with a black-and-white-checkered floor. Lamps from Turkey hang in the front room; those in the back room are of wrought-iron, and from Mexico. There are fresh roses on the table, and cloth napkins. Pottier's cooking is bold and confident, and he uses excellent ingredients, many from local South Jersey markets, to create seasonal dishes like seafood crepes, horseradish-crusted halibut, and Ligurian-style cioppino. Open weekends only off-season. ● ▮ $$$

COLEMAN RESTAURANT AT NORMANDY FARM, *Route 202 and Morris Road, Blue Bell; 215-616-8300.* Under broad wooden beams, where cows once stood for milking, the tuxedoed staff of Coleman Restaurant at Normandy Farm fusses over every table while a fire flickers cozily in a gas-fed hearth. The elegant fabrics, chandeliers, portraits of pedigreed pooches and other old-money trimmings could easily have been plucked from a château. In the kitchen, celebrity chef Jim Coleman creates countryside-meets-country-club cuisine, updating dishes that might have been served in the heyday of this 19th-century estate, using stellar locally produced ingredients. ◗ ● ⊙ $$$

COLLIGAN'S STOCKTON INN, *1 Main Street, Stockton; 609-397-1250.* Built in 1710 as a three-story residence in small-town Hunterdon County, Colligan's Stockton Inn was converted into a tavern later that century. The Stockton had its heyday in the 1930s, when it was frequented by Algonquin Round-tablers fleeing Manhattan and became a hangout during the 1935 trial that convicted Bruno Hauptmann of the Lindbergh-baby kidnapping. Now the bar is frequented by locals, and the restaurant, managed by the Doylestown catering firm Max & Me, offers dishes like a slow-roasted salmon paired with Medjool dates in addition to chef Max Hansen's staples, such as crabcakes and his own smoked salmon. ◑ ● ⊙ $$$

CONTINENTAL, *138 Market Street; 215-923-6069.* The lights, shaped like skewered olives, hint at the lengthy martini list at this "Rat Pack, the Next Generation" restaurant and bar in Old City. Although this, the first of restaurant emperor Stephen Starr's spots, opened in 1995, it remains an anchor of 2nd Street nightlife. (A second location with an oh-so-South-Beach pool on the roof will opened near Rittenhouse Square in 2004.) If the retro cocktails and the beautiful people-watching don't satisfy you, try the seared tuna over mushrooms risotto, or any entrée with the popular wasabi mashed potatoes. ◑ ● ⊙ $$

THE COUCH TOMATO CAFÉ, *102 Rector Street, Manayunk; 215-483-CAFÉ.* Couch Tomato, with its muted color scheme and sparkling red stools, is not a greasy pizza spot designed to feed the boozy masses. Slices, cut from 20-inch pies cooked on pizza stones, are heaped with toppings like eggplant and chicken parmesan. Twenty varieties of salads are topped with homemade dressings; soups are also made in-house. For the lazy, the Couch Tomato does deliver, and it even offers an innovative pickup plan to circumvent Manayunk's nightmarish parking situation: Call ahead with your order and car model, pull into the pickup spot, and honk for curbside service. ◑ ● ⬩ $

COUNTRY CLUB RESTAURANT & PASTRY SHOP, *1717 Cottman Avenue; 215-722-0500.* Sometimes it feels like the average age of the diners here is 70-plus, but the Country Club Restaurant & Pastry Shop's kitchen is still, after 48 years, young at heart, maintaining the Jewish-American comfort classics (blintzes, fluffy matzo-ball soup, roast chicken) while adding a few specials, such as pasta with shrimp in a pesto sauce. All this under the watchful gaze of the obligatory grandmotherly waitress named Millie. ○ ◑ ● ⬩ $$

COYOTE CROSSING, *800 Spring Mill Avenue, Conshohocken, 610-825-3000; and 102 Market Street, West Chester, 610-825-3000.* The first incarnation of Coyote Crossing in Conshohocken, with its spacious patio where the crowd looks like an Abercrombie & Fitch ad clutching margaritas, has been a success since it first opened in 1996. The newer 175-seat West Chester spot is spectacular: a

1930s bank transformed into a double-height tile-and-lattice Mexican hacienda, with a soaring fireplace and rooftop seating for another 100 in summer months. Chef-owner Carlos Melendez's grandmother's chiles de abuelita (poblanos stuffed with shredded pork, pecans and almonds), plus other authentic fish and meat dishes, are on both menus, alongside Americanized thirst-inducers like nachos and enchiladas. Closed for lunch Saturday and Sunday. ◑ ● $$

CUBA LIBRE, *10 South 2nd Street; 215-627-0666.* Hot (Old City), hot (Latino cuisine), hot (those super-cool mojitos): Those are the sizzling ingredients of Cuba Libre, which features chef Guillermo Veloso's twists on Cuban classics. The restaurant's multi-story replication of pre-Castro Havana is designed to make you feel like you're in (not at) the opera, and the theme is furthered by the Cuban coffees, the bar's rum drinks, and the walls upstairs in the La Galleria dining room, where the works of Cuban artists and images of Cuba are exhibited. ● ◐ ☉ $$$

CUCINA FORTE, *768 South 8th Street; 215-238-0778.* Maria Forte's plain ricotta and spinach-ricotta gnocchi are cloud-like, but they aren't the only reason to visit Cucina Forte. The feisty blonde from Molise piques diners' curiosity with her "dream" soup, so named because the recipe came to her in a dream: rich chicken stock, leafy greens, mushrooms, finely chopped vegetables, with a great hunk of pleasantly chewy bread in the center. Veal saltimbocca, covered with prosciutto and a creamy white wine sauce with sage, is a better choice than chicken alla Forte, a sautéed chicken breast crowned with mushrooms, oven-dried tomatoes and lump crabmeat. Not one to hide in the kitchen, Forte enjoys schmoozing in her mirrored dining room. Closed for lunch Saturday and Sunday. ◑ ● ◗ $$

CUCINA PAZZO, *1000 Wolf Street; 215-755-5400.* With the Italian Market a few blocks away, Michael Moss stocks his kitchen at South Philly's Cucina Pazzo with just-off-the-truck ingredients, including free-range chicken and jumbo lump crabmeat. This "crazy kitchen," at the site of the old Priori's restaurant, is cozy but not crammed, with 40 seats in the dining rooms and 10 at the bar; after a face-lift, it has rustic tiled walls, glowing hardwood floors and Tiffany-style lighting. And on the menu: spinach gnocchi in a rich Gorgonzola cream sauce; jumbo shrimp; and veal medallions with portabella mushrooms. Closed Monday; closed for lunch Saturday and Sunday. ◑ ● ◗ $$

DADDYPOPS, *232 North York Road, Hatboro; 215-675-9717.* Daddypops, a whimsical diner in thriving Hatboro, has a counter anchored at each corner by a barber's chair, a mismatched collection of coffee mugs that includes one inscribed "i ♥ intercourse, pa," and cooks who yell out to the old, tired help such admonitions as "Dottie, do your sidework!" And the breakfast is superb: "Eggs in bull's-eye"—two pieces of toast with holes cut in the center into which two eggs are cracked, with the whole mess grilled and served with creamy grits—is a delight. ○ ◐ ● Ⓢ $

D'ANGELO'S RISTORANTE AND LOUNGE ITALIANO, *256 South 20th Street; 215-546-3935.* It might be easy to forget that food is served at D'Angelo's, what with its marvelously trashy summer-on-Ibiza dance scene as well as its favored watering-hole status among graying Rizzo-era nightlifers. But the truth is, we can't forget it, not when we've downed a plate of the gut-busting spaghetti and meatballs served at Sal and Tony D'Angelo's place a block off Rittenhouse Square. With Sal running the front of the house, Tony's free to stay in the kitchen turning out classic, hearty Italian dishes that aren't quite haute but are a long way from red gravy. Try Tony's Special Fettuccine (prosciutto, peas and mushrooms in a white cream sauce), and homemade ricotta ravioli. Closed Sunday; closed for lunch Saturday. ◐ ● $$$

DENIM, *1712 Walnut Street; 215-735-6700.* Denim's nightclub decor is more! more! more!, with a front room of tuffeted denim, a yacht-sized bar ringed by thousands of beaded strands, and, in the rear, a crimson wall of crisscross black-leather straps and antlers that looks like Jean Paul Gaultier doing up the Elk Lodge. Choosing your moment in the madness is the tricky part. Go at eight on a Wednesday, and it can feel like you're the only kids in the candy store. Nine o'clock on a Thursday or Friday feels just about right, though it gets good and loud shortly after 10. Having proved its worth as a nightlife destination, Denim is now focusing energy on dining. The menu is an intriguing mix of Nuevo Latino and Asian flavors, with cross-cultural ceviches, pork tenderloin, rich duck crepe, and the decadent dessert "Chocolate, Peanut Butter, Bananas." Closed Sunday, Monday and Tuesday. ● $$

DEPOT MARKET CAFÉ, *409 Elmira Street, Cape May; 609-884-8030.* Wedged between Cape May's rail station and a bike-rental garage, this bungalow bistro excels in gourmet sandwiches and three-course suppers to go. The owners close shop after lunch to prep for the evening meal, which is delivered in neat black boxes through a window onto an awning-covered deck. (You can stay and eat there, if you like.) Weary antiquers, sandy families, and restaurant servers on their way to work line up for flaky-crusted chicken pot pie and heavenly chocolate bread pudding with caramel ribbons. Closed Sunday. ◐ ● ♦ ❋ $

DEUX CHEMINÉES, *1221 Locust Street; 215-790-0200.* Fritz Blank's cuisine is old-school classic French, and if you're in the mood for some rich standards—sautéed veal loin chops in a cream and Madeira sauce, silky cream-based crab velouté—there's no better place to have them. But Blank's menu isn't frozen in time, and his heart-healthy offerings are some of his most luscious, including a cream-less wild mushroom soup that distills into a bowl the powerful essence of porcini. Do yield to the desserts: From the voluptuous napoleon au bananes to the sensual chocolate crepe, these are fat calories well spent. Closed Sunday and Monday. ● $$$

DILWORTHTOWN INN, *1390 Old Wilmington Pike, West Chester; 610-399-1390.* In spite of being ransacked by the British army after the Battle of the Brandywine, the Dilworthtown Inn has survived gloriously into the 21st century, its colonial ambience intact. Fifteen quaint candlelit dining rooms breathe the charm of uncontrived history, while the seasonal New American menu has included such classics as venison with blueberry cassis demiglace; creamy duck liver pâté flecked with black truffles; and grilled ostrich tenderloin. More conservative standards—Chateaubriand for two, Dilworthtown crabcakes—are done here in the grand manner. A favorite place for big occasions; both jackets and reservations are required. ● $$$

DI PALMA, *114 Market Street; 215-733-0545.* Chef-owner Salvatore Di Palma serves indulgent risottos and hefty cuts of meat as well as dishes that allow Signora to zip up her Versace pencil skirt the next day. (Do wear that skirt in his Euro-sleek dining room, but let someone else attempt the five-course, $55 dégustation.) The current seasonal menus are less experimental than the one that debuted with the restaurant in 1998, not necessarily a bad thing. Figs stuffed with gorgonzola play sweet against salty. A mushroom crepe, tucked around its woodsy filling as neatly as a fitted sheet, is dressed up with teleggio fondue. The tomato sauce on the house-made ricotta gnocchi is discreetly enlivened with a little gorgonzola cheese, a little basil. Excellent service makes customers feel pampered, as do complimentary extras like roasted peppers offered at the start of the meal, and pistachio-anise biscotti at the end. Closed Sunday. ● **$$$**

DJANGO, *526 South 4th Street; 215-922-7151.* Django's young husband-and-wife owners set out to prove that hiring a team of professional interior designers and menu consultants to build a multimillion-dollar grand palace isn't the only path to a memorable dining experience. Their singular vision led them to open a quirky yet serious little BYOB just off South Street where the focus is clearly on one thing—the food. And the food cognoscenti are responding strongly to Bryan Sikora's regional European style; a short-notice reservation here is one of the toughest gets in town. But the enjoyment of dinner here goes beyond the food. Sikora's wife, Aimee Olexy, has put together a well-trained staff of young women who are providing the most sweetly refined service to be found hereabouts. Django is truly an original and may prove to be the standard for a new breed of Philadelphia restaurants where substance takes precedence over style. Closed Monday. ● 🍶 **$$$**

DMITRI'S, *759 South 3rd Street, 215-982-9307; and 2227 Pine Street, 215-985-3680.* With its no-reservation policy, Dmitri's—the funky BYOB Queen Village location, or the more grown-up, full-bar Pine Street spot—can easily turn into a whole evening's investment. But it's is worth the wait. The grilled octopus will call you back again and again: tender and charred, splashed with vinegar and oil, salted, sprinkled with parsley. This is quintessential bargain cuisine. The Mediterranean Meze combination, a $12 bonanza of hummus, tarama salada, tzatziki, baba ghanoush, skordalia and beets, is a meal all by its lonesome. ● ☉ 🍶 (2nd Street location only) **$$**

DONECKERS, *333 North State Street, Ephrata; 717-738-9501.* Chef Greg Gable was surprised when he began cooking at Doneckers and discovered that local farmers driving horse-drawn buggies were showing up (unannounced) with loads of asparagus, cantaloupes and baby turnips for his perusal on spring and summer mornings. But the local produce is the essential ingredient on Gable's seasonal menu, which has included his cream of watercress soup, tempura of asparagus with caramelized baby carrots, and terrine of oxtail with baby turnips. Closed Wednesday and Sunday. ◐ ● **$$$**

ELEMENTS CAFÉ, *517 Station Avenue, Haddon Heights; 856-546-8840.* The flexible menu at Elements Café makes it possible to order standard-size entrées or appetizer-size portions. Take the latter course and try chef Fred Kellermann's panzanella du jour (with flavors like black olives, mushrooms and broccoli rabe); or his caramelized onion and smoked mozzarella tarts. Kellermann was once a pastry chef, so don't skip dessert. Closed Sunday; closed for dinner Tuesday. ◐ ● ◗ $

EL SOMBRERO, *437 Gap Newport Pike, Avondale; 610-268-3553.* This vibrant roadside store lies on the edges of Kennett Square's mushroom-farming community and belongs to a local manufacturer of tortillas and queso fresco. Part restaurant, part groceria, part newsstand, El Sombrero has a menu written in Spanish and English above the register, listing bargain-priced tortas, tacos, burritos and platters. Try a torta, a Mexican sandwich consisting of a big, sweet roll layered with refried beans, avocado, mustard, lettuce, tomato and shredded beef, or a simple, spicy chorizo-filled taco dressed with pickled onions and peppers from the wooden condiment cart in the center of the dining room. On your way out, stock up on dried peppers, fresh papaya, homemade pastries and bargain hot sauces. ◐ ● $$

EL VEZ, *121 South 13th Street; 215-928-9800.* Chichi, but definitely not Chi-Chi's, Mexi-fabulous El Vez is the best of the Stephen Starr canon, surpassing Alma de Cuba, where chef Jose Garces previously cooked. Like Alma, it is sharply focused and brilliantly executed, but El Vez gets the edge for being just plain fun. This Las Vegas-ized take on Tijuana—supersized velvet dining nooks, Charo's face on the bar stools, a wall plastered with postcards, a photo booth in the dining room, a gilded bicycle above the bar—hits the jackpot with roasted corn soup, sopes trio, green chile enchiladas, carne asada, pork chop with mole verde, and guacamole made tableside. Closed for lunch Saturday and Sunday. ○ ◐ ● $$

ERNESTO'S 1521 CAFE, *1521 Spruce Street; 215-546-1521.* With its cream-colored walls and minimalist paintings in a roomy townhouse setting, Ernesto's has of-the-moment polish, plus an inherently Italian warmth. Ernesto himself, the all-American Ernie Salandria, greets you at the door, looking happily proprietary as he watches over his cashmere-clad, Kimmel Center-bound diners. His amped-up trattoria menu includes an appetizer of two homemade butternut squash-stuffed ravioli in brown butter sauce—delicate, nutty and sweet, its paper-thin squares of pasta as wide as its plate. A veal chop special was beautifully grilled and came with classic white beans and bitter greens (which weren't overly bitter or garlicky). Closed Monday; closed for lunch Saturday and Sunday and for dinner Sunday. ◐ ● ☉ $$

EULOGY BELGIAN TAVERN, *136 Chestnut Street; 215-413-2354.* Eulogy—festooned with brewery memorabilia, with solid Belgian tavern food and a long beer list—is above all, owner Michael Naessens says, "a tribute to Belgium's history and quirkiness." This is evident in the second-floor "coffin room," where potent elixirs are served in skull mugs; the decor is accented with burial caskets, and a mix of Gregorian chants and electronica plays. And in a more flippant nod to life in Belgian bars—where artful beer glasses tend to disappear with patrons—Eulogy demands a "shoe deposit" from drinkers who order Kwak ale in the brewery's distinctive vessel. ◐ ● ✪ $$

FADÓ IRISH PUB & RESTAURANT, *1500 Locust Street; 215-893-9700.* This outpost of a small Atlanta chain occupies the space that once housed H.A. Winston. The interiors were crafted in Ireland to replicate a Victorian Dublin pub, an Irish cottage pub, and a traditional Irish pub shop. The full Irish breakfast is served anytime: sausages, rashers, fried eggs, baked beans, black pudding, white pudding, brown bread and a grilled tomato. They cook boxtys here, too—potato pancakes wrapped around fillings like steak and portabellas. ◐ ● ☉ $$

FATOU AND FAMA, *4002 Chestnut Street; 215-386-0700.* Dakar, Senegal, native Fatou N'Diaye named Fatou and Fama, her popular West African restaurant, for her grandmother and mother, who taught her to cook authentic West African and Caribbean dishes. Also popular at the 40-seat BYOB are N'Diave's West African soul-food specialties, such as supa kanja—okra stew with smoked fish—and yassa chicken marinated with onion and lemons. Closed Monday. ◐ ● ⬧ $$

FIESTA MEXICANA, *327 12th Street, Hammonton; 609-704-1611.* You might hear more Spanish than English spoken at Fiesta Mexicana in Hammonton, a modest two-room establishment. Bring your own beer, and try the beef tongue tacos or the exceptionally light tamales. Two people have to work very hard to spend more than $25. ● ⬧ $

FIGS, *2501 Meredith Street; 215-978-8440.* The bright paintings on the saffron walls of Figs and the embroidered pillows lining the windowsill banquette hail from owner Mustapha Rouissiya's native Morocco, as do the restaurant's showpiece meals, tagines. Rouissiya's signature is applying New American flair to traditional North African dishes. At quiet weekend brunches, the menu consists of comfort fare: challah French toast flecked with currants; big, spicy Moroccan omelets; and the neighborhood's best lattes. Closed Monday. ● ⊙ ▮ ◑ $$

FIORAVANTI, *105 East Lancaster Avenue, Downingtown; 610-518-9170.* Fioravanti, a creative BYOB restaurant in the center of Downingtown, offers an astonishing $18 three-course prix fixe between 5 and 6:30 p.m. Monday through Thursday. On a recent evening, chef-owner David Fioravanti dished up warm pureed beet soup with fresh mint, and Malaysian mango shrimp with sticky rice and five-spice carrots, followed by a delightfully homey pound cake made by his mother. The 40-seat dining room, hung with a gallery-like display of art, can be unbearably noisy on weekends; weeknights are serene. Closed Sunday. ◐ ● ▮ $$

FLATSPIN, *2750 Red Lion Road; 215-969-SPIN.* The 94th Aero Squadron, which overlooked the runways of the Northeast Philadelphia Airport for 20 years, has gone into a Flatspin. In aviation lingo, a flatspin is a plane out of control—or an engine-cutting stunt by a maverick pilot. In the restaurant world, Flatspin American Grill and Dance Hall is the new call name of a modern American grill with indoor and outdoor dining areas catering to lunch and dinner crowds; a large bar with a dozen TVs for sports fans; and an indoor/outdoor nightclub that hosts DJs and bands. The menu, developed by Rock Lobster's Patrick Pawliczek, is a collection of the usual pub-suspects. Closed Monday; closed for dinner Sunday. ◐ ● ⊙ $

FORK, *306 Market Street; 215-625-9425.* This Meg Rodgers-designed room, with high-backed banquettes and painted-shade chandeliers in the rear and a minimalist bar out front, manages to be both refined and hip. And the open kitchen produces food that is sleek and fresh and homey and satisfying, all at once. The salads, in their precise sophistication, are a roaring delight for the palate. Seasonal veggies are stars in their own right, from the cream-and-nutmeg-sautéed Brussels sprouts to the French lentils to the buttermilk mashed potatoes. Closed for lunch Saturday and Sunday. ◐ ● ⊙ $$

THE FOUNTAIN RESTAURANT AT FOUR SEASONS, *1 Logan Square; 215-963-1500.* The Fountain is renowned citywide for its polished, thoughtful service and refined French cooking with occasional sparks of innovation. Entering the restaurant from the portal off the lobby, you're greeted sweetly and demurely by a very civil and proper hostess. There's lots of real estate between tables—they could easily make another dining room out of the aisles. The nightly $110 "Spontaneous Taste" menu is a six-course (four savory, two sweet) tasting that shows the kitchen at its best. And after a meal, whether you've indulged in the tasting menu or gone à la carte, there are two things you simply must not miss. Full stomach or not, have the waiter wheel that sparkling cheese cart to your side, and then end your fine evening with hot-out-of-the-oven chocolate soufflé. ◑ ● ☉ $$$$

FRANCO LUIGI'S RESTAURANT, *13th and Tasker streets; 215-755-8900.* Featuring live opera performed by its mostly Curtis-schooled waiters, this friendly South Philly BYOB is more casual than some of its peers: The food is unpretentious, and no one will throttle Grandma for singing along after she's killed the chianti. Standouts include the portabella mushrooms stuffed with extra-sharp provolone, lots of garlic, and broccoli rabe; the tender sautéed calamari in a spicy cherry pepper sauce; and the "Core'n grato"—scallops, lump crabmeat and spinach in a creamy vodka sauce over featherweight gnocchi. Closed Monday. ● ⬩ $$

FRENCHTOWN INN, *7 Bridge Street, Frenchtown; 908-996-3300.* A dressy crowd graces the veranda at the Frenchtown Inn. Typical of chef-owner Andrew Tomko's seasonal brunch choices: eggs Benedict, or North Atlantic salmon with red wine au jus and whipped potatoes. Later on, when brunch gives way to the Grill Room menu, there's no better snack than the ploughman's plate of pâtés and terrines. Closed Monday. ◑ ● ☉ $$$

FRIDAY SATURDAY SUNDAY, *261 South 21st Street; 215-546-4232.* After nearly 30 years, this Restaurant Renaissance holdover remains a familial venture, with a largely local crowd. But the staff treats all comers equally, whether you're interested in old classics, like the cream-and-cognac-laced mushroom soup, or the more current Asian-influenced offerings, like pan-seared salmon with hoisin and ginger. Simple and fresh are the guiding principles. And owner Weaver Lilley's flat $10 markup on every bottle of wine, instead of the traditional 100 to 150 percent gouge, means you get to drink better wine for less money. The Tank Bar upstairs, with its tranquil aquarium, is a favorite watering spot. Closed for lunch Saturday through Monday. ◑ ● $$$

FUJI, *404 Route 130 North, Cinnaminson; 856-829-5211.* Fuji has been sandwiched between cheesy motels on Route 130 for more than 25 years, and those who know about the unassuming spot try their best to keep it a secret. Chef Masaharu "Matt" Ito opened Fuji after a stint at that other Jersey gem, Sagami. Odes have been written to his eight-course kasakei menu—like a snowflake, it's always different—and his sushi bar offerings are just as consistently good. No wonder—he makes early-morning trips to the Food Distribution Center to pick up the freshest fish, and strives to get each roll exactly right, down to the fluffiness of the rice. Closed Monday; closed for lunch Saturday and Sunday. ◐ ● ▮ $$

THE GABLES AT CHADDS FORD, *423 Baltimore Pike, Chadds Ford; 610-388-7700.* A Chester County gem, the Gables at Chadds Ford was once a dairy barn. Now it is a lively bar and restaurant, drawing a well-tanned, well-heeled clientele with big martinis, a wide-ranging wine list, live jazz, and dependably well-executed New American cuisine. The choicest tables are on the flower-filled outdoor patio. ◐ ● ☉ ▮ $$$

GILMORE'S, *133 East Gay Street, West Chester; 610-431-2800.* Gilmore's, from Peter Gilmore, who for 22 years was Georges Perrier's chef de cuisine at Le Bec-Fin, is no Le Bec, and it's not supposed to be. When Gilmore finally defected from the Perrier empire, he was determined to create a French restaurant with a casual, family-friendly atmosphere and impeccable fare. Located in an 1890 townhouse, Gilmore's has a decor that exudes suburban sophistication: dark floral carpeting and drapes, stately arrangements of flowers. But the food—subtle beurre blancs, delicate herb infusions and luscious vegetable purees—recalls trademark Perrier flourishes. Gilmore's crabcake rivals Le Bec's pricier—and tinier—galette any night, and the poached salmon with veal reduction elevates the commonplace to the realm of the extraordinary. It's enough to make patrons book tables months in advance. Closed Monday and Tuesday. ● ↻ $$$

GIRASOLE, *1305 Locust Street; 215-985-4659.* Lean down and inhale the carpaccio caldo, a rosy sunflower comprised of petal-like raw beef slices encircling fresh artichoke hearts, shaved parmesan and roasted garlic. Its heady perfume comes from a gilding of truffle oil. In addition, consider a thin-crusted pizza from the wood-burning oven; seafood bruschetta anchored by thick bread slices; and ravioli filled with ricotta and spinach, draped lightly with tomato sauce. An attractive young staff clad in figure-fitting black gives this restaurant a fresh, sexy, very Italian feel. Closed Sunday. ◑ ● $$

GIUMARELLO'S, *329 Haddon Avenue, Westmont; 856-858-9400.* Giumarello's has been around for more than 15 years, but recently relocated from Haddon Heights to a bigger space with a happening bar and patio seating for 35. Its Northern Italian menu includes grilled veal stuffed with lobster, and crisp potato-crusted halibut. Chef Samuel Giumarello produces a succulent rack of lamb, and a daily crabcake special served with sweet grilled corn sauce or lobster beurre blanc, for which his brother Gian Giumarello (also the pastry chef) recommends a glass of Caymus Conundrum. Closed Sunday and Monday; closed for lunch Saturday. ◑ ● $$

GOVINDA'S GOURMET VEGETARIAN, *1408 South Street; 215-985-9303.* Upstairs from Govinda's deep-green and polished-wood dining room is a space for Bhagavad Gita classes. That Hindu text, along with the study of yoga, inspired Govinda's chef to eat vegetarian—and then to share the cuisine with the masses. Franklin Cameron's mostly vegan menu includes vegetarian standards such as samosas and three-bean chili as well as the peculiarly named "Zucchini Detroit," grilled zucchini and squash seasoned with basil and served over turmeric-infused rice. You'll also find "Congo Asparagus" (asparagus tips sautéed in a ginger-lemon sauce with roasted cashews), "Hawaiian Supreme" (veggies in sweet-and-sour sauce) and "San Francisco Hills Kofta" (vegetarian meatballs in a marinara sauce with pasta). Open Thursday through Sunday. ◑ ● ⓘ $$

THE GRILL, *the Ritz-Carlton, 10 South Broad Street; 215-523-8221.* Former Striped Bass chef Terence Feury now oversees the contemporary American menu of the Ritz-Carlton's formal Grill, bringing a sensibility for local, seasonal flavors and uncomplicated techniques to a strictly traditional, sometimes stiflingly classic dining room. Look for seasonal dishes like duck breast seasoned with pistachio oil, and lamb topped with onion marmalade—and after Feury's five years at the city's seafood mecca, you can trust that the fish choices, such as grilled swordfish smothered with peppers, will be excellent ones. Closed for lunch Saturday and Sunday. ◑ ● $$$

HAMILTON'S GRILL ROOM, *8 Coryell Street, Lambertville; 609-397-4343.* Hamilton's Grill Room, the outstanding BYOB in Lambertville, sits right next to a quaint canal, but its shady courtyard offers no view. No one minds, because the focus is on the stellar raw ingredients that executive chef Mark Miller employs: giant shrimp served with anchovy butter, and thick hunks of tuna topped with mango chutney. Inside, diners relax in one of four dining rooms: the Delaware Room, adorned with floor-to-ceiling pastoral murals; the Grill Room, with modern Mediterranean decor; the Bishop Room, named for its eclectic collection of religious symbols; and the Gallery, with a nude mural and the restaurant's most popular table, nestled in the woman's, ahem, embrace. ● $$$

HAPPY ROOSTER, *118 South 16th Street; 215-963-9311.* It's the same room that once housed a notorious chauvinist realm in which unattended women weren't allowed. But today the stained-glass rooster in the window casts a different light into this upscale old watering hole, falling as it does on the smiling presence of owner Rose Parrotta at work behind the bar. Top-notch food comes from the tiny kitchen downstairs; the menu is written on a big blackboard held up for patrons' perusal. What hasn't changed is the manly-man dark-wood-and-leather decor. Closed Sunday. ◐ ● $$

HORIZONS CAFÉ, *101 East Moreland Road, Willow Grove; 215-657-2100.* Owner/chef Rich Landau is "in love with anyplace the sun shines brighter than it does here." That predilection shows up in his café's bright walls and Latin music, and in the menu of seitan, tofu and veggies that are smoked, spiced, and glazed with mingled flavors imported from warmer climes, such as chipotle aioli (which combines Mexican and Provençal) and saffron/green olive sauce (Spanish and Mediterranean). The "tapas for two" comes with cakey flatbread to dip into edamame hummus, and tequila-grilled hearts of palm; the sopa de tortilla is a mild green chile broth with ancho chile grilled seitan steak, red beans, roasted corn and avocado. And the vegan (no animal products, including dairy) desserts taste sinful even if they're not. Closed Sunday and Monday. ● $$

HOSTARIA DA ELIO, *615 South 3rd Street; 215-925-0930.* Regulars return to Elio Sgambati's inviting Queen Village restaurant for astonishingly delicate veal-filled cannelloni with tomato-cream sauce, reminiscent of Rome, and a stack of paper-thin, lightly breaded fried eggplant in marinara sauce. Ask how it is prepared, and "Secreto!" the proprietor will insist, refusing to divulge how the eggplant, like the cannelloni, could be so satisfying and yet so light. It is equally pointless to pursue the secrets of the sweet-potato gnocchi in a cream sauce with strands of spinach, or the chianti gravy on the excellent filet mignon. Italians prefer fresh fruit for dessert, and in this regard, Sgambati has another secreto: The half-cantaloupe that looks like such a prudent choice hides, in its hollowed-out center, a potent shot of triple sec. Closed Monday. ● ⬧ $$

ILLUMINARE, *2321 Fairmount Avenue; 215-765-0202.* If you peer through Illuminare's plate-and-stained-glass front window, only the banquettes of the small front room, the curved bar, and the open kitchen are visible. There is more beyond the kitchen's brightly burning wood stove: a cozy dining room with a fireplace, semicircular brocade booths, and polished wood above and below. Outdoors lies a sparkling courtyard filled with miniature lights, with a 50-year-old magnolia tree as its centerpiece. The centerpiece of the menu is the brick-oven offerings, but pastas and seafood dishes are also popular. Closed Monday. ◑ ● ⊙ $$

IL PORTICO, *1519 Walnut Street; 215-587-7000.* As neighboring Le Bec-Fin trumpets a recent top-to-bottom renovation, it might be time for Alberto Del Bello to spruce up the most swank of his three establishments. A well-trod carpet and slightly dull chandeliers shouldn't distract from the tall, lemony arugula salad with fresh artichokes and shaved parmesan; the soft twin polenta cakes with earthy portobellos; the snappy house-made tagliolini with wild boar; or the spicy seafood risotto, with its sprawl of perfectly cooked langoustines, calamari, mussels, shrimp, tuna, salmon and other fish across a wide white plate. ◑ ● $$$

IO E TU RISTORANTE, *1514-20 South 9th Street; 215-271-3906.* Whoever declared Philadelphia the most hostile city in America never met Concetta Varallo, a South Philly native who treats every customer, tourist or local, like a vip. Concetta's Italian-born husband, chef Giovanni Varallo, extends hospitality in the form of Italian and Italian-American dishes, as well as some entirely his own. In the latter category is a luscious warm radicchio "salad": shredded bitter radicchio, crumbled bacon and lump crabmeat, in a balsamic cream sauce. Crabmeat reappears as a stuffing for mussels or clams, in spaghetti, as a topping for veal, even tucked into a steak. House-made potato gnocchi holds its own against its neighborhood rivals. The wine list holds possibilities for conservative or expansive spenders. Closed Monday. ● $$

average entrée price: $ under $12 $$ $13 to $20 $$$ $21 to $30 $$$$ more than $30

JACK'S FIREHOUSE, *2130 Fairmount Avenue; 215-232-9000.* Much celebrated chef Jack McDavid hasn't lost his Southern drawl or his overalls despite his more than 20 years in Philadelphia. His home-style cooking can be found at the Down Home Diner, his outpost in Reading Terminal, but his Firehouse (housed, yes, in a fire station, complete with fireman's pole and imposing doors that open onto a sidewalk café) is about "haute country cuisine": black-eyed pea and hog jowl soup, crawdads and macaroni with spicy tomato sauce, and buffalo with moonshine sauce. ◑ ● ☉ $$

JAKE'S RESTAURANT, *4365 Main Street, Manayunk; 215-483-0444.* No food within miles of Manayunk approaches this level, and Bruce Cooper's success was long ago ratified by the stylish crowd. If foie gras is your weakness, yield to it here. Pan-seared and buttery, with mellow caramelized pineapple vinai-grette, it just edges out the veal-stuffed pan-fried Chinese dumplings as my favorite appetizer. Speaking of favorites, potatoes are Cooper's most cherished food, and the best way to have them is mashed, studded with lobster, and nudged up against succulent sautéed veal tournedos. The small bar that fronts the restaurant is a chic place for pre- or post-dinner cocktails. ◑ ● ☉ $$$$

JAMAICAN JERK HUT, *1436 South Street; 215-545-8644.* Island ambience pre-vails on the tented veranda decorated with colorful potted annuals at the Jamaican Jerk Hut, especially on weekends, when live bands play. Bring your own Red Stripe beer to accompany chef-owner Nicola Shirley's jerked chicken Caesar salad and curried lobster. Closed Sunday when weather is cool. ◑ ● ♦ $$

JOHNNY BRENDA'S, *1201 Frankford Avenue; 215-739-9684.* Johnny Brenda's, named for longtime owner and 1940s boxer John Imbrenda, is now run by Standard Tap's Paul Kimport and William Reed. Small tears in the red-and-white-striped linoleum floor still offer glimpses of vibrant tiling beneath, and a hole in the dark wood paneling reveals the original tin walls match-ing the ceiling. But the flames in the open kitchen, where flank steak and marinated octopus are grilled, distract from these flaws. Have a drink—there are 13 local beers on tap, including Victory Mad King, Yards Love Stout, and Sly Fox ESB—and relive most of the decades the bar has seen with the well-stocked jukebox. Closed Sunday. ◑ ● ❂ $

JOHNNY MAÑANA'S, *4201 Midvale Avenue; 215-843-0499.* At the intersection of Midvale and Ridge avenues, a 10-foot-long chili pepper announces Johnny

Mañana's. If you miss the pepper, the Mexican cantina and margarita bar, modeled on some New York favorites, also has a vibrant south-of-the-border paint job. And the flavors at Johnny's are as eye-popping as the decor, starting with the fiery complimentary salsa and addictive freshly fried tortilla chips. Prices are mild, though. Mexican basics—tortillas, tacos, burritos—are under $10, and entrées peak at around $20. ○ ◑ ● $$

JONES, *700 Chestnut Street; 215-223-5663.* There can be a massive wait at Jones—on a Saturday evening, as much as two hours for a table. Sounds horrible, right? Wrong. And this is one of the keys to Stephen Starr's success— his restaurants always have bars that make the wait for tables part of the fun. Sample a funky cocktail, and comment on the decor: "It looks like the Brady Bunch's living room" is what every diner seems to say at least once while gazing at the faux-sandstone walls and fireplace. The affordable menu is just as nostalgic. Get the macaroni and cheese; tuna tacos; fried chicken and waffles; Cobb salad; or roast turkey Thanksgiving dinner with all the trimmings. If the kitsch becomes too much, skip the Tang sorbet. ◑ ● ⊙ ✪ $$

KARMA, *114 Chestnut Street; 215-925-1444.* It was like karma, the way it happened: New Delhi native and Wharton MBA Munish Narula was searching for an Old City spot in which to open an Indian restaurant. At the same time, popular eatery Shivnanda shut its doors for good—leaving what would have been a painful void for Indian food lovers. Instead, Narula opened Karma in the same space, giving his new spot a modern flair, with abstract art on its bright, multi-hued walls. Chef Dominic Sarkar—imported from a luxury New Delhi hotel—has created an eclectic menu of favorites from throughout the subcontinent: classics like tandoori chicken and biryani, and such seldom-seen dishes as paneer tikka masala and tandoori cauliflower. ◑ ● $$

KHAJURAHO, *Ardmore Plaza, 12 Greenfield Avenue, Ardmore; 610-896-7200.* Khajuraho's extensive and surprisingly inexpensive lunch buffet offers all the Indian standards: yogurt-and-lemon-marinated tandoori chicken, chicken tikka masala, lamb rogan josh. What's unusual—besides the erotic artwork of the Kama Sutra on the walls—are the harder-to-find dishes chef-owner Bharat Luthra includes, such as potato and okra-based aloo bhindi and broiled eggplant baingan bartha. In the evenings, a full menu of northern and southern Indian entrées is available at this popular BYOB. ◑ ● ⊙ ⬧ $$

KISSO SUSHI BAR, *205 North 4th Street; 215-922-1770.* Dining at Kisso is a little like having your kid's portrait drawn at a street fair. Nothing can change the fact that the work is being done individually, piece by piece; if you don't have patience in you, don't get in that line. But if you have a Zen center and can wait with the rest of the young, hip and black-clad for beauty to slowly evolve, you will find no better sushi in town than the killer maki—broiled eel, cucumber, scallion and salmon skin—at Kisso. Closed for lunch Saturday and Sunday. ◑ ● ▮ $$

KONAK, *228 Vine Street; 215-592-1212.* Service at Konak, the reincarnation of Voorhees's Authentic Turkish Cuisine—while polite and helpful in describing (and pronouncing) the unfamiliar entrées—can be leisurely and haphazard. But a seat in the large, high-ceilinged, spring-sunshine-yellow dining room is a soothing place to wait. And eventually your Turkish-garbed waiter will bring crisp, flaky phyllo pockets of spinach and feta; eggplant stuffed with peppers and pine nuts; and the chef's special, a hummus and smoky-spicy pastrami plate dotted with bursting grape tomatoes. When entrées like Emperor's fish (delicate tilapia grilled with olive oil, spinach and pine nuts) and kabobs of every variety—even mussels—emerge from behind the ornate wooden kitchen doors, followed by syrupy desserts and Turkish coffee, you'll forget about the delay. Closed Monday. ◑ ● ◉ $$

KRAZY KAT'S, *the Inn at Montchanin Village, Route 100 and Kirk Road, Montchanin; 302-888-4200.* Krazy Kat's, just north of Wilmington in the precisely restored Inn at Montchanin, has a simultaneously elegant and hilariously tongue-in-cheek decor. The formal oil portraits that line the walls are of dogs and cats. The napkins are embossed with a crow and a Holstein. A cutout of a Victorian-clad she-cat covers one restroom door; a correspondingly dapper tom adorns the other. Wilmington's elite comes here to business-lunch and fine-dine, on creative French and Asian-accented cuisine. Closed for lunch Saturday and Sunday. ○ ◑ ● $$$

KRISTIAN'S RISTORANTE, *1100 Federal Street; 215-468-0104.* Reservations are essential, even on a Monday night, because 30-something Kristian Leuzzi is cooking better than ever in the restaurant that his family built to showcase his talents. Listening to the soft Sinatra music playing in the dining room, you might look to the singer's song list for titles to describe dinner. The chilled seafood appetizer? "You're Sensational." The osso buco, fragrant with fresh rosemary, on saffron risotto? "Too Marvelous for Words." You'll want to finish every bite of the pappardelle noodles with mushrooms, topped with a sliver of crisped duck confit. "They Can't Take That Away from Me." The attentive service? "Someone to Watch Over Me." Closed Tuesday; closed for lunch Saturday, Sunday and Tuesday. ◑ ● $$$

LA BOHÈME, *246 South 11th Street; 215-351-9901.* La Bohème doesn't need to advertise to attract customers; a pair of inviting storefront windows trimmed in white lights does the job. Inside, couples lean over tabletop lanterns to clink wineglasses and share bowls of mussels. Brick walls, dark wooden banquettes, and bistro tables are the setting for dishes that include French, Spanish and Moroccan flavors. The steak frites is a densely flavorful cracked peppercorn-rimmed filet topped with pungent gorgonzola. ● ♨ ☉ $$$

LA CAMPAGNE, *312 Kresson Road, Cherry Hill; 856-429-7647.* Grape arbors and terraces make magic of the summer season, and a hearth blazes during the chilly months. If you hadn't just turned off a bustling suburban artery, this 150-year-old farmhouse, with its rustic appointments, could be in Provence. Chef Eric Hall's talents reinforce the reverie; his classic dishes are emboldened by the flavors of the South of France. So the escargots en croûte are scented with hazelnut, sauced with roasted fennel butter and saffron vanilla. The tender, luscious rack of lamb has lavender in its shallot and herb crust. Owner John Byrne runs a cooking school on the premises and has published a recipe book of La Campagne favorites, all of which helps to attract a food-savvy crowd. Closed Monday. ◑ ● ♨ $$$

LACROIX AT THE RITTENHOUSE, *the Rittenhouse Hotel, 210 West Rittenhouse Square; 215-790-2533.* Chef Jean-Marie Lacroix, who spent two decades at the Four Seasons Hotel, has created what may be the most ambitious menu in the city. He experiments, sometimes wildly, with food pairings, while remaining rooted in traditions from his native Dijon. Lacroix's menu format offers mix-and-match three-, four- and five-plate options, plus dessert, for between $58 and $75. Dishes are organized into four suggested courses, but the chef leaves a great deal of discretion to the diner. The wine list and 4,000-bottle wine cellar are outstanding, and the seasonal foods coming out of Lacroix's kitchen—from an amuse-bouche of tuna tartare and truffled dandelion, to skate with surprising mix of orange hollandaise sauce and caviar, presented on a wedge of pink grapefruit—are impeccable. ○ ◑ ● ⊙ $$$

LA FAMIGLIA, *8 South Front Street; 215-922-2803.* With its marble floors, heavily framed portraits, breathtaking wine list and tuxedoed European service, La Famiglia might be called the Le Bec-Fin of the city's Italian restaurants. Sumptuous as the setting is, it's hard to justify $26 for a bowl of gnocchi, no matter how ethereal; $36 for a whole baked fish; $85 for rack of lamb for two; or $15 for a scoop of apple cobbler from the dessert cart. But people do: The dining rooms are nearly filled even during Sunday-night dinners. If money is no object, by all means pull the cork on a Biondi-Santi Brunello di Montalcino Riserva, a Vietti Barolo Le Rocche, or an amarone from Masi. Closed Monday; closed for lunch Satuday and Sunday. ◑ ● $$$$

LA LOCANDA DEL GHIOTTONE, *130 North 3rd Street; 215-829-1465.* The late Giuseppe Rosselli's cantankerous pronouncements against food stupidities (and food critics) never obscured the fact that his restaurant provided nascent Old City with some of its first great eats. This is homey food, rustic food, the Italian food of Rosselli's father and grandfather, who were both chefs, and it has First Friday-ites packing the sidewalk, waiting for tables. The candle-in-a-chianti-bottle humbleness of the small, crowded room is the perfect setting for plates of gnocchi; osso buco; and wild mushroom-stuffed crepes sauced with porcini-essence béchamel. Closed Monday. ● ▮ ⊖ $$

L'ANGOLO, *1415 Porter Street; 215-389-4252.* A charming oasis in a sea of double-and triple-parked cars, L'Angolo may be the best of all the new wave of BYOB restaurants, and is value-priced to boot. Credit for this small miracle goes to owner Davide Faenza, a native of Gallipoli, down in Italy's heel, and his wife Kathy, who makes the desserts. The seduction begins just inside the front door, when you spy the glorious assortment of room-temperature cooked vegetables that includes zucchini, bell pepper, eggplant, carrots, potatoes, onions and beets, plus chickpeas and frittata. Order antipasto misto as an appetizer, and you'll get some of everything, a platter large enough to share. A happy din fills the 36-seat dining room divided by a brick archway, as couples pass plates back and forth across the table: "Try my lobster ravioli." "Isn't this calamari incredible?" Excepting the specials, every entrée is under $18. Closed Monday; closed Saturday and Sunday for lunch. ◑ ● ▮ $$

LANGOSTINO'S, *100 Morris Street; 215-551-7709.* This small, noisy, lace-curtained dining room, stark white save for a few framed posters, sits at the end of a rowhouse block that stops at a retaining wall for I-95. Most of the dishes are simple gifts: mussels and clams, red or white, with a spicy zip; handmade potato gnocchi in a light tomato-basil or gorgonzola-mascarpone sauce; a fine veal scallopini with mushrooms and artichokes. But what reels in the Center City crowd are the grilled langostinos, four to an order for $28.95, a plate-filling display rounded out by black olives and tomatoes. The meat, tasting like a cross between lobster and shrimp, is sweet and addictive, if dearly priced. ● ♦ $$

LAULETTA'S GRILLE, *1703 South 11th Street; 215-755-5422.* Joe Lauletta was a waiter for years before taking command of his own stove. It took plenty of sweat equity to reclaim an abandoned luncheonette near his boyhood home, but the result is cool and understated, in the manner of Northern Liberties or Old City. Sit at the counter by the open kitchen and let the wood-burning grill influence at least a couple of courses: perhaps calamari with lemon and olive oil, or meaty portabella mushroom slices topped with chopped tomato, garlic and basil. The grill contributes greatly to the standout meat dish, pork tenderloin with full-flavored fig-onion relish and cannellini beans. ● ♦ ✸ $$

LA VIOLA, *253 South 16th Street; 215-735-8630.* A popular spot for pre-theater dining, sometimes booked out from 5:30 to 7:30 weeks in advance, La Viola is petite and unpretentious. The understated whitewashed walls and basic white table coverings provide a simple setting—which doesn't prevent the waiters from being indulgent and attentive in a manly, Italian way. They'll double-check that you're enjoying the superb porcini insalata, grilled calamari with seafood-infused dipping sauce, and savory osso buco (which you are). Chef Pedro Beltran prepares even the more straightforward dishes with flair: Chicken marsala is rich with wine, and linguini with red sauce is more South Philly than Rittenhouse Square. Closed for lunch Saturday and Sunday. ◑ ● ♦ ✸ $$

LE BAR LYONNAIS, *1523 Walnut Street; 215-567-1000.* Whereas Le Bec-Fin has Big Special Occasion written all over it, Le Bar Lyonnais, named for Georges Perrier's hometown of Lyon, is elegant without reservations, the kind of place to drop in for pre-theater drinks (and tobacco) or post-opera dining. All the refinement of the first floor makes it down the stairs, but the very act of descending creates the more cozy embrace of a pub—and what pub food! Heavenly, hearty onion soup, delicate fish terrines, bordelaise-sauced filet with pommes frites, exquisite desserts from Perrier's pastry kitchen—there is no going wrong. This is the next best thing to being upstairs in the Big House—and, in its own small and charming way, better. Closed Sunday; closed for lunch Saturday. ◗ ● $$$

LE BEC-FIN, *1523 Walnut Street; 215-567-1000.* The name is idiomatic for "the fine palate," and Philadelphia owes Georges Perrier a debt of gratitude for putting us on the culinary map. For more than 30 years Philadelphians have looked to Le Bec, crowned with one award after another, as the consummate elegant dining experience. Though Mobil toyed with its stars, and Perrier took his waitstaff out of tuxes, that position remains impregnable. Every detail is opulent, from the recently renovated dining room to the classic French cuisine that perfectionist Perrier has continued to hone and refine. The service makes you feel like something special is going on—and that you're in on the secret. The prix fixe lunch, which includes the over-the-top dessert cart, is one of the best meal deals in town. Closed Sunday; closed for lunch Saturday. ◗ ● $$$$

LE CASTAGNE, *1920 Chestnut Street; 215-751-9913.* At modern, minimal Le Castagne, a glass facade reveals a cavern of black, softened by white gauze curtains and warmed by textured rose walls. Waiters in salmon-colored shirts blend into this background, leaving the focus on food. Lengthy menu descriptions such as arancini di patate e capesante con salsa di peperoni gialli e rossi—that's potato and bay scallop croquettes served in a red and yellow pepper sauce—translate into five courses of simply prepared and elaborately plated offerings full of northern Italian flavors. Closed Sunday; closed for lunch Saturday and Sunday. ◗ ● $$

LE MAS, *503 West Lancaster Avenue, Wayne; 610-964-2588.* Georges Perrier changed the name of his first Main Line restaurant foray from "Le Mas Perrier" to "Le Mas" to fit the more casual vibe of this spot, with a sunny decor designed to conjure up images of the South of France. A convenient spot for power-lunchers from the Western suburbs, Le Mas has a French-based menu that features both a burger and an elaborate bouillabaisse. The spacious lounge, with its large stone fireplace and big screen TV, is a popular place to enjoy stone-fired pizzas and signature cocktails like the "Flirtini." A weekday happy hour offers complimentary hors d'ouerves. (Guests can BYOB on Sunday evenings.) Closed Monday; closed for lunch Saturday and Sunday. ◗ ● $$$

LE PETIT MITRON, *207 Haverford Avenue, Narberth; 484-562-0500.* What makes Petit Mitron so enticing is the same quality that makes it occasionally infuriating: its unbridled Frenchness. Chef Patrick Rurange, trained in Lyons, presides over this room with its framed French holiday postcards, which could have been rocketed over to downtown Narberth from the 7th arrondissement. There are glass cases of proud little meringues and cakes, and the half-moon-shaped lemon cookies seem to be nothing but air, sugar, and a tart river of citrus filling. On Sundays, the croissants are as flaky (and as irresistible) as the Styles section of the *New York Times.* But come before noon, when these Gallic doors slam shut. Closed Monday. ○ $

A LITTLE CAFÉ, *Plaza Shoppes, 118 White Horse Road East, Voorhees; 856-784-3344.* Early diners will find great value at A Little Café, a compact BYOB. Chef-owner Marianne Cuneo Powell, known for generous portions and globally inspired dishes, includes high-end offerings like rack of lamb in her $19.95 three-course prix fixe, available between 5 and 6 p.m. Tuesday through Friday. Closed Sunday and Monday; closed for lunch Saturday. ◐ ● 🍶 $$$

LITTLE MARRAKESH, *1825 Limekiln Pike, Dresher; 215-643-3003.* Dresher BYOB Little Marrakesh calls to mind the homeland that owner Terry Manfa remembers: brass lamps, hand-engraved tabletops, Berber carpets, fezzes for the waiters. On Friday and Saturday nights, a $25 seven-course prix fixe includes the restaurant's popular Atlas bastilla, Moroccan phyllo dough stuffed with shredded chicken, eggs and toasted almonds, and topped with cinnamon and powdered sugar; fragrant chicken and lamb tagines; and belly dancers, who go well with a full-bodied red. Closed Monday. ● 🍶 $$$

LOBSTER TRAP, *5300 North Park Drive, Pennsauken; 856-663-3537.* A former concession stand in Cooper River Park has become the Lobster Trap, an exceedingly friendly seafood restaurant and piano bar with an abundance of rosebushes rimming a large outdoor terrace. It's not fancy, but there's no need to fancy up fresh grilled salmon, sautéed mussels, or Maine lobster plucked from the tank. When one is tucked into a terrace table, watching sailboats on the water and kids flying kites along the shore, it's easy to forget that lunch is over and it's time to get back to work. ◐ ● $$

LOIE, *128 South 19th Street; 215-568-0808.* Loie, a cool, casual brasserie on 19th Street, is a restaurant-hot spot with a straightforward timeline. There is dinner, a very good dinner, then the party, starting at 10 p.m. The menu, which is the same at lunch and dinner, is divided between sandwiches, entrées, and plats du jour—homey picks like Monday's coq au vin that keep the regulars happy. Steak frites, a hearty, surprisingly tender hanger steak with roasted shallots, would do any French brasserie proud, and the Loie burger, tall but evenly cooked, with the perfect balance of sharp Maytag blue cheese and sweet caramelized onion, is a favorite. These options are refreshingly priced, too. For dessert, go for the crème brûlée—or better yet, skip it, and have another glass of one of the excellent French or Australian wines on the list. Closed for lunch Monday. ◑ ● $$

LOLITA, *106 South 13th Street; 215-546-7100.* Casually chic, modern Lolita features a 12-foot photo of a calla lily, long walls of exposed brick, an open kitchen, and glass pendant lamps from local artisan Hot Soup. Marcie Turney, formerly chef at Valanni and Audrey Claire, and partner Valerie Safran planned Lolita long before Stephen Starr's El Vez moved in catty-corner. Neighborhood pricing—dinner for two is about $55—is a big draw for little Lolita. Bring along blue agave tequila to amp up your pitcher of homemade virgin margaritas—perfect alongside the rustic tamales with black beans, manchego, sauteed mushrooms, and achiote chicken; grilled pork chop with Mexican corn, huitlacoche, and avocado-tomatillo salsa; and tres leches chocolate cake. ● ♦ ⊖ $$

LOS CATRINES & TEQUILA'S BAR, *1602 Locust Street; 215-546-0181.* At Los Catrines, housed in an opulent mansion at 16th and Locust streets, the presence of a grand mahogany bar transforms fresh margaritas into a decadent experience. Drama is on the menu: Owner David Suro commissioned dramatic murals of Oaxacan farmers and skeleton families for the walls, and the dining rooms have dark woodwork and 20-foot ceilings. But Suro's menu still points to the earthbound origins of this haute Mexican cuisine, with extra-spicy tortilla soup, tamarind and ancho-coated filet mignon, whole red snapper covered with green olive and caper salsa, and rich and mysterious mole poblano. ◑ ● $$

MAGGIANO'S LITTLE ITALY, *1201 Filbert Street, 215-567-2020; and 205 Mall Boulevard, King of Prussia, 610-922-3333.* A table of three may be disappointed to learn that the $23.95 all-you-can-eat three-course special is available only to groups of four or more—Maggiano's is all about "more"—but don't worry; you certainly won't go hungry. With two locations in the Philadelphia area, this chain restaurant has established itself as the casual, comfortable place to carb up for the next marathon, with full orders of pasta weighing in at more than a pound. Order three entrées for three people, and you'll end the meal with a doggie bag: in one case, half a half-order of shrimp arrabiata, several spinach-stuffed manicotti, and more than two pounds of chicken parmesan. ◐ ● $$

MAMMA MARIA, *1637 East Passyunk Avenue; 215-463-8410.* Maria Di Marco briefly had a TV cooking show on WYBE (Channel 35), but she is best known for her $50 prix fixe, a parade of homespun dishes that includes a roasted vegetable antipasto, vegetable soup, a trio of pastas in three sauces, a fish or meat entrée, a salad-fruit-cheese course, Italian cream cake, a carafe of Carlo Rossi house red or white, and an assortment of cordials that includes homemade grappa, limoncello and mandarina. Big feeds like this are best enjoyed in a boisterous dining room, but on a Tuesday night, the restaurant was empty, and the meal had a perfunctory feel. Closed for lunch Saturday and Sunday. ◐ ● ♦ $$$

MARGARET KUO'S, *175 East Lancaster Avenue, Wayne; 610-688-7200.* Behind Margaret Kuo's grandly pillared facade are two distinct restaurants—one Chinese, one Japanese. In the Dragon's Lair dining room, named for the hand-carved stone dragons positioned at its entrance, antiques from mainland China, set the scene for Chinese dishes as simple as chicken lo mein or as showy as crispy whole fish Hunan-style. On the upper level, the Akari Room is a clean-lined triumph of Japanese design and carpentry, with an inviting sushi bar, cozy booths, and two tatami rooms. Although the menu has many adventurous options, suburban families with mainstream tastes are the core audience, and the menu is amply stocked with simple stir-fries that can also be ordered for takeout. ◐ ● ⊙ ♦ $$

MATYSON, *37 South 19th Street; 215-564-2925.* You may know Matt Spector and Sonjia Bidegain Spector: He's the former executive chef at Trust and Novelty; she's been in the kitchen at several of Stephen Starr's spots. Now the husband-and-wife team have lent their names to Matyson, an attractive American BYOB on a block of Center City skyscrapers. Midday, the restaurant draws business types lunching on entrée-size salads topped with grilled shrimp and chorizo or polenta and wild mushrooms, and a variety of gourmet sandwiches served with greens or crisp french fries. At dinner, Matt cooks up seasonal entrées like braised lamb shank with parsnip puree, while Sonjia turns out such intriguing desserts as honey crepes with poached pears, and cranberry bread pudding. Closed Sunday; closed for lunch Saturday. ◐ ● ▮ $$

MAX'S, *602 Route 130 North, Cinnaminson; 856-663-6297.* Route 130, one of the ugliest and deadliest stretches of highway in the Philadelphia region, has landed one of the area's classiest BYOBs: Max's in Cinnaminson, a vision in 19th-century brick. Polished old wide-plank floors run through the intimate dining rooms; walls are burnished in subtle golds and greens, and tables are draped in quiet damask. The pacing at Max's is unhurried, but the tempo picks up with the food: Bruce Lim's seasonal Continental menu has included handmade spinach, pine nut and raisin ravioli with beurre parmesan; fricassee of Maine lobster with golden caviar and lobster sauce; and Peking duck breast with ginger honey sauce. Closed for lunch Saturday and Sunday. ◐ ● ▮ $$$

MAYFAIR DINER, *7353 Frankford Avenue; 215-624-8886.* Now that medical researchers have lifted their full-on egg-eating ban, one of life's greatest, simplest breakfasts can be enjoyed semi-worry-free: two eggs over easy, with a side of bacon, home fries, and buttered white toast. Perhaps this shouldn't be consumed every day, but when you've got to have it, go to Mayfair Diner, where, since 1932, in a low-slung, stainless-steel-booth-lined building, two eggs are perfectly cooked in a small frying pan and served by pink-dressed ladies named Betty. If that's not enough, scarf down any one of the 22 classic desserts—all available 24/7. ○ ◐ ● $$

MÉLANGE CAFÉ, *1601 Chapel Avenue, Cherry Hill; 856-663-7339.* In chef/owner Joe Brown's kitchen, Southern cuisine meets Italian cooking. A bottle of olive oil sits on each table of this BYOB; sweet-potato cheesecake is on the dessert tray. There are endless combinations of ingredients, Brown says, but he prides himself on his crawfish. There's also crab ravioli and (more authentically) jambalaya, rich with crawfish, clams, mussels, shrimp and andouille. Closed Monday. ◐ ● ▮ $$$

MELOGRANO, *2201 Spruce Street; 215-875-8116.* Eight months of renovations and a sunny coat of yellow paint turned a vacant corner grocery into Melograno, a so-simple-it's-chic BYOB with a dining room out of *Real Simple*: tall windows, bare tables, strands of faux berries overhead, a few well-placed objects along the plain walls. And this splendid simplicity carries over to the plate. Flavor and texture combinations seem instinctive for chef Gianluca Demontis, who chooses fine ingredients, tinkers minimally, and presents them beautifully. The roasted artichoke appetizer, centered on the plate with its stem pointing skyward, is surrounded by grill-marked sea scallops and drizzled with lemon and olive oil. Touches of balsamic vinegar and truffle oil highlight two saucer-size roasted portabella mushroom caps paired with soft goat cheese bristling with toasted pine nuts. Meanwhile, Demontis's wife/dining room manager, Rosemarie Tran, skillfully manages the throng of Rittenhouse Square residents willing to wait an hour—or longer—for a table. Closed Monday. ● ▮ $$

MIXTO, *1141-43 Pine Street; 215-592-0363.* Floor-to-ceiling plate-glass windows reveal exposed brick walls, a sweeping wooden staircase, wrought-iron accents, and an extensive breakfast-lunch-dinner menu. Chef Miguel Leon of the Four Seasons in Venezuela and former La Tierra Colombiana chef Freddy Mosquera serves up fried plantains, rice and beans, paella, and a melt-in-your-mouth rodizio, plus American-style steak and seafood entrées—or you can simply stop in for an authentic caffe con leche. ○ ◐ ● ⊙ $$

MIXX, *Borgata Hotel, Casino & Spa, 1 Borgata Way, Atlantic City; 866-692-6742, 609-317-1000.* This Latin-Asian club-restaurant was conceived by Aaron Sanchez, son of Mexican restaurateur-cookbook author Zarela Martinez, and Edwyn Ferrari, who did a turn at Manhattan's penultimate sushi shrine, Nobu. The dining room, which morphs into a dance club around 11 p.m. on weekends, has black and white and red all over, with a vaguely Asian-industrial aesthetic. There are bare tables, chopsticks and forks at every place setting, and servers outfitted in white tees and cargo pants. And the moderately priced menu of modern nibbles—poached lobster ceviche in a delicious sweet-hot passion fruit-habanero pepper marinade; poblano pepper and onion rings as wide as bangle bracelets, enrobed in puffy tempura batter—is aimed squarely at younger gamblers. ● $$

MOJO, *223 North Washington Avenue, Margate; 609-487-0300.* Mojo has obvious pretensions. The motto: "Where SoHo Meets The Shore." But attitude aside, Mojo represents a completely new direction in Shore dining and nightlife. It's nice to sit at the smooth white bar, drink a Negroni, and listen to a jazz singer croon. The dining room, with its blond-wood floors, cobalt-blue glasses and bright orange walls, is extremely attractive and surprisingly comfortable; the wine list may be the best at the Shore, with lots of Italian selections; and the service in the dining room is without airs. Mojo publishes a full page of specials each day, and these offerings are the best bets: spinach ravioli tossed with kalamata olives and shaved Parmigiano-Reggiano; a timbale of tuna tartare; and grilled opakapaka filet. ● $$$

MOONSTRUCK, *7955 Oxford Avenue; 215-725-6000.* No longer a trend-setter but still vigorous after more than a quarter-century, Moonstruck delivers several noteworthy dishes: vegetable soup with emerald fava beans, tubettini pasta and a confetti of fresh basil pesto; house-made ravioli filled with chard and three cheeses, topped with a chunky tomato-basil sauce; and an elongated Milanese-style veal chop, pounded to tenderness and dredged in herbed cheese crumbs before cooking. Also a treat: unusual wines by the glass, such as the 1996 Cannonau Meloni from Sardinia. ● $$$

MORIMOTO, *723 Chestnut Street; 215-413-9070.* So many diners request chef Masaharu Morimoto's tasting opus that the restaurant recently opened a 15-seat private room (with private sushi chef) reserved for omakase parties. Translated literally, "omakase" means "leave yourself in my hands." And those who splurge for the Iron Chef's $80, $100 or $120-plus tasting do so, even when presented with Japanese delicacies such as cod sperm. The slightly-less-adventurous experiment with from-the-menu flavors like the five-spice lobster; sake-steamed grouper; and wasabi tiramisu. Closed for lunch Saturday and Sunday. ◑ ● $$$

MOSHULU, *Penn's Landing, 401 South Columbus Boulevard; 215-923-2500.* The largest and oldest four-masted sailing ship still afloat, the Moshulu, which turned 100 in 2004, is again docked in Philadelphia. The redesigned restaurant aboard it evokes the South Seas destinations once familiar to the ship's crew, with wicker, bamboo and indulgent colors, but executive chef Ralph Fernandez offers a closer-to-home New American menu with worldly touches: honey-glazed Pekin duck with potato gnocchi; smoked salmon with asparagus strudel; and sesame-crusted ahi tuna. More casual options and a view of the river are available on the multi-level deck, complete with Tiki sculptures. ◑ ● ⊙ $$$

MR. MARTINO'S TRATTORIA, *1646 East Passyunk Avenue; 215-755-0663.* Husband-and-wife owners Marc and Maria Farnese shun publicity, never advertise, and limit their hours of operation to dinner only, Friday through Sunday. This all heightens the air of exclusivity that surrounds Mr. Martino's, which is actually a sweet, down-to-earth establishment that has been serving uncomplicated, modestly priced dishes for 12 years. Maria cooks, and Marc oversees the dining room, a lovely approximation of an antique Old World café. The charm of this space draws plenty of dating pairs, as well as customers nostalgic for roasted red peppers, sautéed broccoli rabe, baked ricotta with olives and sliced dry sausage, veal tortellini with gorgonzola-tomato sauce, or cavatelli with tomato pesto. Open Friday to Sunday. ● 🍴 ⑤ $$

MS. TOOTSIE'S, *1314 South Street; 215-731-9045.* Southern hospitality is on the menu at Ms. Tootsie's. The waiters and waitresses call everyone by name: Honey, Sweetheart, Darling. "Tootsie" is owner Keven Parker's mother, Joyce, whose cooking inspired this kudzu-and-copperhead-colored BYOB. The kitchen serves up three kinds of fried (chicken, whiting and catfish) with okra, candied yams and collard greens on the side. Every meal starts with hot biscuits and ends with a Tootsie Pop. Closed Monday and Tuesday; closed for lunch Wednesday and Thursday. ◑ ● 🍴 $$$

NAN, *4000 Chestnut Street; 215-382-0818.* Kamol Phutlek has a pedigree in Philadelphia that traces back to our first great restaurant years of the '70s, when he worked the back of the house at the seminal La Panetiere with Steven Poses. Over the decades, first at Poses's Frog, later at his own Alouette, Phutlek refined his beautiful French-touched Thai cuisine, and it endures in this simple room. His sautéed sweetbreads embody the sophisticated intricacies of the Frog-Alouette heritage, layered in squares of puff pastry on creamy leeks, their sauce now evolved to a port-based version. From the Thai warmth of basil-scented red curry to the French standard escargot in puff pastry with garlic butter, Nan embodies Philadelphia's first fusion, alive and well. Closed Sunday and Monday; closed for lunch Saturday. ◑ ● 🍴 $$

NEXT, *223 South Street; 215-629-8688.* Next doesn't look like a BYOB. First, it's on South Street, where every other sign advertises frozen drink specials and happy-hour deals. And then there's the design—not homey and "intimate" (read: cramped), but modern and spacious. If you're looking for a cocktail, though, you'll have to head across the street to co-owner Rich Podulka's North

Lounge. If you're looking for an eclectic menu, trust executive chef Terry Owens, who serves up ever-changing entrées that are by turns Southern-influenced (bacon-wrapped monkfish with risotto carbonara and black-eyed peas) and South Asian (house-cured gravlax with ginger, coriander and lime). Closed Monday. ● ⊙ ♦ $$

NORTH BY NORTHWEST, *7165 Germantown Avenue; 215-248-1000.* This Mount Airy hot spot attracts big crowds with its big-name performers, so come early for dinner, which includes one of the city's finest macaroni and cheeses and a mean fried chicken salad. With NXNW's venerable selection of local brews, a dozen bottled wines south of $40, and dangerously smooth spiked raspberry lemonade, you'll be on the maple dance floor before dessert arrives. Closed Sunday and Monday. ● $$

N. 3RD, *810 North 3rd Street; 215-413-3666.* This funky bar and restaurant has quickly become the neighborbood common room of choice for newcomers to Northern Liberties. And with veteran chef Peter Dunmire in the kitchen, it's not just a place for a Pabst. Most of the week, Dunmire turns out upscale bar food, but Thursday through Sunday, he offers more ambitious options, like pan-seared rainbow trout with a fragrant lemon-basil-caper beurre blanc. ● ⊙ $$

NUNZIO'S RISTORANTE RUSTICA, *706 Haddon Avenue, Collingswood; 856-858-9840.* For almost 20 years, chef Nunzio Patruno was a well-known figure in the Center City culinary scene, cooking in the kitchens of his popular Monte Carlo Living Room and Club and Primavera Restaurant. Now you'll find him in Collingswood, where he has opened the 120-seat Nunzio's Ristorante Rustica. Housed in a former nickelodeon-turned-hobby shop on Haddon Avenue, Nunzio's is notable for its piazza-style decor, reasonably priced pastas, risottos and grilled entrées (like pollo tarantino, grilled chicken breast topped with crabmeat and asparagus in a white wine sauce)—and free parking. Closed for lunch Saturday and Sunday. ◑ ● ♦ $$

OASIS, *1709 Walnut Street; 215-751-0888.* Sushi chefs watch attentively over the buffet tables at Oasis, ready to refresh the slate of sushi, sashimi and maki as soon as you've made your selections. For a traditional meal in the minimalist dining room, add a bowl of steaming udon or miso soup and a handful of edamame to your tray. Or browse the chafing dishes, where you'll find American-Chinese favorites like beef and broccoli, egg rolls, and

General Tso's chicken. Other offerings include everything from shrimp to fruit cocktail. ◑ ● $$$

THE OLD GUARD HOUSE INN, *953 Youngsford Road, Gladwyne; 610-649-9708.* The Old Guard House Inn, still vigorous after more than two decades, remains the epitome of tradition-minded fine dining. In a log-walled room reminiscent of a chalet hideaway, Continental classics like Dover sole and roast duck are treated with respect, not as clichés. Owner Albert Breuers honors his German roots by including sauerbraten and Wiener schnitzel, but he may have scandalized locals when he first dared to serve his excellent lump crabcake with a Thai red curry sauce. Closed Sunday. ● $$$

OLD HOMESTEAD, *Borgata Hotel, Casino & Spa, 1 Borgata Way, Atlantic City; 866-692-6742, 609-317-1000.* With curving, polished wood walls and gallery lighting, Old Homestead, Borgata's most architecturally stunning restaurant, looks more like an art museum. Its cuts of meat are predictably monstrous—the $72 porterhouse for two is nearly three inches thick, perfectly medium rare and neatly trimmed of fat, but the steak lacks any hint of seasoning. Service issues plague this outpost of the celebrated New York restaurant, and high prices are a turnoff—but the New York-supplied cheesecake is excellent. ● ◉ $$$$

OMBRA, *Borgata Hotel, Casino & Spa, 1 Borgata Way, Atlantic City; 866-692-6742, 609-317-1000.* Ombra, a wine-cellar hideaway down a flight of stairs from the casino floor, boasts 25 offerings by the glass and many intriguing small-plate possibilities, plus high-roller entrées like a $160 double-cut, dry-aged Florentine-style porterhouse for two. Dinner in the dining room or at the lively bar is a feast of wines, cheeses and lush flavors like fried olives, fat green Sicilian olives lightly jacketed with crisp bread crumbs, hiding a soft, pungent filling of gorgonzola and crushed walnuts; and insalata frutti di mare, a generous helping of cool calamari, shrimp, mussels, clams, cubed potatoes and celery, dressed with fruity olive oil and fresh parsley. Closed Sunday and Monday. ● $$$

PALM, *the Bellevue, 200 South Broad Street; 215-546-7256.* The Palm, Philadelphia's outpost of the nationwide chain, is a chance to dine with the city's movers and shakers: Their faces deck the walls of this power-lunch spot off the lobby of the Bellevue building, and the lunch hour is populated by the city's celebs, each angling for the best table. The food is as establish-ment as the caricature decor, and the kitchen does the basics best: lobster bisque, veal piccata, and, of course, steaks. Closed for lunch Saturday and Sunday. ◐ ● $$$

¡PASIÓN!, *211 South 15th Street; 215-875-9895.* Much-acclaimed chef Guillermo Pernot literally wrote the book on ceviche (the James Beard award-winning ¡Ceviche!). Pernot claims to have more than 100 ceviches up his sleeve, and each night he offers five different ones here. Think ahi tuna in coconut milk, ginger and jalapeño—a wonderful mix of cool, sweet and spice that's served in a coconut shell; shrimp with blackened tomatoes, pep-pers and onions in a spicy garlic sauce, and topped with popcorn in the Ecuadoran tradition; and salmon with very spicy onion rocoto sauce, served with thin, crispy yucca fries. But the restaurant, with its tranquil dining room, is more than just ceviche, from the elegant pisco sour cocktails and Latin wine list to the cabrito, baby goat braised with yellow and black mus-tard seeds and served on a banana leaf. ● $$$

PATOU, *312 Market Street; 215-928-2987.* When he was a young boy living on the French Riviera, Patrice Rames would tie sardines in fishnetting and use them as bait to catch squid, which his mother would stuff with spinach, rice, pork and Italian sausage, and then roast. That preparation of squid is on the menu at the vast Patou, which Rames opened to evoke the tastes and sights of a youth lived along the Mediterranean—and gave his childhood nickname. The open kitchen also features a lobster tank; its residents might find their way to the grill, to the rotisserie, paired with arugula as a topping for pizza, and into the inevitable bouillabaisse as well. Closed for lunch Sat-urday and Sunday. ◐ ● ⊙ ◎ $$$

PEACE A PIZZA, *4 Station Road, Ardmore, 610-896-4488; 1132 Lancaster Avenue, Rosemont, 610-525-3025; 522 West Lancaster Avenue, Wayne, 610-293-6988; 143 South Gulph Road, King of Prussia, 610-962-9900; and 291 Main Street, Exton, 484-875-5800.* Peace a Pizza began selling thin-crusted gourmet pizzas by the slice to Main Line college students in 1996. The local company now has seven locations that specialize in far-out pies (black bean taco pizza or Buffalo wing-blue cheese pizza, anyone?) and well-executed basic pizzas. Hmmm—what's in those brownies next to the register? Noth-ing more mind-bending than chocolate chips. ◐ ● $

PENNE, *3611 Walnut Street; 215-823-6222.* The Inn at Penn's unfocused and short-lived Ivy Grille has given way to this specialty pasta restaurant, the name a play on its University City location. And the terrazzo-topped pasta bar has ringside seats for patrons who want a close-up look as Roberta Adamo fashions tender potato gnocchi, ricotta cavatelli, ravioli and quill pasta by hand. (American-born but grandmother-trained, Adamo also makes the scrumptious pignoli-studded amaretti that sometimes come gratis at meal's end.) Chef Ed Vadden oversees the rest of the modern Italian menu, and the desserts are commissioned from Miel, Robert Bennett's haute pâtisserie. The affordable wine list emphasizes Italy, by the glass, flight or bottle. Closed for lunch Saturday and Sunday. ◑ ● $$$

PETIT 4 PASTRY STUDIO, *160 North 3rd Street; 215-627-8440.* Petit 4 is more Old City than Left Bank, with its retro dinette tables and chairs. But this storefront space's small, beautiful individual tarts have a French flavor; in one, a poached peach, pink tinged with pale purple veins, flavors vanilla pastry cream. Custom cakes, for weddings and other occasions, range from classic to inventive; one popular style is decorated with icing that's formed to look like elegant folds of draped fabric. ○ $

PHILADELPHIA FISH & COMPANY, *207 Chestnut Street; 215-625-8605.* Before we had the new Old City, we had 2nd and Chestnut and its little radiating constellation of restaurants, with Philadelphia Fish & Company, two decades plus and counting, one of the steady lights. Because of its location blocks from Independence Hall and its attractive but casual ambience, it reels in a lot of tourists. Locals and businesspeople know it as a place to get dependable but innovative seafood—and the incredibly juicy $6 ground sirloin burger on a brioche roll that's hiding on the bar menu. Closed for lunch Sunday. ◑ ● $$

PHO XE LUA, *907 Race Street; 215-627-8883.* Saturday lunch at Pho Xe Lua in Chinatown puts you in the company of dozens of teenage and young-adult Asians, eating enormous platters of Vietnamese food (there are also some Thai options) at the speed of light. Service is just as brisk, as the waiters serve up raw fresh flank steak with lime juice, sautéed chicken with lemongrass on rice, snails with coconut and basil, and grilled pork balls on vermicelli. To wash it down, order a fresh mango milkshake if you're timid, or a red bean, mung bean and Jell-O combination if you're brave. Closed Wednesday. ◑ ● $

average entrée price: $ under $12 $$ $13 to $20 $$$ $21 to $30 $$$$ more than $30

PICNIC, *Shops at the Left Bank, 3131 Walnut Street; 215-222-1608.* As the name promises, Anne-Marie Lasher's Picnic has everything you could need, including vintage baskets priced $18 to $35. Salads such as niçoise, sandwiches, and the chili-spiked coleslaw are the most popular items here. Lasher, formerly of Fork, opened Picnic in response to the growing takeout trend: "I didn't know a single 20-year-old who knew how to cook." Lasher won't picnic without her chickpea-and-olive-studded Greek cucumber salad and her garlic-cumin-paprika-spiced Moroccan eggplant salad. Follow her lead. And if it's raining, there are café tables available. Closed Sunday. ○ ◑ ● $

PIF, *1009 South 8th Street; 215-625-2923.* The big deal about this petite bistro is nothing more than classic and contemporary French food in an ultra-casual luncheonette-like setting. The space itself recalls the French predilection for simplicity, with dried bouquets of roses hanging in the curtained window. When full, Pif becomes as warm, loud and crowded as any well-priced café in Paris's Latin Quarter. The menu changes nightly. On one evening, the chalkboard may feature medallions of foie gras with red grape compote; on another, it might be succulent duck confit over potato galette, or entrecôte with mushroom fricassee. A bulb of roasted garlic stuffed with petit-gris escargots and hazelnuts has become Pif's signature dish. At dessert time, regulars demand the demitasse of chocolate custard. Closed Tuesday. ● ▲ $$$

PLACES! BISTRO, *39 Conestoga Road, Malvern; 610-647-8060.* The terrace garden at Places! Bistro at the People's Light & Theater Company is so meticulously maintained that the restaurant proudly displays citations from the Pennsylvania Horticultural Society. Executive chef Michael Merlo's commitment to freshness ensures that the food is equal to its setting; he employs seasonal vegetables for the daily soup and flawless greens for the salads. Theater patrons already know how good this restaurant is; it deserves a wider audience. Closed Monday; closed for dinner Sunday. ◑ ● ⊙ ◒ $$$

PLATE, *105 Coulter Avenue, Suburban Square, Ardmore; 610-642-5900.* Plate's dining room, painted warm vanilla and chocolate tones, with an orange concrete floor, evokes a Pottery Barn store, and executive chef Tom Harkins's menu complements the comfy atmosphere with unfussy entrées, most priced under $18. At lunch, gourmet pizzas with smoked salmon and goat cheese or skirt steak and feta fill the stone oven; at dinner, the focus turns to garlic-roasted chicken and smoked pork chops, plus turkey meatloaf and mac-and-cheese. Kids get a special menu—chicken fingers, french fries, homemade doughnut holes coated tableside with cinnamon and sugar. ◑ ● $$

THE PLOUGH AND THE STARS, *123 Chestnut Street; 215-733-0300.* High ceilings, a blazing hearth and a perfect pour of Guinness are the hallmarks of this Old City haunt.The oak-smoked salmon, Irish bacon, and garden mint in vinegar are imported regularly straight from Ireland. Weekend brunches feature a traditional breakfast of Irish bacon, sausage, tomato, mushrooms, eggs, potato pancakes, black and white pudding and beans. ◑ ● ⊙ $$$

POD, *3636 Sansom Street; 215-387-1803.* Stephen Starr's space-age Pod was Philadelphia's introduction to something that was old hat in London and New York: the sushi conveyor belt. Paired with the white plastic decor and the possibility of changing the lighting in the "pod" in which one is seated (Fuchsia! Aqua!), the conveyor belt gives Pod a Disney World-for-adults feel. But patrons have tired a bit of the toys, having learned that not all sushi looks appetizing when lit with apple-green lights. Instead, they come for the Asian fusion dishes, the well-selected sake list and the elaborately plated desserts. Closed for lunch Saturday and Sunday. ◑ ● $$$

PORCINI, *2048 Sansom Street; 215-751-1175.* It's not for the claustrophobic: The wee dining room can barely hold the 40 customers shoehorned in by brothers David and Steven Sansone during peak periods. Regulars (and they are legion) gladly sacrifice personal space for chef Steven's elemental cooking, much of it from the grill. Carefully charred calamari with lemon and olive oil is especially appreciated during the gray months of the year. Fresh pasta dishes are a hallmark, as are the porcini and other mushrooms that appear over chicken and veal, in ravioli fillings, or with wide pappardelle noodles. The chef is a fount of information about Italian wines, so don't hesitate to call ahead for advice. Closed Sunday. ● ♦ $$$

THE PRIME RIB, *1701 Locust Street; 215-772-1701.* The jackets-required steakhouse in the Warwick Hotel is as old-school as they get, transporting diners to a romantic supper club from a long-gone era. With high-back leather chairs, Louis Icart lithographs, ice-cold martinis, thick aged steaks, and buttery-smooth jazz with Philadelphia veterans like Kenny Gates on piano, the Rib is the perfect place to woo or be wooed. ● $$$

RADICCHIO CAFÉ, *402 Wood Street; 215-627-6850.* Seafood gets star billing, but is nearly upstaged by the astonishingly beautiful diced tomatoes, unblemished arugula and smoky grilled mushrooms that appear with so many dishes at this 40-seat gem a few blocks north of Market Street. Raw materials this good need minimal enhancement: a splash of fruity oil, a few drops of balsamic vinegar, a squeeze of lemon or a handful of shaved parmesan. Look to the blackboard for market finds such as sepia, a squid-like mollusk commonly known as cuttlefish, or decadent additions like lobster ravioli in tomato-cream sauce. Dover sole, striped bass and other whole fish are deftly filleted tableside. If New York strip steak is a special, it is likely to be served as a pretty arc of slices, with a pinch of grated Parmigiano Reggiano sprinkled over. Now that's a cheesesteak. Closed for lunch Saturday and Sunday. ◐ ● ▲ $$

RALPH'S ITALIAN RESTAURANT, *760 South 9th Street, 215-627-6011; and* **Jimmy Rubino's Ralph's of South Philadelphia,** *Butler Pike and York Street, Ambler, 215-619-4550.* The Italian-American menu might as well be chiseled in granite: greens and pastina soup, clams casino, mussels in red or white sauce, manicotti, eggplant parmigiana, spaghetti with every conceivable topping (except pesto or sun-dried tomatoes), and 15 possibilities under the heading of veal. Since 1900, Ralph's well-worn South Philly rooms have been hosting family groups numbering 10 or 12 or 20, and there is never a risk that an entrée will upstage Nonna on her birthday. A waiter may lean down and ask your seven-year-old, "Have you decided what you want?" as if she's a grown-up. The Ambler location is equally retro. Closed for lunch Saturday and Sunday. ◐ ● ◉ (Philadelphia location) $$

RANGOON, *112 North 9th Street; 215-829-8939.* Co-owner Christine Goyaw is quick with a smile and advice on the menu, because who, after all, knows anything about Burmese food? Rangoon is in Chinatown, but the distinctive cuisine of Burma shares as much with neighboring India as with China, and its most characteristic element is curry. Noodle dishes, especially creamy coconut noodle soup, are also hallmarks. The menu includes traditional Chinese, Thai and Indian dishes, and a bargain $5.50 lunch special is served Monday through Friday. ◐ ● $$

RAT'S, *16 Fairgrounds Road, Hamilton; 609-584-7800.* Rat's is J. Seward Johnson's obsessive vision, opened in 2000 and named against all advice for his favorite character in the children's book *The Wind in the Willows.* Johnson is an heir to the Johnson & Johnson fortune, and an artist known for his eerily lifelike statues. Rat's has a colorful French country vibe of Monet reds, blues, yellows and lavenders; rustic tables and chairs are juxtaposed with *Beetlejuice*-style circular banquettes. But while Rat's is whimsical, and even silly at times, its executive chef, Eric Martin, has serious ambitions. He presides over a French menu that employs organic produce in almost every dish—produce is supplied by Johnson's own Spring Hill Farm, in nearby Hopewell. Closed Monday. ◑ ● $$$$

RAY'S CAFÉ AND TEAHOUSE, *141 North 9th Street; 215-922-5122.* The windows are beaded with moisture, and the clear glass globes and siphons on the counter burble and steam like a hypnotic chemistry experiment. The coffee prices in this crowded little cafe will snap you awake, though, because you can spend $8 on a cuppa Jamaican Blue Mountain, and the same on a top-grade green tea. These are connoisseur's cups, and the best part is the presentation, unique miniature still-lifes of sugar and cream, delicate porcelain and gilded petit fours. The green tea is a Zen moment of rusticity, cradled in an earthen cup, with serving pieces of tactile wood and bamboo. The food has the same pure and nourishing qualities, whether steamed or stir-fried, with seasonal vegetables at its heart. The dumplings are a marvel, and you can get a sampler of all five: pork and napa, pork and leek, shrimp, vegetable, and curried chicken. ◑ ● ⸙ $

RED HEN CAFÉ, *Ironstone Village, 560 Stokes Road, Medford; 609-953-2655.* With its beet-red upholstered walls and Chagall prints, the charming 30-seat Red Hen Café is our local equivalent of the Russian Tea Room—with much better food. Owner Bill Roka works the room in the evenings, while his co-owner and wife, chef Tracey Slack, formerly of La Campagne, handles familiar Eastern European dishes with finesse, from smoked trout to veal schnitzel with spaetzle. All are eminently compatible with any vouvray or riesling you might bring. The apple strudel, sour cherry crepes, Hungarian cheese pie and other desserts are made in-house. Closed Monday and Tuesday. ◑ ● ⸙ $$

RESTAURANT 821, *821 North Market Street, Wilmington; 302-652-8821.* The typical tasting menu at Restaurant 821, a 90-seat Mediterranean restaurant, is six courses, but chef and co-owner Tobias Lawry has one devoted (and hungry) customer who travels annually from Indiana for a 12-course feast. That meal, like all of the restaurant's tastings, is a spontaneous creation, highlighting the best of that day's ingredients. For those who aren't traveling as far—or eating as much—Lawry offers combinations like peppery seared tuna with tomato conserve and roasted egglant; chilled white corn and truffle soup; and sherry-braised short ribs atop blue cheese ravioli. Closed Sunday; closed for lunch Saturday. ◐ ● $$$

RAVENNA, *Center Point Shopping Center, 2960 Skippack Pike, Worcester; 610-584-5650.* In a spacious dining room with an open kitchen and a double-sided fireplace, 33-year-old chef-owner Shawn Sollberger turns out crisp chicken livers with dried cherries and pine nuts, a poor man's foie gras sweetened with balsamic syrup; hand-formed cappellacci pasta filled with butternut squash, tossed with fresh sage leaves, butter and parmesan; and fresh tagliatelle in a Bolognese meat ragu. There is a Caesar salad for stubborn souls who would never, ever consider the panzanella—Tuscan bread salad with tomato, cucumber and red onion. Veal osso buco, a special every Saturday night, falls effortlessly from the bone. Sous-chef Pete Kaiser and Sollberger make all of the enormously appealing desserts, which include a warm apple tart with pumpkin ice cream, and creamy chocolate panna cotta served with amaretto cookies. Closed Sunday; closed for lunch Saturday. ◐ ● ◢ $$

RED SKY, *224 Market Street; 215-925-8080.* It's hard to miss Red Sky while walking down Market Street—there's a long, luminous red ceiling floating 25 feet above the lounge and dining area, casting a hot-pink glow out the front windows onto the sidewalk. But food and atmosphere get equal play. Chef Michael Salvitti, formerly of Audrey Claire, has created an ambitious New American menu: pan-seared foie gras with caramelized onions and shiitake mushroom-stuffed crepes with port wine reduction; ginger-crusted red snapper with long-grain black rice and miso broth. The dessert menu is, wisely, all chocolate, all the time. ● $$

RISTORANTE LA BUCA, *711 Locust Street; 215-928-0556.* The fish cart makes its rounds at lunch as well as dinner, so that customers at this venerable white-tablecloth basement hideaway near Washington Square can judge for themselves whether the Chilean sea bass, the Dover sole or the langoustine looks most alluring. Chef-owner Giuseppe Giuliani is a minimalist with seafood—only lemon and olive oil on the whole fish, perhaps adding a bonus of lump crabmeat to a pan-crisped fillet. Tortellini in chicken broth, concave orecchiette ("little ears") with broccoli rabe and sautéed mushrooms, and Italian rum cake are as no-nonsense as the waiters, who are outfitted in black tie even at lunch. Closed Sunday; closed for lunch Saturday. ◑ ● $$$

RISTORANTE MEZZA LUNA, *763 South 8th Street; 215-627-4705.* The wineglasses sparkle (there is a bar, but you can also BYOB); the table linens are blindingly white. Meticulous housekeeping makes the first good impression at Mezza Luna, a sophisticated room with sunflower-yellow walls and a blue ceiling suggesting an evening sky. Then, dinner makes the lasting one. Exceptional baby clams, tiny and tender, steamed with white wine and garlic, are a must on their own or with spaghetti. Ricotta gnocchi in gorgonzola cream sauce are positively ethereal. And don't forget the vitello "Champagne," surrounded with artichokes, wild mushrooms and a champagne cream sauce, with a side of green beans and a delightful fried potato croquette. Closed Monday; closed for lunch Saturday and Sunday. ◑ ● $$

RISTORANTE PANORAMA, *14 North Front Street; 215-922-7800.* Ordering at Panorama is never easy, because it involves choosing from temptations like arugula salad with Italian blue cheese and walnuts in a roasted pear-white balsamic vinaigrette, porcini risotto with white truffle oil, or a host of house-made pastas. Part of the fun is matching the 120 wines by the glass with each course. Closed for lunch Saturday and Sunday. ◑ ● $$$

RISTORANTE PESTO, *1915 South Broad Street; 215-336-8380.* When the waiter—South Philly slick, with a smooth Italian accent—arrives tableside to rattle off the specials at Ristorante Pesto, close your menu. It will take all your concentration to remember, and choose between, the options. Among the most popular of the recited choices: the crabmeat-and-mozzarella-stuffed portabella mushrooms. From the awninged outside, the restaurant looks like any carbs-and-red sauce joint south of the Italian Market. But inside, Pesto's minimalist dining room is designed to spotlight the food: pizzas from the wood-fired oven; a whole branzino or Dover sole, filleted table-side by a friendly, if slightly clumsy, waiter; and sweet-tart limoncello sorbet, served in a chilled champagne glass. Closed Sunday; closed for lunch Saturday. ◑ ● ▮ $$

RISTORANTE VALENTINO, *1328 Pine Street; 215-545-6265.* Valentino is a regular haunt for Antiques Row shop owners and shoppers. The dining room—a former frame shop—is candlelit to a ruddy glow and bordered by an open kitchen, with a clay tile roof, sculptural wrought ironwork in the windows, and crimson walls painted with trompe l'oeil curtains. From the menu, choose from simple Caprese and Caesar salads, followed by crabmeat-stuffed homemade ravioli with pink vodka sauce; veal or chicken paillard dressed with fresh herbs and lemon vinaigrette; or al dente linguini with sardines, raisins, roasted garlic and fennel, and pine nuts. ◐ ● ▮ $$

RITZ SEAFOOD, *910 Haddonfield Berlin Road, Voorhees; 856-566-6650.* First, owner Daniel Hover opened a fresh fish market in the shadow of Voorhees's Ritz 16 movie theater. But "people were too busy for that," Hover says. At his retooled Ritz Seafood, now a 40-seat BYOB, reservations are a must, and the menu boasts tongue-tingling Asian creations like wasabi-stuffed sea scallops. Hover's favorite isn't on the menu, but the Thai-style devilfish is a constant special. He wok-fries the hard-to-come-by Malaysian fish, then glazes it with tamarind and chili to add a fiery "wow factor." Bring a pinot noir or a light red zinfandel to put out the fire. Closed Monday and Tuesday. ● ▮ $$$

ROUGE, *205 South 18th Street; 215-732-6622.* Many Rittenhouse Square dwellers treat this hip bistro as an extension of home. You'll see patrons seated in the sidewalk café calling to friends walking through Rittenhouse Square, making plans to meet up later for a drink at—where else?—Rouge. Beyond the cosmopolitans, though, is a creative kitchen helmed by talented Michael Yeamans. Quietly toiling away in the kitchen, he turns out such delectable plates as tuna tartare with wakane seaweed and wasabi sesame chips, and striped bass with corn risotto. But don't miss the burger, either. ◐ ● ◉ $$$

ROUX 3, *4755 West Chester Pike, Newtown Square; 610-356-9500.* Happy hour at Roux 3 in Newtown Square is doubly so: From 5 to 6:30 p.m., it's possible to order two courses for $15, along with drink specials. But the food is worth a trip on its own merits. The American-eclectic menu includes such disparate temptations as a duck confit crepe and steak frites. There's a full bar, but patrons can BYOB. Closed for lunch Saturday and Sunday. ◐ ● $$$

ROYA RESTAURANT, *1823 Sansom Street; 215-557-0808.* Roya Restaurant bills itself as a house of kabobs, but that's only the beginning of its Persian plate delights. Appetizers like borani, a creamy mix of sautéed spinach, yogurt and garlic, and kashk-o-bademjan, a thick dip of roasted eggplant, grilled onion, garlic and yogurt, are served with flatbread peeled off the wall of the round oven up front. Kabob sandwiches are wrapped up in the same delicious loaves. Traditional Persian dishes include ghormeh sabzi, a piquant stew of boneless leg of lamb with kidney beans and Persian dried lime in a green veil of minced cilantro, parsley and leeks. Desserts, made on the premises, include warm brownies and cookies as well as more traditional Middle Eastern sweets, like baklava and vanilla ice cream scented with saffron rosewater. Closed Sunday. ◐ ● $$

ROYAL TAVERN, *937 East Passyunk Avenue; 215-389-6694.* Like the wonderful Standard Tap in Northern Liberties, the Royal, in Bella Vista, has a great jukebox, local beers on tap, and thoughtful food that can be eaten with your hands. Salads and sandwiches are superb; the first are liable to feature beets, and the second could be a smoked-duck club. There are deep-fried foods, too, but in this case, it's crab fritters. ● ◉ ✪ $

ROY'S, *124/134 South 15th Street; 215-988-1814.* Don't ask for a pu pu platter or pineapple ham at Center City's new Hawaiian restaurant, Roy's. This is "aloha" cuisine, a mix of French, Asian and High Californian: Mongolian charred venison, lemongrass-crusted day-boat scallops, ahi tartare. Try for a table on the soaring mezzanine level of this 1940s bank, for views of the Union League across the street—and don't miss Roy's creative wine list. ● $$$

R$_X$, *4443 Spruce Street; 215-222-9590.* A funky bistro whose idea of comfort food is black cod with ginger, sweet potato mash and crispy long beans, West Philly's R$_X$ (say it "R.X.") is the new canteen for yuppies and Penn professors who've moved into the neighborhood in recent years. Owner Greg Salisbury, who's worked at the Ritz-Carlton in Philadelphia, poured his life savings into converting this former drugstore into a nouveau American restaurant, painstakingly preserving a mahogany display case that runs the full length of one side. Closed Monday; closed for lunch Saturday and Sunday; closed for dinner Sunday. ◐ ● ◉ ◗ $$

SAGAMI, *37 West Crescent Boulevard, Collingswood; 856-854-9773.* Sagami serves the meat-and-potatoes of the sushi world. Not literally, of course, but don't go to this bustling, low-ceilinged, darkly lit BYOB expecting to find, say, spotted sardine just flown in from the Sea of Japan that morning, or some crazy maki roll combination that might cause an authentic sushi chef to commit hara-kiri. Instead, expect happy-go-lucky owner and head sushi chef Shigeru Fukuyoshi to cut pristine slices of the favorites—yellowtail, tuna, flounder, scallop, sea bass. Each piece possesses a distinct flavor and impeccable texture that bear witness to Fukiyoshi's 27-plus years of experience in choosing and preparing the best specimens. Closed Monday; closed for lunch Saturday and-Sunday. ☾ ● ▮ $$$

SALOON, *750 South 7th Street; 215-627-1811.* Saloon's signatures are dark wood wainscoting, stiff drinks, and chophouse cuts of meat. Though the Italian side of the menu can be disappointing, service is excellent, and dinner is mostly pleasurable. Try the calamari in zimino, tender squid rings sautéed with spinach, garlic and white wine, served in a light broth dotted with pieces of tomato; veal Mondelaise, two pounded scallopini, one atop the other, with sage, prosciutto and melted mozzarella in between, surrounded by a marsala sauce brimming with smoky-tasting mushrooms; pumpkin crème brûlée; and limoncello, served in a martini glass filled to the brim. Closed Sunday; open for lunch Thursday and Friday. ☾ ● ✆ $$$

SALT, *253 South 20th Street; 215-545-1990.* Salt, the sleek, beautifully designed 40-seater near Rittenhouse Square, is lucky to has a chef who takes chances few chefs in the city are willing to. Highlights of a recent dinner from the seasonal menu included a delicious Spanish mackerel tartare served atop beetroot gelée; sturgeon caviar in a horseradish crème fraîche; and a chilled green tomato soup. But that's not to say Salt doesn't do the classics: A perfect hanger steak shares a plate with flavorful mustard spaetzle, and the tender lamb loin is paired with a brilliant artichoke puree. ● $$$

SAMBA CHURRASQUERIA & NIGHT CLUB, *714 West Girard Avenue; 215-625-7900.* Rodizio is a decidedly vegetarian-unfriendly Brazilian tradition: an all-you-can-eat feast of meats cooked over an open flame. At this Girard Avenue restaurant and nightclub, chefs deliver the grilled goods on skewers hot from the barbecue, slicing the meats directly onto your plate. In addition to traditional cuts of beef, Samba offers charcoal-smoked chicken, quail, pork, lamb, veal and shrimp. (A grilled vegetable version is available.) The price also includes the salad bar, and a samba spot on the large dance floor. Closed Monday and Tuesday. ● $$$

SANSOM STREET OYSTER HOUSE, *1516 Sansom Street; 215-567-7683.* Twice a week, Sansom Street Oyster House owner Cary Neff drives his beat-up pick-up to Philadelphia International Airport to collect nearly 600 pounds of the freshest oysters, just air-freighted in from a Washington State supplier. Icy-cold, briny, expertly shucked (these careful pros leave the oyster liquor in the shell so you can slurp it down)—there are often 10 varieties on hand here. And the raw bar plateau provides quite an assortment—cherrystone clams from New Jersey, oysters, shrimp, house-smoked mussels, snow crab legs, easily enough for two. Or opt for that Philadelphia fish-house classic: fried oysters and chicken salad. Closed for lunch Sunday. ◑ ● $$$

SAVANNAH, *1836 Callowhill Street; 215-557-9533.* Savannah isn't reminiscent of that romantic Spanish moss-strewn city. It's Southern the way Atlanta is Southern—its cosmopolitan facade hides a down-home sensibility. (Sautéed shrimp over penne has a touch of moonshine.) Chef Richard Venussi says it's American and Caribbean soul food that even a Southern grandma would love. He loves the Jamaican jerk chicken served with warm black bean salsa, green jalapeño rémoulade, white rice and an orchid, on a white plate. Closed Monday. ● $$$

SAVONA, *100 Old Gulph Road, Gulph Mills; 610-520-1200.* While this luxurious seafood house is still decked in Frette linens, Savona's chef-partner, Dominique Filoni, now leans toward the French Riviera as well as its Italian counterpart. (He is, after all, from St. Tropez.) That said, his lobster risotto with fresh peas, slender tagliatelle with scampi, and lobster-langoustine mousse ravioli are mighty classy carbs. Ligurian seafood stew and branzino baked in a salt crust with rosemary maintain ties to Italy. Ice creams and sorbets are glorious in both countries, so it's debatable which inspired the espresso ice cream and the cherry sorbet. ● $$$$

SHIROI HANA, *222 South 15th Street; 215-735-4444.* In the same spot since 1984, Shiroi Hana stands out from the pack of sushi places scattered around Center City. Not only does it serve incredibly fresh fish, but the chefs' presentation is impressive. The Dragon Roll (eel, avocado and cucumber) snakes diagonally across its plate and has two orange fish eggs for eyes. The teardrop sections of the Shiroi Hana Roll (tuna, yellowtail, avocado, smelt roe, cucumber and scallion) radiate out from a pile of orange roe like petals from a pistil. Closed for lunch Saturday and Sunday. ◑ ● $$$

SHOGUN/SERENDIPITY CAFE, *1009 Arch Street; 215-592-8288.* Under one Chinatown roof, Philadelphians can now find a sushi bar, a coffee bar, and a bar with a valid liquor license. The sushi bar is part of Shogun (where patrons can BYOB), a pan-Asian restaurant whose palate is less fusion than fission: Diverse national tastes are kept curiously apart, with kim chi, udon, and Chinese smoked fish scattered across the menu. There is in this schizophrenia an evocation of a food court, but no mall has been so warmly decorated, with concrete, mosaic and hardwood floors and colorful walls. Up front, the Serendipity Cafe is adorned with the works of local artists and equipped with an Internet-ready iMac, with sidewalk seating outside. There are beautiful cakes (the mango-passion fruit is wonderful) from bakeries including the Pink Rose Pastry Shop; Asian milk sorbets made on-site (taro and avocado among them); and a variety of cold tea drinks. Serendipity is also one of the few places where café sua, the Vietnamese combination of strong French-roast coffee and sweetened condensed milk, can be sipped or taken to go, either warm or iced. Closed for lunch Saturday and Sunday. ◐ ● $$

SIMON PEARCE, *1333 Lenape Road, West Chester; 610-793-0948.* Diners drink in the bucolic river view from Simon Pearce, on the Brandywine near West Chester, but this dining room above a touristic glassblowing workshop makes a pleasant destination even without a flotilla of Canada geese drifting by. A recent dinner included arugula and grilled pear salad with goat cheese and shredded duck confit, ultra-rich bay scallop risotto with wild mushrooms, and crème brûlée. Wine lovers with non-drinking partners will rejoice at the two dozen wines by the glass. If the occasion calls for a gift, an attached retail shop sells beautiful pottery and glassware. ◐ ● $$$

SIRI'S THAI FRENCH CUISINE, *2117/2119 Route 70 West, Cherry Hill; 856-663-6781.* The entrance to Siri's is a pâtisserie, so dinner begins with a glimpse of the sweet confections that wait at meal's end: mango and coconut mousse layered in pretty squares, a buttery macadamia nut torte, the sugary symmetry of layered triple chocolate mousse, all made by owner Siri Yothchavit, who has presided over this little haven of exotica for seven years. But getting to dessert is the best part. Whether classically prepared, like the pad Thai—bright-flavored fried-noodle comfort food—or fused, like the crisp, spiny little deep-fried corn and shrimp fritters or the silky Thai herb-perfumed cream of asparagus soup afloat with crabmeat, the dishes are a snapshot of one of the world's most elegant cuisines. Closed for lunch Saturday and Sunday. ◐ ● $$$

SPEZIA, *614 West Lancaster Avenue, Bryn Mawr; 610-526-0123.* Young husband-and-wife team Kevin and Monica Couch (he's the executive chef; she creates pastries) are crafting ethereal fare in this lovely storefront BYOB, with its neutral stucco walls, fresh orchids, and fine touches like Riedel glassware (for an additional $7 per table). The menu changes frequently, using ingredients from top-notch locals Wells Meats and Green Meadow Farms, but you might sample prosciutto di Parma with black Mission figs, baby greens and truffle oil, or a grilled quail salad, or spinach pappardelle with duck-leg confit in buttery sage sauce. A five-course tasting menu is also available for $58, and it often includes a luscious foie gras course (a huge, generous lobe), and ends with sumptuous crème brûlée. Closed Monday. ● ┃ $$$

SPRIGS, *3749 Midvale Avenue; 215-849-9248.* At Sprigs, a casual, warm East Falls bistro, you'll find three generations: Chef Howard Green turns out affordable options like tender roast chicken with rice pilaf and slivers of fried onion, while his mother, restaurant owner Sally Ferry, mans the bar, and his daughter Myranda greets customers with a hesitant smile and a tiny taste of fresh tomato bruschetta. Closed Monday; closed for lunch Saturday and Sunday. ◐ ● ☉ $$

SPRING MILL CAFÉ, *164 Barren Hill Road, Conshohocken; 610-828-2550.* Spring Mill County Park, a spot of green along the Schuylkill River in Conshohocken, engulfs the Spring Mill Café. Bring your own beaujolais, take a table on the porch or deck of the two rustic buildings of this country French restaurant and art gallery, and share the generous sampler of country pâté, truffled chicken liver pâté, and shredded pork pâté, served with grainy mustards and tiny cornichons. Follow with a Moroccan-style lamb tagine with sinus-clearing harissa paste, or one of the daily specials, and watch the stars come out. Closed Monday. ◐ ● ┃ $$$

STANDARD TAP, *901 North 2nd Street; 215-238-0630.* Northern Liberties' Standard Tap screams neighborhood bar: It's dark, and it has a nice selection of beer on tap, a jukebox cranked to ear-splitting volume, and enough secondhand smoke to scare the guys in the cigar lounge at Holt's. The menu, though, crafted by ex-Fishmarket chef Carolynn Angle, takes bar food to new heights; no greasy wings here. Where else can you eat perfectly fried smelts with a garlicky rémoulade or a moist pork sandwich with fennel jus while slamming back a Yards ESA during a game of darts? ● ☉ $$

STATION GRILL, *West and Greenwood avenues, Jenkintown; 215-885-9000.* Housed in the Jenkintown train station, Station Grill offers traditional American bistro fare—Buffalo turkey wings, hearty cheeseburgers, grilled sirloin, teriyaki salmon, and "drunken chicken" (half a honey-basted, roasted bird served over fried potatoes and onions)—in a unique space dominated by a large wooden bar that seats 30, surrounded with eight mahogany booths softened by plump pillows and cushions. On the lower level, you'll find a private dining room in the restaurant's wine cellar. Closed for lunch Saturday and Sunday. ◐ ● $$

STELLA BLU, *101 Ford Street, West Conshohocken; 610-825-7060.* Stella Blu bills itself as an Italian restaurant, but it's one that, at times, suffers from an identity crisis. Despite this, the small, charming dining room, painted a happy shade of blue with an astral motif, is certainly buzzing. Stella Blu's menu is huge for such a small place, with many entrées over the $20 mark, and it's perhaps too ambitious. (There are five chicken dishes alone.) Still, chef Ralph Pallarino is talented, particularly when he moves toward the unfussy and straightforward. His forte is clearly fish; he offers at least four different seafood specials each night. Closed Sunday. ◐ ● $$$

STONEHOUSE BISTRO, *552 Washington Crossing Road, Newtown; 215-860-7888.* This 300-year-old Bucks County house on 14 acres originally belonging to William Penn is home to the Stonehouse Bistro, on- and off-premise catering, and extensive banquet facilities, including a 300-person outdoor tent with chandeliers and fountains. The Bistro's open kitchen turns out an eclectic menu that includes meatloaf and mashed potatoes, the "Seafood Tower"—three tiers of chilled clams and oysters, shrimp, mussels—and whole Maine lobster stuffed with seafood salad. But the outdoor patio is Stonehouse's biggest attraction. The 60-person seating area is bordered by two gazebos; the rest of the bluestone patio is landscaped with pear trees, and even a small bridge over a tiny creek. ● ☉ $$

STRIPED BASS, *1500 Walnut Street; 215-732-4444.* Despite the six-month renovation, when Striped Bass reopened under Stephen Starr's management in 2004, some things about the decade-old landmark were unchanged: The patrons, still crowded at that corner bar. The polished marble columns and soaring ceilings. The open kitchen, bustling beneath the sculpture of a leaping fish. The polished waitstaff serving in the dramatic dining room. The focus on seafood. In the kitchen, Alfred Portale of New York's Gotham and Christopher Lee of Oceania preside over a menu that remains primarily seafood, with a host of influences: Asian (miso-marinated black cod with a sake yuzu emulsion), Peruvian (striped bass ceviche) and New Yorker (Portale's grilled steak with bone marrow and Dijon custard, straight from Gotham's menu). ● $$$$

SUEDE LOUNGE, *120 Market Street; 215-923-5570.* It's luxury, not just liquor, that Suede Lounge sells: The lounge, which spans three Market Street storefronts, has suede-covered couches, slate floors, a Brazilian granite bar, and not one but two soothing waterfalls. To be found on executive chef Sean Joyce's tapas menu: buttermilk-marinated, hazelnut-crusted calamari, and duck-confit crepes with a port wine reduction. Closed Monday. ◑ ● $$

SUILAN, *Borgata Hotel, Casino & Spa, 1 Borgata Way, Atlantic City; 866-692-6742, 609-317-1000.* Suilan (pronounced "sway-lahn"), created by Susanna Foo, is a calm, cream-walled cocoon amid the slot machines of the Borgata. The beautiful dining room captures the understated luxury of Foo's Center City restaurant, with soft ivory table linens, arcing orchid branches, a backlit display of shapely tetsubin teapots, and twisty wall sconces that resemble origami Slinkys. And the kitchen also has strong ties to the flagship, ensuring that beloved dishes like the pan-fried lobster dumplings and spicy Mongolian lamb are faithfully replicated, though both get a Borgata tweak: Suilan patrons can gild their $16 trio of dumplings with Beluga caviar for a $20 supplement, while the always-wonderful lamb dish ($28) is scaled up in size to yield an even bigger bounty of thinly sliced lamb, creamy Chinese eggplant, shiitake mushrooms, fennel, ginger, scallions, and fresh jalapeño peppers. Closed Tuesday and Wednesday. ● $$$$

SUSANNA FOO, *1512 Walnut Street; 215-545-2666.* The dining room here is quiet, just the soft murmur of classical music. Silk lanterns, hand-crafted bamboo woodwork, and mirrors with sterling silver leaf forming ancient Chinese symbols for prosperity and longevity come together to create a warm and serene space for Susanna Foo's ingredient-driven cuisine. There's a nice interplay of French and Asian influences, one that is bringing new flavor combinations to old dishes. After more than 15 years, Susanna Foo's continues to show the country how wonderful the flavors of Chinese cooking can be when New World thinking is applied to the very best ingredients. Closed for lunch Saturday and Sunday. ◑ ● ◉ $$$

SWANKY BUBBLES RESTAURANT AND CHAMPAGNE BAR, *10 South Front Street; 215-928-1200.* Here you can test the claim that bubbly and sushi are the perfect match. Stainless steel chopsticks adorn the place settings in this long, narrow room, which has cracked-glass-topped tables along one side and a curvy yellow bar along the other. Maki and sashimi make up half the menu, and the rest is pan-Asian dishes served family-style. The sushi standbys are here, plus unusual vegetarian combos—the Mexican Roll is cilantro, tomato, scallion, kappa, avocado and spicy sauce; the Gomae Roll is steamed spinach and sweet chili sauce-and rolls with beef and chicken. Try the Tunafornia Roll, a California Roll draped with slabs of tuna, or the Unaju, two filets of broiled eel served over sesame-seasoned sushi rice. ● ○ $$

SWEET VIDALIA, *122 North Bay Avenue, Beach Haven; 609-207-1200.* Sweet Vidalia's 115-seat dining room is attractive, with soft, soothing earth tones and a bank of cozy booths, and the service at this BYOB is, well, sweet and charming, if sometimes a bit unexperienced. But food is the focus here, and Sweet Vidalia's amazingly poised chef-owner, 25-year-old Michael O'Meara, is bold and willing to experiment, as with the menu's namesake item: a big roasted Vidalia stuffed with domestic puy lentils and red onions, topped with what the chef calls "red onion marmalade." Nothing here is frou-frou, just a fresh escape from the usual Shore fare. Closed Monday through Thursday off-season. ● ▮ $$$

TACCONELLI'S, *2604 East Somerset Street; 215-425-4983.* A Monday phone call to Tacconelli's Pizzeria in Port Richmond won't get a live person on the line, just an answering machine telling you that the place is closed Monday and Tuesday and Wednesday and to call first thing Thursday to reserve a pie for that night. Reserving pizza? It may be a gimmick meant to fuel desire, or perhaps it's true that there's only so much capacity in the brick oven. Either way, these garlicky, thin-crusted pies are on the mark. The signature white pie, strewn with spinach and chopped tomatoes, carries enough garlic to put Buffy out of business. Open Thursday through Sunday. ● ▮ ○ $

TANGERINE, *232 Market Street; 215-627-5116.* From the street, Stephen Starr's Moroccan Tangerine is intentionally nondescript, beckoning people in the know. Inside—especially in the spacious renovated lounge—find a sophisticated, middle-aged city crowd sipping cocktails like the "Strawberry Blonde" (a combination of Italian strawberry liquer and Blanc de Blanc champagne). Despite the move away from a strictly Tangier decor, family-style North African-influenced dishes are still passed around the atmospheric dining room. ● $$$

TAQUERIA VERACRUZANA, *908 Washington Avenue; 215-465-1440.* A tidy spot at the edge of the Italian Market, Taqueria Veracruzana has a bustling sit-down and takeout scene from 7 a.m. until midnight. Servers scurry among tables of Mexican families and gringo foodies, ladling out home-squeezed tamarind juice, delivering plates of chiles rellenos stuffed with mild asadero cheese, soft corn tacos filled with savory roasted chicken or steak, and pork tamales that send up clouds of steam when their corn-husk wrappers are peeled away. Order a side of smoky, almost chocolatey refried pinto beans, and layer on the chunky green salsa. ○ ◑ ● ▮ ◔ $

TARTINE, *701 South 4th Street; 215-592-4720.* At Tartine, the menu is a small card inscribed in neat French: "pissaladière," "quiche classique," "steak au poivre," and a few more Gallic classics. This is cuisine familiale, or home cooking, from chef/owner Yves Longhi, a blue-eyed, white-haired, Versailles-born septuagenarian. The chef often takes leave of his kitchen to greet diners and refill wineglasses alongside his partner, maître d' Suzie Di Rienzo. (There is a wine list, but patrons can also BYOB.) Appetizers include palourdes farcies, a half-dozen carpet-shell clams anointed in garlic, butter and fresh chopped parsley; salade de boeuf; and moules (of course). Chicken du jour might be à la charcutière—marinated in a subtly tart sauce of white wine, Dijon mustard, capers and gherkin bits. Steak au poivre is a tender rump cut ringed by a peppery crust and accompanied by marvelous, grease-free pommes frites. Closed Monday. ● ◔ $$$

TECA, *38 East Gay Street, West Chester; 610-738-8244.* Teca is a paninoteca and an enoteca—and a discoteca. The small West Chester Euro-boîte looks like it belongs in Rome, with a mahogany facade, which is open to the sidewalk in summer, and a 12-seat wine bar featuring dozens of wines by the glass. Along with toasted panini, you can dine on platters of imported prosciutto, bresaola (cured filet), Austrian speck (a peppered prosciutto) and mortadella. Teca also makes salads topped with shaved parmesan and fresh lemon; serves up olive ascolane (stuffed, fried olives); and offers plates of Tuscan pecorino, tallegio, and other Italian and French cheeses. Closed Sunday. ◑ ● $$

TEIKOKU, *5492 West Chester Pike, Newtown Square; 610-644-8270.* Japanese-Thai Teikoku makes the best of roadside construction, turning a sterile box that once housed Bobby's Seafood into one of the area's most majestic spaces. Teikoku, which means "empire" in Japanese, effectively tears down the wall between Japanese and Thai cuisines. There are separate menus for each, with sushi on one and curries on the other—which means eel "flaming dragon rolls" can be followed by a spicy lime-dressed calamari salad, or even rack of lamb. Closed for lunch Sunday. ◐ ● $$$

TEN STONE, *2063 South Street; 215-735-9939.* With real estate prices around Graduate Hospital soaring, the area's nightlife is gentrifying as well: Witness Ten Stone, a low-key corner bar and restaurant so named because "ten stone" is the approximate weight of a keg of beer—140 pounds. A chalkboard built into the exposed brick wall lists the well-chosen beer selection, including 15 drafts, such as Victory Golden Monkey, La Chouffe, Dogfish Head, and the Belgian-style Brewers' Art. The menu is brief and bar-food-heavy, but the three-cheese risotto fritters, filet mignon cheesesteak, and ham and cheese on a soft pretzel do soak up the beer stylishly. ◐ ● ⊙ $

TERRACE RESTAURANT AT LONGWOOD GARDENS, *U.S. Route 1 and Route 52, Kennett Square; 610-388-6771.* Most people don't go to Longwood Gardens for the cream of mushroom soup, pan-fried crabcakes with rémoulade sauce and a glass of Chaddsford wine, but maybe they should. The Terrace Restaurant at Longwood Gardens is an exceedingly understated dining room in the midst of this American Versailles created by Pierre S. du Pont. Indoor greenery is minimal, and during a lunch visit, the dining room was nearly as hushed as a library. Reservations are advised for lunch, served daily, or dinner. You must pay admission to the gardens to access the restaurant, but the upside is no guilt whatsoever about ordering the triple chocolate mousse dessert, because you can walk it off on the magnificent grounds: 1,050 acres of gardens, woodlands and meadows, plus four acres of greenhouses. Dinner served Tuesday, Thursday and Saturday in season. ◐ ● $$

TIERRA COLOMBIANA, *4535 North 5th Street; 215-324-6086.* Fluorescent purple lights and neon palms guide hungry diners to a festive space beneath a Latin dance hall, located at the edge of North Philadelphia's barrio. Inside, a jukebox plays the latest Latino pop tunes, and the Spanish-speaking waitstaff gently points newcomers to house specialties: fried green plantains, marinated octopus, platters piled high with yellow rice, pinto beans, steak, arepas (Colombian corn patties), avocado, thick slices of maduros (sweet plantains)—and fried eggs. Though the selection of tropical fruit smoothies is tempting, the giant pitchers of fruity sangria do a better job of washing down these seriously huge meals. ○ ◐ ● ⊙ ♦ $

TRATTORIA SAN NICOLA, *668 Lancaster Avenue, Berwyn; 610-296-3141.* It's a pity that so many martinis go down here, because the wine list—almost exclusively Italian, with nearly every bottle priced under $30—brims with food-friendly varieties like crisp Orvieto and fruity, medium-bodied Montepulciano. And while chef-owner Vito Giannandrea's customers order plate after plate of Caesar salad, his roots in coastal Bari are better expressed by a starter of roasted peppers with a spicy kick, or pasta e fagioli soup ladled from a copper pot, or mussels. Specials are worth a listen, particularly if the magically light lasagna that layers crepes, rather than pasta, is available. The two dining rooms, accented simply with Italian culinary objects and a few colorful paintings, exude a rustic coziness. Closed Sunday; closed for lunch Saturday. ◐ ● $$

TRATTORIA PRIMADONNA, *1506 Spruce Street; 215-790-0171.* Where better to dine before a night at the theater than a restaurant called Primadonna? This former generic Chinese restaurant has been transformed into a charming neighborhood spot, with terra-cotta sconces, bright murals, and a six-seat wooden wine bar. Don't miss the crispy calamari served with spicy shellfish marinara, the rustic antipasto plate, the champagne-sautéed flounder alle Sofia Loren (sic), or the homemade fennel and pistachio biscotti served with mascarpone—perfect with a glass of house prosecco. The waitstaff also randomly chooses a prima donna from each evening's customers to dine in a regal throne and delight in a free meal. Order from the bar, or BYOB. Closed for lunch Saturday and Sunday. ◐ ● $$

TRAX CAFÉ, *27 West Butler Pike, Ambler; 215-591-9777.* Good buzz about barbecued baby back ribs and spicy slaw led us to a handsomely renovated SEPTA station at Ambler and the compact white-tablecloth BYOB inside called Trax Café. Those ribs are good, but chef-owner Steve Waxman has plenty of fine-dining skills up his sleeve, amply demonstrated by a gorgeous roasted red pepper-fresh mozzarella-pesto appetizer, terrific crabcakes, and feather-light wild mushroom ravioli in pesto cream sauce. The fig tart, made in-house, is worth a trip on the R5. Closed Sunday and Monday; closed for lunch Saturday. ◐ ● ♦ $$$

TRE SCALINI, *1533 South 11th Street; 215-551-3870.* With all the charm of a mirrored-and-paneled finished basement, Tre Scalini will never wow anyone with its decor. With the first or second course, though, first-timers realize that the delicate gnocchi and other homemade pastas of chef-owner Franca Di Renzo are the focus, along with the familial warmth of her daughter, Francesca, and husband, Alberto. You'd expect to find no-frills peasant dishes like broccoli rabe over grilled polenta in this unassuming rowhouse devoted to south-central Italian cuisine, but there are plenty of others with uptown flair: quail with sage and garlic; squid-ink pasta with shrimp; a huge veal chop with shiitake mushroom sauce. The tab is higher than at most other BYOBs in this neighborhood, which matters not to Di Renzo's disciples. Closed Monday. ● ▮ $$$

20 MANNING, *261 South 20th Street; 215-731-0900.* In the early evening, 20 Manning is a sleek dinner spot, with an Asian-inspired menu and a long communal table that dominates the dining room. But as the night progresses, the bar becomes the focus as the restaurant is slowly transformed into Lounge 20. The white tablecloths are removed, and the upholstered cubes and low tables tucked into the corner become the most coveted place to kick back with a drink. In warm weather, the café tables—under heat lamps and equipped with blankets for chillier spring evenings—on the wide sidewalk are popular. ● ◐ $$

269° FAHRENHEIT KISSEN TEMPURA BAR, *604 North 2nd Street; 215-413-1606.* Yes, this sister establishment of Old City's Kisso Sushi Bar offers the popular Alex's Maki (broiled salmon, scallion, tobiko, avocado and cucumber) and Kevin Maki (asparagus, crabstick, masago, scallion and broiled salmon) available at the original Kisso. 269°'s menu has these and more, like the Kissen Tempura Maki, with tuna, salmon, yellowtail and whitefish coated with thin slices of potato or noodles and deep-fried in relatively healthy brown rice oil (as are all of 269°'s tempura offerings). And 269° looks as good as its food—Kima Design did the space-age white and orange interior. ◑ ● $$

VALANNI, *1229 Spruce Street; 215-790-9494.* Owners George and Valerie Anni go to the head of the class with Valanni, an A-plus effort at Mediterranean-Latin fusion. A 14-seat bar serves as the nucleus of their cozy, dimly lit restaurant, a place to savor the electic by-the-glass wine list or high-octane cocktails like the "Brazilian pop," an elixir of mango-pomegranate juice and champagne served in a tall, slender cylinder. Banquettes line the walls in the rear of the single dining room, candles burn on tables for two near the front windows, and the clientele—dining on entrées like roasted duck atop a sweet potato mash dotted with brandied cherries—is as varied as the decor of sophisticated black surfaces, hip exposed brick, comfortable bar stools, and a quirky purple-and-blue striped wall. ● ✪ ⊙ $$

VALLEY GREEN INN, *Valley Green Road at Wissahickon Creek; 215-247-1730.* The pillared veranda of the stately Valley Green Inn, on car-free Forbidden Drive in Fairmount Park, is an urban Eden. A glass of pinot grigio and a salade Niçoise on a sun-washed afternoon, when painters and horseback riders convene along the creek, is an idyllic experience—in part because cell phones don't work here. Inquiries about the resident waterfowl have prompted the inn to post a note on its website: "The ducks which live in the Valley Green area are not the same ducks on our menu." ◑ ● ⊙ $$$

VETRI, *1312 Spruce Street; 215-732-3478.* Dinner in Vetri's intimate 35-seat confines is like a perfect moment that stretches across two hours, because each dish springs from chef-owner Marc Vetri's training in Italy, amplified by the return trips he makes several times each year. Observance of the seasons means that extraordinary winter dishes such as shaved raw baby artichokes with arugula and fondue, and spinach gnocchi with smoked ricotta and brown butter, are in residence year-round. Singular Italian wines and startling desserts, such as one in which hot olive oil is poured through a circle of chocolate onto a scoop of rosemary ice cream, make Vetri a restaurant that appeals to the intellect as well as the senses. This is one of the most coveted reservations in town. Closed Sunday. ● $$$$

VIENTIANE CAFÉ, *4728 Baltimore Avenue; 215-726-1095.* The hot-climate cuisines of Thailand and Vietnam rely on kaffir lime leaves, lemongrass, ginger, and sweat-inducing chili paste to chase torpor from the table. The adorable Vientiane Café. a 25-seat BYOB with jadeite-green walls and homey cabbage-rose tablecloths, does it well, and inexpensively: Three-course lunches are available for $7.95, while at dinner, entrée specials like spicy duck with pungent Thai basil are a mere $13.95. Closed Sunday. ◑ ● ♦ $

VIVO ENOTECA, *108 North Wayne Avenue, Wayne; 610-687-6558.* In Italian, "enoteca" means "place where one buys wine," and Vivo Enoteca's hipster-dark bar inspires diners to do just that. The by-the-glass wine list has a few interesting selections, like La Villa Prosecco and 2001 Castello Di Poppiano, but is underwhelming, with a fairly standard array of chardonnays, pinot grigios and Italian reds. The by-the-bottle wine list, however, has clearly been chosen with great care, with mostly Italian and California selections. And the service has nice little touches. Wines were served in miniature decanters, and the bubbly prosecco in tall, silly glasses. Vivo Enoteca's dinner menu is made up of small plates, but is no match for the wines. The dessert menu, though, includes a delicious pine-nut tart. Closed Sunday and Monday. ● $$

WHITE DOG CAFÉ, *3420 Sansom Street; 215-386-9224.* On the menu at the White Dog Café: innovative New American cuisine and wide-ranging social activism. Located in a Victorian brownstone in University City, the more-than-two-decade-old restaurant is a maze of intimate, comfortable dining rooms. Newly arrived Chef Michael O'Halloran—a sous-chef here in the mid-1990s—has updated the restaurant's local-produce-dependent menu with dishes like five-spiced Peking duck breast with a raspberry-ginger glaze and anise-black pepper beef carpaccio. But the White Dog's commitment to social projects—supporting local farmers, sponsoring dinner discussions and organizing community outreach—remains unchanged. ◐ ● ☉ ✪ $$$

WILD TUNA, *Chesterbrook Village Shopping Center, 500 Chesterbrook Boulevard, Wayne; 610-695-8862.* Chef Anthony Bonett is behind the mostly seafood menu at Wild Tuna, balancing modernisms like a tuna trio appetizer (rare seared tuna, Mediterranean-style tuna salad, and tuna tartare with diced melon and cucumber) with suburban standards such as crab-stuffed shrimp with hollandaise sauce. Bonett's wife makes the splendid apple tart. On Fridays and Saturdays, owner Richard Robinson, a co-founder of Rock Lobster, brings in a DJ. The decor, sadly, is nondescript. Closed for lunch Saturday and Sunday. ◐ ● $$

THE WOODEN IRON, *118 North Wayne Avenue, Wayne; 610-964-7888.* When Chris Dutton, Steve Brady and Jim Flanigan opened the golf-themed Wooden Iron restaurant in Wayne, they were thinking "upscale country club." And with specialties like wild mushroom ravioli with porcini cream, crabmeat, spinach and chives, they're turning out more ambitious American food than you'll find at most golf resorts. There's a handsome dark mahogany bar and framed golf prints, and Dutton's and Brady's wives furnished the place with appropriately cushy forest-green banquettes. In stock and waiting for rocks, or not, are 40 single-malt scotches, 50 vodkas, and 100 specialty martinis, such as Flanigan's Love Potion #9—Charbay blood-orange vodka, Cointreau, Chambord, a splash of grenadine, and orange and pineapple juices. In addition to the California-heavy wine list starting at $21, there are 14 approachable wines by the glass—hence the happy-looking crowd gathered at the bar every evening. Closed for lunch Saturday and Sunday. ◑ ● $$$

WORD OF MOUTH, *729 Haddon Avenue, Collingswood; 856-858-2228.* Chef Greg Fenski does many things well at Word of Mouth, but his mashed potatoes are positively haunting: laced with horseradish alongside a New York strip steak, or with fresh herbs to accompany a nicely seasoned but somewhat chewy rack of lamb. The house-made gnocchi with grilled shrimp and a full-bodied garlic-tomato-basil sauce is a winner, as is the duck quesadilla. Closed Monday: closed for lunch on Sunday. ◑ ● ⫯ $$$

YANGMING, *Haverford Avenue and Conestoga Road, Bryn Mawr; 610-527-3200.* High-style Chinese elegance has transformed an 18th-century tavern into a special-occasion destination for Main Line crowds. Yangming, whose name means "sunshine, bright and happy," serves up creative Chinese/Continental fusion, with Westernized dishes, like rigatoni in garlic lemon saffron sauce with sautéed chicken tenders, as well as fragrant classics like spicy General Tso's chicken. Closed for lunch Sunday. ◑ ● $$$

YANN, *122 South 18th Street; 215-568-5250.* Stepping into Yann requires that you forgive its awkward window space, which is too high for passersby to properly ogle the glistening individual tartes Tatin and dark-chocolate "Jefferson" pastries that are posed gorgeously within. Once inside, you'll find that Yann's opera cake, a slim rectangle of ganache, almond cake and chocolate cream, is like eating velvet, and the apricot tart is a pile of golden fruit on a cloud of pastry cream, with tulle-thin pastry. French-born Yann Machard, who owns Symphony wholesale bakery in Moorestown, also serves baguette sandwiches and salads at the back bar and in the mellow-yellow upstairs dining room. Closed Sunday. ○ ◑ ⫯ $

ZEKE'S MAINLINE BAR B QUE, *6001 Lancaster Avenue; 215-871-7427.* On nights when it's too hot to fire up the Weber, head to Overbrook for Zeke's Mainline

Bar B Que, and bring home a trunkful of pulled pork, slow-cooked brisket and meaty pork ribs. Owner Prentice Cole—a former *Daily News* photographer, wine merchant, and onetime City Council candidate—serves it up with made-from-scratch hot and sweet sauces, fresh coleslaw, collard greens, house-baked cornbread and sweet-tart lemonade. ◑ ● ⬩ ◓ $$

INDEX : **BY CUISINE**

INDEX : **BY NEIGHBORHOOD**

ACKNOWLEDGEMENTS

No meal is complete without dessert. (I'm thinking specifically of the clementine and candied ginger semifreddo at Django.) And no book is complete without deserts for those who made it possible. My gratitude to photographer Zoey Sless-Kitain; researcher Karrie Gavin; copy maven Sandy Hingston; and designer Andrew Zahn, who achieved the most important thing for a book about food—he made it look almost appetizing enough to eat.

It took *Philadelphia* magazine editor Larry Platt and Temple University Press's director Alex Holzman and senior acquisitions editor Micah Kleit to envision a partnership between the magazine and the press, but it took the cooperation of both staffs to make this first book in that partnership a reality: *Philadelphia* magazine chairman D. Herbert Lipson and publisher David H. Lipson Jr.; senior editor Amy Donohue and executive editor Benjamin Wallace, who edited—and wrote—many of the pieces included in this collection; food critic Maria Gallagher and the many foodies—Daniel Bergman, Teresa Banik Capuzzo, Kathleen Fifield, Victor Fiorillo, Lawrence Goodman, Sasha Issenberg, Rebecca Kenton, Lauren McCutcheon, John Mariani, Francine Maroukian, Blake Miller, Daniel Morell, Roxanne Patel, Richard Pawlak, Stephen Rodrick, Caroline Tiger, Jason Wilson and Stephen Yeager—who have informed the magazine's food coverage; and Temple's patient director of production Charles Ault and publicity manager Gary Kramer.